The Secret Door to Understand Bible Prophecy

THE SECRET DOOR
to Understand
Bible PROPHECY

~A WARNING TO GOD'S PEOPLE~

by
APOSTLE STAN JOHNSON

*This book has been purposely made thin using near-Bible paper, in the typical Bible size of 6 x 9, to make it easy to carry with your Bible as a handy reference.

Printed by:
Kingery Printing Company
3012 S. Banker
Effingham, IL 62401

Copyright © 2018, Stan Johnson

ISBN#978-1-945693-26-7

All Rights reserved under International Copyright Law. Written permission must be secured from the publisher/author to use or reproduce any part of this work.

Unless otherwise noted, all Scripture is taken from the New King James Version® Copyright © 1982 by Thomas Nelson. Used by permission. All rights reserved.

TABLE OF CONTENTS

PREFACE vii

INTRODUCTION ix

Chapter 1
FIRSTFRUITS: KEY TO
THE SECRET DOOR 1

Chapter 2
THE HARVESTS 3

Chapter 3
THE FEASTS 7

Chapter 4
TABERNACLES: THE NEW
JERUSALEM ARRIVES 11

Chapter 5
WORLD GOVERNMENT
IS GOD'S PLAN 14

Chapter 6
144,000 FIRSTFRUITS 26

Chapter 7
THE NAME ON
THE FOREHEAD 31

Chapter 8
TWO WITNESSES
(Not Enoch and Elijah) 34

Chapter 9
THE DAY AND THE HOUR 48

Chapter 10
MORNING STAR 51

Chapter 11
NATIONS 56

Chapter 12
PROPHECIES IN THE
FEASTS OF THE LORD 59

Chapter 13
MARRIAGE SUPPER
OF THE LAMB 72

Chapter 14
TRUMPETS: ATONEMENT:
TABERNACLES 84

Chapter 15
THE JUDGMENT
SEAT OF CHRIST and the
GREAT WHITE THRONE 105

Chapter 16
PARABLES OF JESUS 112

Chapter 17
OVERCOMERS vs.
REMNANTS 121

Chapter 18
SEVEN EARLY SIGNS
TO SPOT THE
BEAST/ANTICHRIST 129

Chapter 19
DO ALL PROPHECIES FROM
GOD COME TO PASS? 138

Chapter 20
MY TESTIMONY 156

PREFACE

What is behind that Secret Door? It's a mystery until we can use the Key, open the Door and look inside. Isn't it wonderful to experience that "AH-HA!" moment of discovery?

God sees us as so much more than we see ourselves. He knows us in all of our sin. He knows all we have done. He can see our potential as Kings, as part of His Family. He wants us to be fulfilled. Proverbs 25:2 says,

"It is the glory of God to conceal a thing: but the honour of kings is to search out a matter."

This is not a perfect book. It is a mystery we have been shown in part. Others will contribute as we learn from the Lord more of the clues He has set in the path before us. It is exciting and fun to discover the answers to the secrets He has set before us. Scripture from the KJV Bible will be used. You can believe it, or twist it! Some will refuse to believe the verses. They may say, "I don't believe it is a hint. I don't believe it is a clue." This is much like observing activities around us like earthquakes, hurricanes, volcanos, and massive fires and refusing to attribute any of them to God actively seeking to get our attention. They would rather refer to "Mother Nature."

You will see a brief overview of the Secret Door to Understand Bible Prophecy first with little explanation. Most of the rest of the book will be used to explain the points made initially. You are about to understand the future like you never have before! You SHOULD expect to read new information you have never considered. You may even DISAGREE with some points. That's OK. Scriptures will be given for almost every point made as we move through the book. After all, one of the reasons you are reading this is to gain new information. You want to learn more about God and His plans for us and the entire world.

JOB 33:15, "In a DREAM, in a vision of the night, when deep sleep falleth upon men, in slumberings upon the bed; Then he openeth the ears of men, and SEALETH THEIR INSTRUCTION."

God told my wife, Leslie, in 2007, that He was going to give me this Secret Door. The Secret Door To Understand BIBLE PROPHECIES!

DREAM GIVEN TO LESLIE FOR STAN— NOVEMBER 23, 2007

Stan was speaking to a small group about Bible prophecy. They were listening intently and very supportive and in agreement. A man at the back of the room, dressed in a white button-down shirt, a graying beard and hair just below the ears began to speak to Stan. He seemed to be Jewish. He was very kind to Stan and complimented him on his understanding of Bible prophecy. After all the accolades of kind and encouraging words, he said, "If you will study the Feasts, God will show you the SECRET DOOR TO UNDERSTAND BIBLE PROPHECY."

While talking to my friend on the phone, suddenly I saw two books and what appeared to be a supernatural door connecting them book-to-book. This supernatural door looked like a stick of butter suspended between two books except it was not butter; it was a yellow-time-tunnel. It was a secret door between the Torah of Moses and John's Book of Revelation! The time-tunnel was slightly blurred, showing these two books are linked. They were written thousands of years apart, but I was shown they are linked spiritually. There is a secret, spiritual door between the books. The vision occurred in less than a blink of an eye. It happened so fast I didn't even say anything about it at the time. I was in a conversation, but the knowledge was imparted just that quick, and I kept talking. Now I will explain the secret door I was given.

My suggestion is that you read every word on BOTH charts before beginning to read the book and refer to the charts often as you read. Check for updated charts at:

http://www.prophecyclub.com/document-downloads.html

INTRODUCTION

I am going to start by giving you the key to the Secret Door! These were the last secrets revealed to me, but I will give them to you first! Hearing about the Secret is the easy part, understanding it will take most of the rest of the book. Enjoy!

You will also notice I make the same point repeatedly. This is not an accident; this is to help solidify the information in your mind as we go along. Most of the information you are about to read is going to be new. The repetition, as with memorizing Scripture, is helpful.

KEY

The KEY to the secret door is the word "FIRSTFRUITS!" This is the KEY word that links the two books together to open the Secret Door to Understand Bible Prophecies.

SECRET DOOR

The SECRET DOOR to UNDERSTAND BIBLE PROPHECY is linking the word FIRSTFRUITS in the Feasts of Leviticus 23:10-13 to the word FIRSTFRUITS in Revelation 14:4. The Secret Door is linking the Feasts given to Moses to the Prophecies given to John the Revelator. The TORAH links to REVELATION. That's it! The Torah is the first five books of the Bible. REVELATION is the last book of the Bible. If you could understand what was just written, you could stop reading now. It will take most of the rest of the book to explain the Key and Secret Door.

The understanding of the Key to the Door is found in the word FIRSTFRUITS in Revelation. It is the FINAL FULFILLMENT of the FIRSTFRUITS given to Moses. It is not the "shadow or rehearsal." It is the final fulfillment, the conclusion, the point, the REASON the Feast of Firstfruits were given to Moses in the first place.

God gave Moses the Feasts and commanded that they be observed, because within them was the SECRET TO UNDERSTAND THE LAST SEVEN MONTHS. It is to allow His Chosen People, people chosen above all the people of the earth, to understand the prophecies of the last days.

The more a person is familiar with the Feasts and Revelation, the more of what you are about to see will excite you. The purpose of the Feasts is to put the prophecies of Revelation into proper order. The purpose of the Feasts is to give order and sequence to the prophecies found in the Bible, especially REVELATION.

Chapter 1
FIRSTFRUITS:
Key to the Secret Door

FIRSTFRUITS

The word, FIRSTFRUITS, found in the Feasts and REVELATION IS THE DOOR!

LEVITICUS 23:10, *"... When ye be come into the land which I give unto you, and shall reap the harvest thereof, then ye shall bring a sheaf of the firstfruits of your harvest unto the priest: And he shall wave the sheaf before the LORD, to be accepted for you: FIRSTFRUITS on the morrow after the sabbath the priest shall wave it."*

REVELATION 14:4, *"... These were redeemed from among men, being the FIRSTFRUITS unto God and to the Lamb."*

The word FIRSTFRUITS in LEVITICUS 23:10, also found in REVELATION 14:4, is the benchmark that sets the timing and sequence for BIBLE PROPHECIES in Revelation and those concerning the last seven months!

Having studied prophecy for 40 years, taught it for 30 years, and hosted a radio and sometimes television program on it, I cannot tell you the hundreds of times I said that Jesus returns the next time as the Lion of the Tribe of Judah and puts his foot down on the Mount of Olives. I discovered in the process of receiving this book that that is NOT TRUE!

Now that you know THE DOOR, the journey begins here. These next verses say Jesus arrives as a "Lamb" on "Mt. Zion" with the 144,000 witnesses. These 144,000 are 12,000 Israelites from each of the 12 tribes described in Revelation, chapter 7.

REVELATION 14:1, 4, 5, *"And I looked, and, lo, a Lamb stood on the mount Sion, and with him an HUNDRED FORTY AND FOUR THOUSAND, having his Father's name written in their foreheads. ... These are they which were not defiled with women; for they are virgins. These are they which follow the Lamb whithersoever he goeth. These were redeemed from among men, being the FIRSTFRUITS unto God and to the Lamb. And in their mouth was found NO GUILE: for they are WITHOUT FAULT before the throne of God."*

On the seventeenth day of the first month is the Feast of Firstfruits. The next day [the morrow] the high priest waves a barley cracker made of a sheaf (a handful) of barley flour mixed with oil WITHOUT LEAVEN before the Lord. This is a SHADOW PICTURE for a future and final fulfillment when the 144,000 are resurrected to Mt. Zion having no sin. These 144,000 Jewish males clothed in white robes, *"follow the Lamb whithersoever he goeth."* This is one of the greatest events in Bible prophecy! They are the Secret Door! Firstfruits is the Key word, and these 144,000 Jewish male virgins are the Secret Door of Prophecy. In understanding them, one can understand the secret to all end time Israelite Bible prophecies!

Jesus was the Firstfruits of "THEM THAT SLEPT." Whereas, these 144,000 "redeemed from the earth" are the Firstfruits of "THE HARVEST." They are the FIRST TO BE RESURRECTED for the END TIME HARVEST. These servants of God are the first to receive their new glorified eternal bodies since Jesus arose. Hence, "Firstfruits."

They are the FINAL FULFILLMENT of the Firstfruits Barley Harvest. Said another way, the reason the Feast of Firstfruits was given to Moses was to one day reveal the FINAL FIRSTFRUITS, the 144,000!! They will get to announce, "This is it! This is the year in which Messiah returns!" This is an amazing thing God does for His chosen people!

The Feasts linked to Revelation show us the Secret Door to Understand Bible Prophecy. Jesus arose on Firstfruits, STOPPING THE PROPHETIC PLAY OF THE FEASTS until He returns on Firstfruits with the 144,000. The prophetic play of the Feasts BEGINS AGAIN WHEN THE 144,000 appear on Mt. Zion and the Feasts begin to play prophetically for the final time.

1 CORINTHIANS 15:20-23, "But NOW IS CHRIST RISEN FROM THE DEAD, AND BECOME THE FIRSTFRUITS OF THEM THAT SLEPT. For since by man came death, by man came also the resurrection of the dead. For as in Adam all die, even so in Christ shall all be made alive. But every man in his own order: CHRIST THE FIRSTFRUITS; AFTERWARD THEY THAT ARE CHRIST'S AT HIS COMING."

This is the verse which tells us the next time Jesus returns is ON FIRSTFRUITS! Surprised? This is only the first of many surprises you are about to experience in this book. I will back them all up with Scripture, so you know you are not being misled.

On the first day of Firstfruits, the high priest is commanded to take a sheaf of fine barley flour, add olive oil, and bake it without leaven. A sheaf is a handful, so it makes a barley-cracker about the size of a large cookie. Barley represents the Israelites or the Children of Israel. For ease of typing, henceforth, I will refer to the Children of Israel as "Jews." We all know that Judah was only one of the 12 tribes, but it is easier for the sake of writing to refer to all the 12 tribes as Jews.

When we see the Lamb standing upon Mount Zion with the 144,000, we will know the day, and many times, the very hour the following will be fulfilled:

The resurrection of the dead in Christ

The Euphrates River dried to prepare the way of the kings of the east

The three unclean spirits like frogs released to gather the tares and grapes

The day Jesus returns!

The day the Beast and False Prophet will be cast into the Lake of Fire

The day those dead or alive IN CHRIST will be judged

The day the dead NOT in Christ will be judged

The day the old heaven and the old earth pass away

The day Lucifer is chained in the bottomless pit for 1,000 years

The day and hour the New Jerusalem descends out of heaven and much more ...

Chapter 2
THE HARVESTS

THE WHEAT AND BARLEY HARVESTS

On Pentecost the high priest is commanded to take two tenth deals of fine wheat flour. A tenth deal is about six pints or a quart and a half. He then mixes the wheat flour with oil and LEAVEN. He bakes these two lumps of leavened wheat flour making two large loaves of wheat bread about the size of two medium-sized watermelons and waves them before the Lord.

Wheat is a shadow picture for Christians, just as Barley is for Israelites. The reason we know Wheat represents those washed in the blood of Jesus is because of these verses.

MATTHEW 13:25-30, "... his enemy came and sowed TARES among the WHEAT ... Wilt thou then that we go and gather them up? But he said, 'Nay; lest while ye gather up the tares, ye root up also the wheat with them. LET BOTH GROW TOGETHER UNTIL THE HARVEST: and in the time of harvest I will say to the reapers, 'GATHER YE TOGETHER FIRST THE TARES, and bind them in bundles to burn them: but gather the WHEAT into my barn.'"

The Barley Harvest of 144,000 will be resurrected on Firstfruits. Exactly 50 days later on the Feast of Pentecost the Wheat Harvest is resurrected. The wheat represents those who were washed in the blood of the Lamb. This is the fulfilment of "the dead in Christ shall rise first." This is the *"multitude, which no man could number, of all nations, and kindreds, and people, and tongues, stood before the throne."* You recall in Acts, Pentecost was the Feast in which the Holy Spirit appeared in the upper room. People were filled with the Holy Spirit, began to speak in tongues and saw tongues of fire sit upon people.

The following Scriptures are describing the Christian-Wheat Harvest standing before God. "Therefore, are they BEFORE THE THRONE," refers to the Christians, saved and washed in the Blood of the Lamb.

REVELATION 7:9-14, "After this I beheld, and, lo, a GREAT MULTITUDE, which no man could number, of all nations, and kindreds, and people, and tongues, STOOD BEFORE THE THRONE, and before the Lamb, clothed with white robes, and palms in their hands; ... These are they which came out of great tribulation, and have WASHED their robes, and made them white in THE BLOOD OF THE LAMB. Therefore are they BEFORE THE THRONE OF GOD, and serve him day and night in his temple: and he that sitteth on the throne shall dwell among them."

To be admitted to the Marriage Supper one must be without sin. Notice the Barley Harvest was a small crop of only 144,000. They were admitted because they were "of the first year" and "without fault before the throne of God," whereas the Wheat is admitted because they were washed in the Blood of the Lamb. The Blood of Jesus will admit far more than those without fault. In the prophetic picture, the wheat and tares grow together until the harvest.

The harvest is the end of the world, specifically the Feasts of Trumpets.

MARRIAGE SUPPER OF THE LAMB

The Barley and Wheat Harvests are the only two groups invited to the Marriage Supper of the Lamb.

> REVELATION 19:9, "... Blessed are they which are called unto the MARRIAGE SUPPER OF THE LAMB..."

> REVELATION 20:6, "Blessed and holy is he that hath part in the FIRST RESURRECTION: on such the second death hath no power, but they shall be priests of God and of Christ, and shall reign with him a thousand years."

The reason we know the Barley and Wheat harvests are called the FIRST RESURRECTION is because they are the first to be resurrected as a GROUP. They are resurrected on two different feasts, but ascend as one group to the Marriage Supper of the Lamb on Pentecost.

Look closely at, "... a LAMB stood on the MOUNT SION, and with him an hundred forty and four thousand ... These are they which FOLLOW THE LAMB whithersoever he goeth."

> REVELATION 14:1, 4, 5, "And I looked, and, lo, a LAMB stood on the MOUNT SION, and with him an HUNDRED FORTY AND FOUR THOUSAND, having his Father's name written in their foreheads. ... These are they which were not defiled with women; for they are virgins. These are they which follow the Lamb whithersoever he goeth. These were redeemed from among men, being the FIRSTFRUITS unto God and to the Lamb. And in their mouth was found NO GUILE: for they are WITHOUT FAULT before the throne of God."

Notice, the Barley follows "Jesus as the LAMB." Notice, He has not been to the Marriage Supper yet. He has not been crowned KING OF KINGS yet. He has NOT returned yet on a white horse in the air as the Lion of the Tribe of Judah. He returns in the air as the Lion on Trumpets. He is walking on Mt. Zion as a LAMB on the Feast of Firstfruits. He is waiting for the precious fruit of the earth. He is waiting exactly fifty days for the Christian-wheat harvest to fully ripen. Then, TOGETHER, they will go watch Jesus be brought "near before" the Father, where Jesus will be crowned and made KING OF KINGS!

> DANIEL 7:13, "... the Son of man [Jesus] came ... to the Ancient of days [Father], and they brought him NEAR BEFORE HIM. And there was given him dominion [Crowns, Vesture and a white horse], and glory, and a kingdom, that all people, nations, and languages, should serve him: his dominion is an everlasting dominion, which shall not pass away, and his kingdom that which shall not be destroyed."

At that Wedding Supper, the Barley and Wheat harvests get three things:— Glorified Bodies, White Wedding Garments, A White Horse.

This is NOT about us, this is about Jesus. We get the rest of our rewards on the day of Trumpets after the burning of the tares and crushing of the grapes about four months after the Marriage Supper. More later ...

The Wedding Supper is the Coronation of Jesus, the Crowning of Jesus. The Ancient of Days (The Father) changes him from being the "Prince of the kings of the earth" to "King of Kings and Lord of Lords!"

We don't get crowns at the Wedding Supper. We get our crowns on the day of Trumpets, the Judgment Seat of Christ. This will be the day Jesus returns as He

THE SECRET DOOR TO UNDERSTANDING BIBLE PROPHECY

said, *"My reward is with me."* Trumpets is the day we can cast our crowns at his feet saying,

> *"Thou art worthy, O Lord, to receive glory and honour and power: for thou hast created all things, and for thy pleasure they are and were created" (REVELATION 4:11).*

The Father, the Anient of days, presides at the Wedding and gives Jesus many crowns and a vesture dipped in blood with *"KING OF KINGS AND LORD OF LORDS"* written on it. His thigh will have thereon the same name of King of Kings and Lord of Lords. He will also receive a white horse. This is a wonderful picture of the Wedding Supper as was described in Daniel 7:13.

What blood is Jesus' Wedding Vesture dipped in? You recall when Mary went to the tomb of Jesus and thought she was talking to a gardener. Jesus told her not to touch him yet.

> *JOHN 20:17, "Jesus saith unto her, 'TOUCH ME NOT; FOR I AM NOT YET ASCENDED TO MY FATHER: but go to my brethren, and say unto them, I ascend unto my Father, and your Father; and to my God, and your God.'"*

We can conclude that Jesus must have gone to heaven to dip his Wedding garment in his sacrificed blood in preparation for his Wedding Day. He appeared before His disciples. Three days later, He told Thomas to feel his scars. Over 500 saw him after his resurrection when He walked around for another 40 days.

The Bible doesn't directly say his Vesture is dipped in his own blood, but the Blood of Jesus is the only thing which washes sin away, and the Vesture of Jesus would certainly not have anything else upon it. It is NOT the blood of the tares or grapes yet, as the Marriage is four months before Armageddon.

> *REVELATION 19:13, 14, "And he was CLOTHED with a VESTURE DIPPED IN BLOOD: and his name is called The Word of God. And the armies which were in heaven followed him upon WHITE HORSES, clothed in fine linen, white and clean."*

GRAPE HARVEST

The grape harvest arrives about four months after the Wedding Supper on the Feast of Trumpets. We return with Jesus for the grape harvest on white horses at Armageddon. There we will watch our new Husband Jesus destroy His enemies with the Morning Star. This Morning Star is like a light sword coming out of his mouth. The Morning Star is instant judgment, destroying both body and soul. Those hit with the Morning Star are turned to shivers or ashes.

At the grape harvest, along with Jesus, there are two other destroying angels. These angels have a sharp sickle, which is apparently not the Morning Star. Ezekiel was told the birds will eat the dead people killed at Armageddon. Birds can't eat ashes. Jesus burns the tares to ashes with the Morning Star, but the two angels use sickles to cut them to pieces; thus, shedding blood. That is not to say that the Morning Star, which could also be something like a very powerful laser, could not also be used to cut and slice. We know for sure the Morning Star turns people to ashes and a sickle cuts and slashes, releasing the blood of the grapes.

> *EZEKIEL 39:4, "Thou shalt fall upon the mountains of Israel, thou, and all thy bands, and the people that is with thee: I WILL GIVE THEE UNTO THE RAVENOUS BIRDS of every sort, and to the beasts of the field TO BE DEVOURED."*

REVELATION 14:14-20, "And I looked, and behold a WHITE CLOUD, and upon the cloud one sat LIKE unto the Son of man [Not Jesus], having on his head a golden crown, and in his hand a SHARP SICKLE. And another angel came out of the temple, crying with a loud voice to him that sat on the cloud, Thrust in thy sickle, and reap: for the time is come for thee to reap; for the HARVEST of the earth is ripe. And he that sat on the cloud thrust in his sickle on the earth; and the earth was reaped. And ANOTHER ANGEL came out of the temple which is in heaven, he also having a SHARP SICKLE. And another angel came out from the altar, which had power over fire; and cried with a loud cry to him that had the sharp sickle, saying, 'Thrust in thy sharp sickle, and gather the CLUSTERS OF THE VINE OF THE EARTH; for her GRAPES are fully ripe.' And the angel thrust in his sickle into the earth, and gathered the VINE OF THE EARTH, and cast it into the great WINEPRESS of the wrath of God. And the WINEPRESS was trodden without the city, and BLOOD CAME OUT OF THE WINEPRESS, even unto the horse bridles, by the space of a thousand and six hundred furlongs."

JOEL 3:12, "Let the heathen be wakened, and come up to the valley of Jehoshaphat: for there will I sit to JUDGE ALL THE HEATHEN ROUND ABOUT. Put ye in the SICKLE, for the [grape] harvest is ripe: come, get you down; for the PRESS IS FULL, THE FATS OVERFLOW; for their wickedness is great. Multitudes, multitudes in the valley of decision: for the DAY OF THE LORD is near in the valley of decision. The sun and the moon shall be darkened, and the stars shall withdraw their shining. The LORD also shall roar [Trumpets] out of Zion, and utter his voice from Jerusalem; and the HEAVENS AND THE EARTH SHALL SHAKE: but the LORD will be the hope of his people, and the strength of the children of Israel."

Chapter 3
THE FEASTS

TRUMPETS—GATHERING FOR ARMAGEDDON

About four months after the Feast of Pentecost, on the first day of the seventh month, is the Feast of Trumpets. In verse 15, Jesus warns He is about to return like a thief in the night. In verse 16, the tares are gathered for Armageddon. Please notice the word "garments." What group will get to wear garments, the Wheat or the tares? Since we know Jesus is referring to Himself as returning *"as a thief,"* to whom is He speaking when He is warning them not to lose their garments? The Wheat or tares? What is the point Jesus is trying to make here? WHO is He warning not to lose their garments? Why is there a warning a day or so before Armageddon not to stop watching and lose your garments?

> REVELATION 16:14-16, *"For they are the spirits of devils, working miracles, which go forth unto the kings of the earth and of the whole world, to gather them to the battle of that great day of God Almighty. Behold, I COME AS A THIEF. Blessed is he that watcheth, and keepeth his GARMENTS, lest he walk naked, and they see his shame. And he gathered them together into a place called in the tongue Armageddon."*

The burning of the tares and crushing of the grapes is on the Feast of Trumpets. Jesus returns after sunset; hence, *"thief in the night"* with the Barley and Wheat harvests for Armageddon. The tares are burned, and the grapes are gathered into the great winepress of the wrath of God and crushed. Blood pours out of the winepress for about 200 miles. After the burning of tares and the pressing of grapes, it is the Judgment Seat of Christ and the remaining Wheat resurrected dead or remaining alive are given their crowns and rewards.

Fifteen days later on Tabernacles, they are gathered into the barn, the New Jerusalem. Meaning, if you are not burned or sliced to death and remain standing after the burning and crushing, you made it! You have escaped! You are left standing! (Except the nations of course.) Trumpets IS the Judgment Seat of Christ. Jesus judges those IN CHRIST, dead or alive, on Trumpets. Ten days after Trumpets, on the Feast of Atonement, is the Great White Throne. Jesus judges ALL the dead NOT IN CHRIST.

> LUKE 21:36, *"Watch ye therefore, and pray always, that ye may be accounted worthy to escape all these things* [the burning and crushing] *that shall come to pass, and to STAND before the Son of man."*

On Trumpets the Judgment is set. No one else gets saved, no one else falls away. Those who are unjust are unjust still; those who are holy are holy still. The judgment is set. The living tares have been burned and the living grapes have been crushed.

The living Barley and Wheat from the Marriage of the Lamb are united with the rest of the Wheat. *"Those who are alive and remain."* Those who survive the burning along with all the dead, going back to Adam, are gathered before their proper Judgment. It will be the Great White Throne for those NOT in Christ or the Judgment Seat of Christ for those IN Christ.

> *"We* [saints] *must all appear before the judgment seat of Christ"* (2 CORINTHIANS 5:10).

By Trumpets, the sun will have been out for three days. The earth is frozen. Anyone alive is forced to move underground to seek escape. All moisture in the atmosphere has been frozen and has fallen to the earth in the form of 75-pound hailstones.

From the throne it is said, *"Behold, it is done;" "It is finished;"* and the *"Kingdoms of this world are become the kingdoms of our Lord and of his Christ."* There is no more sin. No one else gets saved. No one else falls away. The judgment is set. The Day of Atonement arrives in nine days on the tenth day of the seventh month.

Those familiar with the Feasts may wonder why there is no mention of the Ten Days of Awe. *The Secret Door to Understand Bible Prophecy* is a book about what the KJV Bible says about prophecy. The words "days" and "awe" do not appear in the same verse in the KJV. This traditional interpretation is not discussed for this reason. Traditions often get in the way of our understanding of the true Word of God. Jesus spoke of traditions in eight verses in the gospels— ALL of them were negative examples of tradition. Other traditional interpretations not backed by Scripture will not be covered as well.

> *MARK 7:8a, 9b, "For laying aside the commandment of God, ye hold the tradition of men ... Full well ye reject the commandment of God, that ye may keep your own tradition."*

> *MARK 7:13a, "Making the word of God of none effect through your tradition ..."*

ATONEMENT: OPENING THE BOOKS

Atonement is a one-day feast. On this day, all souls that are NOT in Christ are judged in two ways. They are judged to see if their name is in the Book of Life, and they are judged according to their acts written in their Books of Works.

This is NOT a judgment by fire as in Trumpets. This is judgment by books. Everyone appearing at the Great White Throne is dead hence, "I saw the dead." Those not in the Book of Life are tossed into the Lake of Fire, but the judgment is based upon books, not fire.

The Books of Works and the Book of Life are all opened. Some people may have many books of works. This means everybody, all the way back to Adam, that is NOT in Christ must give an account of their life.

> *REVELATION 20:12-15, "And I saw the DEAD, small and great, stand before God; and the BOOKS were opened: and another book was opened, which is THE BOOK OF LIFE: and THE DEAD WERE JUDGED out of those things which were written in the books, ACCORDING TO THEIR WORKS. And the sea gave up the dead which were in it; and death and hell delivered up the dead which were in them: and they were judged every man ACCORDING TO THEIR WORKS. And death and hell were cast into the lake of fire. This is the second death. And WHOSOEVER WAS NOT FOUND WRITTEN IN THE BOOK OF LIFE WAS CAST INTO THE LAKE OF FIRE."*

Some think the "good" will report before Jesus at the Judgment Seat of

Christ, and the "bad" will report before the Great White Throne. Not true. These verses say that whether it is those who are IN Christ at the Judgment Seat of Christ or those who are NOT IN Christ at the Great White Throne, ALL GOOD AND BAD WILL REPORT TOGETHER on their respective judgment day.

MATTHEW 13:47-50, "Again, the kingdom of heaven is like unto a net, that was cast into the sea, and gathered of EVERY kind: Which, when it was full [Judgment Seat of Christ], *they drew to shore, and sat down, and gathered the GOOD into vessels, but cast the BAD away. So shall it be at THE END OF THE WORLD: the angels shall come forth, and sever the wicked* [tares] *from among the just* [wheat], *And shall cast them into the furnace of fire: there shall be wailing and gnashing of teeth."*

Jesus is the judge, not the Father. (2 CORINTHIANS 5:10).

JOHN 5:22, "For the Father judgeth no man, but hath committed all judgment unto the Son."

Whatever sin is not covered by a garment is revealed for those IN Christ and for those NOT in Christ at their respective Judgment day. All people see all the sins of those not covered with a garment. Many are shamed by their sins!

REVELATION 3:18, "I counsel thee to buy of me gold tried in the fire [Morning Star burning], *that thou mayest be rich; and white raiment* [white garment], *that thou mayest be clothed, and that the SHAME of thy nakedness do not appear* [Sins are covered]*;..."*

REVELATION 16:15, "Behold, I come as a thief. Blessed is he that watcheth, and keepeth his garments, lest he walk naked, and they see his SHAME."

DANIEL 12:2, 3, "And many of them that sleep in the dust of the earth shall awake, some to everlasting life, and some to SHAME and everlasting contempt. And they that be wise shall shine as the brightness of the firmament; and they that turn many to righteousness as the stars for ever and ever."

Whosoever is not found written in the Book of Life is cast into the Lake of Fire, which for most people is soul-death. The Beast and the False Prophet are cast into the Lake of Fire at this point and tormented "day and night forever." They do NOT get SOUL-DEATH, but rather ETERNAL TORMENT. The Bible calls it "perdition."

REVELATION 20:10, "And the devil that deceived them was cast into the lake of fire and brimstone, where the beast and the false prophet are, and shall be TORMENTED DAY AND NIGHT FOR EVER AND EVER."

Lucifer, the devil, is cast into the bottomless pit on Trumpets (REVELATION 20:1, 2), falling helplessly for the next 1,000 years without the ability to deceive the nations until he is loosed to gather the nations for their destruction. The nations are not allowed to live past the 1,000 years, *"...shall NOT BE LEFT TO OTHER PEOPLE, but it shall break in pieces and CONSUME ALL THESE KINGDOMS, and it shall stand forever"* (DANIEL 2:44). Who are the nations? They are all those who are not of the Barley or Wheat Harvests. They are the corners not harvested.

Those who worshiped the Beast, his image, or received his Mark or the number of his name are also cast into the Lake of Fire with the Beast and

False Prophet, and likewise, DO NOT RECEIVE SOUL-DEATH, but are tormented eternally.

Those whose name was not found in the Book of Life are now, *"ashes under the souls of your feet."* Both body and soul are dead. They are, *"as though they had not been."*

> MALICHI 4:3a, *"And ye shall tread down the wicked; for they shall be ASHES UNDER THE SOLES OF YOUR FEET..."*

> ISAIAH 10:18, *"And* [Morning Star] *shall consume the glory of his forest, and of his fruitful field, BOTH SOUL AND BODY: and they shall be AS WHEN A STANDARDBEARER FAINTETH."*

> OBADIAH 1:16, *"For as ye have drunk upon my holy mountain, so shall all the heathen drink continually, yea, they shall drink, and they shall swallow down, and THEY SHALL BE AS THOUGH THEY HAD NOT BEEN."*

Chapter 4
TABERNACLES:
The New Jersusalem Arrives

The New Jerusalem, the golden city clear as glass or crystal arrives on the fifteenth day of the seventh month at evening, but there is *"no night there,"* prepared as a bride adorned for her husband. *"Behold, I make all things new."* The old heaven and the old earth have passed away five days previously on Atonement, and there is no more sea. The new earth is a smooth round ball except for the one mountain of the Lord upon which the New Jerusalem sits.

The sun went out about 72 hours before Trumpets, the day Jesus returns and the sun never relights as Jesus literally is the light of the world.

REVELATION 21:25, "And the gates of it shall not be shut at all by day: for THERE SHALL BE NO NIGHT THERE."

REVELATION 21:23, "And the city had no need of the sun, neither of the moon, to shine in it: for THE GLORY OF GOD DID LIGHTEN IT, AND THE LAMB IS THE LIGHT THEREOF".

We are in our glorified bodies with our crowns, wearing white garments. We may enter our eternal homes made of clear-gold. We can drink of the River of Life and may eat of the Tree of Life; however, we don't need either of these as our bodies and lives are glorified and eternal. The Barley and Wheat and all the rest of those whose names were in the Book of Life are in the barn enjoying eternity with us and Jesus! The nations are not admitted into the New Jerusalem.

REVELATION 22:14, 15, "Blessed are they that DO HIS COMMANDMENTS, that they may have RIGHT TO THE TREE OF LIFE, and may enter in through the gates into the city. For without [not admitted to the New Jerusalem] *are dogs* [the nations], *and sorcerers, and whoremongers, and murderers, and idolaters, and whosoever loveth and maketh a lie."*

REVELATION 21:10-12, 16a, 18b, "And he carried me away in the spirit to A GREAT AND HIGH MOUNTAIN, and shewed me that GREAT CITY, THE HOLY JERUSALEM, descending out of heaven from God, Having the GLORY OF GOD: and her light was like unto a stone most precious, even like a jasper stone, clear as crystal; And had a wall [Nations not admitted] *great and high, and had twelve gates, and at the gates twelve angels* [to keep the nations out], *and names written thereon, which are the names of the twelve tribes of the children of Israel:... And the city lieth foursquare, and the length is as large as the breadth: ... and the city was pure gold, like unto clear glass."*

MILLENNIUM—1,000 YEARS WITH THE NATIONS

The nations are those people who didn't take the Mark, but didn't receive Jesus either. They can live for 1,000 years if they don't break a law, but are ALL destroyed at the end of the 1,000 years.

LEVITICUS 23:22, "And when ye reap the harvest of your land, THOU SHALT NOT MAKE CLEAN RIDDANCE OF THE CORNERS OF THY FIELD when thou reapest ..."

We as the Barley and Wheat live for eternity. I once heard eternity explained this way. Imagine a bird flies by the Rock of Gibraltar every 1,000 years and brushes one side of his beak on this large rock. Eternity will have only just begun when the rock has worn away.

We never work again, age again, get hungry or hurt. We can look and see Jesus face to face. We can move through time and space at the speed of thought (so says Dean Braxton in his Prophecy Club DVD, *I was Dead for an Hour and 45 Minutes*). The disc is available at **ProphecyClub.com** or instantly viewable at **WatchProphecyClub.com**

THE SECRET DOOR SUMMARY
1,000 Piece Jigsaw Puzzle Box

The secret door of prophecy is like a 1,000-piece jigsaw puzzle. The Israelites were given the top of the box with the picture on the front, but not the pieces inside. The Gentiles, those reading REVELATION, were given the pieces, but not the picture.

CROSSWORD PUZZLE

The secret door is also like a crossword puzzle. Moses was given the feasts, which is like the grid-squares. John, the revelator, was given the questions-text. One cannot solve the crossword puzzle without the other.

KEY

The KEY is the single word FIRSTFRUITS found in both the Feasts and the Book of Revelation. The KEY REVEALS the Secret Door to Understand Bible Prophecy that links the Feasts to Revelation. The more you are familiar with the Feasts and Revelation, the more you will understand the secret door of prophecy and how to understand the prophecies, most of which are found in Revelation.

ISRAELITES

The Israelites have kept the Feasts. They have lived them, taught them, and carried them for around 3,500 years. However, since they didn't have the pieces [revelation] in the box looking at the picture on the front of the box was limited. They have the crossword-grid, but not the questions and can't fill in the puzzle.

Every Torah teacher says the Feasts are a *"shadow of things to come,"* knowing they are a "rehearsal," you will rejoice once you see the fulfillment of shadow-picture and the purpose of the rehearsal!

NON-ISRAELITES

The Non-Israelites, Christians or Church have the pieces of the puzzle— the prophecies of Revelation. But, it is as if the box filled with small puzzle-pieces was thrown in the air like a deck of cards and scattered all over. The Gentiles find the pieces saying, "Wow! Look at that! Look what God has given us! Oh, thank You, God!" But they can't put them in order. They can't see the picture, nor fit them into the crossword-grid.

It's like they have the questions to the crossword puzzle, but not the grid. They don't know the order, sequence or timing of the prophecies. They can't fit the answers together without the grid. The Feasts are the picture and the grid. The prophecies of Revelation are the pieces and the questions to the grid.

This frustration has brought division in the Church. They know they have something of great importance, but can't fit the pieces together— until now!

THE SECRET DOOR TO UNDERSTANDING BIBLE PROPHECY

Now, the picture and the pieces can be matched to put the puzzle together. The crossword-grid and the questions can be matched to solve the puzzle. This will set the Children of Israel and the Church FREE! The Israelites will rejoice to finally discover the Secret in the Feasts, and the Church can fit the pieces together!

Chapter 5
WORLD GOVERNMENT IS GOD'S PLAN

I must cover the next topic before explaining more of the Secret Door. I must give an overview of where the world is headed according to Bible prophecy. Bible prophecy can be confusing if we look at it only through a bugs-eye view. Sometimes, we must step back and look at it from a birds-eye view. This is a very simple overview of what the Bible says we will see between now and the return of Messiah.

The Bible says God has put on the hearts of evil people in high places to form a world government, which He will use to bring a test to all men. They must answer the question, "Which God will you choose? Jesus or the Beast?" There will be several wars. At the end of them, the tares, controlled by the Beast/Lucifer, think they can defeat Jesus and set up his Beast Kingdom. The final battle, which the Beast and the kings of the earth lose, is called Armageddon.

THE ILLUMINATI

The world government plan was hatched on May 1, 1776. God directed a German philosopher, Adam Weishaupt, and four others in Inglostady, Bavaria, to form a group called the Illuminati. They were joined by elite bankers whose goal was to form a world government. They thought this was their idea, but it was God's plan to bring the world of sin to final destruction. Just as God hardened the heart of Pharaoh to show His power to the world, God has placed a grand plan in the heart of evil men in high places to destroy themselves and their world government and make Jesus King of Kings and Lord of Lords!

> REVELATION 17:12, "And the TEN HORNS which thou sawest are TEN KINGS, which have received no kingdom as yet; but RECEIVE POWER AS KINGS ONE HOUR WITH THE BEAST."

> REVELATION 17:17, "For God hath put in their hearts to fulfil his will, and to agree, and give their kingdom unto the beast, until the words of God shall be fulfilled."

Evil always thinks it has the advantage if it has the wealthiest, smartest people join its group and swear by some dastardly, secret oath to keep the plan secret.

The Bible says that God sits in the heavens and laughs at their plans, (Psalm 2:2), because He not only knows the smallest thoughts of their heart, but He controls them and their counsel. The Bible says that God gives wisdom and might. He changes the times and the seasons and removes Kings and sets up Kings. He knows what is in the darkness, and the light dwells with Him. (Summarized from Daniel 2:21).

> PSALM 2:2-4, "The KINGS OF THE EARTH SET THEMSELVES, and the rulers take counsel together, against the LORD, and against his anointed, saying, Let us BREAK THEIR BANDS ASUNDER, and cast away their cords from us. HE THAT SITTETH IN THE HEAVENS SHALL LAUGH: the Lord shall have them in derision.

This was taken from: *https://illuminati.am/globalist-agenda/*

"SINCE THE EARLIEST BEGINNINGS OF THE ILLUMINATI, BEFORE THE WRITING OF OUR ETERNAL OATHS OR THE UTTERANCE OF OUR VOWS AS HUMANITY'S PROTECTORS, OUR ORGANIZATION HAS ADVOCATED FOR THE ULTIMATE GOAL OF A GLOBALIST EARTH.

OUR VISION FOR THE FUTURE IS A UNIFIED PLANET WITHOUT NATIONAL BORDERS, GOVERNED BY THE BEST AND THE BRIGHTEST OF THE HUMAN SPECIES, IN WHICH ALL PEOPLE, IN ALL PLACES, CAN LIVE IN ABUNDANCE."

A GLOBALIST SOCIETY WOULD MEAN THE ABANDONMENT OF DIVISIONS BETWEEN COUNTRIES AND AN END TO THE MILLENNIA OF WARS FOUGHT OVER LAND AND ITS ASSETS. IT IS AN END TO THE HOARDING AND STOCKPILING OF EXCESS RESOURCES BY ONE COUNTRY, WHILE ANOTHER COUNTRY'S PEOPLE STARVE. IT IS THE IDEA THAT ALL HUMANS ARE BOTH INDIVIDUALS AND ALSO PART OF AN EXTENDED SPECIES FAMILY, AND THAT NO HUMAN SHOULD BE LEFT BEHIND SIMPLY BECAUSE OF THE RANDOM CHANCE OF WHERE THEY WERE BORN.

IN THE CURRENT AGE OF WAR, THE RICH MUST HOARD THEIR SUPPLIES TO ENSURE THE SAFETY OF THEIR CHILDREN THROUGH THIS TIME OF CHAOS. THEIR OBELISKS AND FACTORIES CAN ONLY BE BUILT THROUGH THE WORK OF NECESSITOUS MASSES.

BUT A DIFFERENT AGE IS NEARLY UPON US: A POST-LABOR CIVILIZATION MAINTAINED BY AUTONOMOUS MACHINERY AND POWERED WITH UNLIMITED ENERGY. IN THE COMING AGE OF ILLUMINATIAM, ALL WHO SEEK RICHES RECEIVE THE RICHES THEY DESERVE."

Those 224 words outline their plans which God has placed on their heart to make a global Communist-based government—"FROM EACH ACCORDING TO HIS ABILITY, TO EACH ACCORDING TO HIS NEEDS" is a slogan popularized by Karl Marx in his 1875 Critique of the Gotha Program. The principle refers to free access and distribution of goods, capital and services. Take from the haves and give to the have-nots.

The whole purpose is to gain control of the world to force a decision from every person—either you take the Mark or lose your head.

About 3,500 years ago, in Daniel, chapter 2, God told Nebuchadnezzar, the King of Babylon, that He would allow four kingdoms upon the earth. We call them world governments. Throughout human history there will be four, and only four, world governments. These were represented by Gold, Silver, Brass and Iron. Gold was Nebuchadnezzar/Babylon, Silver was the Medes and Persians, Brass was the Grecian Empire and Iron was the Roman Empire, or today, we refer to them as the European Union.

These verses tell of the rise of the four world governments. In the days of the fourth and final world government, Jesus will put down all four world governments, NOT leaving ANY of them alive, except those in His eternal Kingdom.

DANIEL 2:32-35, "This image's head was of fine GOLD, his breast and his arms of SILVER, his belly and his thighs of BRASS, His legs of IRON, his feet part of iron and part of clay. Thou sawest till that a stone was cut out without hands, which smote the image upon his feet that were of iron and clay, and brake them to pieces. Then was the iron, the clay, the brass, the silver, and the gold, broken to pieces together, and became like the chaff of the summer threshingfloors; and the wind carried them away, that NO PLACE WAS FOUND FOR THEM: and the stone that smote the image became a great mountain, and filled the whole earth."

DANIEL 2:40, "And the fourth kingdom shall be strong as iron: forasmuch as iron breaketh in pieces and subdueth all things: and as iron that breaketh all these, shall it break in pieces and bruise."

DANIEL 2:44, "And IN THE DAYS OF THESE KINGS SHALL THE GOD OF HEAVEN SET UP A KINGDOM, WHICH SHALL NEVER BE DESTROYED: and the kingdom shall NOT BE LEFT TO OTHER PEOPLE, but it shall break in pieces and consume all these kingdoms, and it shall stand for ever."

Four kingdoms are listed in the dream of the statue given to King Nebuchadnezzar. The head of Gold is Nebuchadnezzar's kingdom, followed by a second inferior kingdom of Silver, and a third kingdom symbolized by Brass. Our concern is the fourth kingdom of Iron, and then later, Iron and Clay. The scriptures say, *"in the days of these kings shall THE GOD OF HEAVEN SET UP A KINGDOM, WHICH SHALL NEVER BE DESTROYED."* The fourth world government, which is the next world government, will be the final world government.

During the reign of this fourth world government, God will destroy all remnants of all four kingdoms, going back to the first one. That means ALL people going back to Nebuchadnezzar will be destroyed like chaff being carried away by the wind. *"No place will be found for them,"* except those whose name is in the Book of Life. That includes the nations which survive the tribulation, but are destroyed at the end of the Millennium (or 1,000 years). This is a short way to say that only those with their names in the Book of Life will live eternally.

Nebuchadnezzar reigned about 2,400 years ago. This prophecy of four world governments stretches from Nebuchadnezzar, King of Babylon, until Jesus destroys the four kingdoms and sets up His eternal Kingdom in the near future. That is not bad news, but rather good news! Jesus destroys this world of sin and sets up a Kingdom of righteousness where there is no death, nor sorrow, nor sickness and where we live in love for eternity!

Daniel 2:40 says, "The fourth kingdom shall be strong as iron: forasmuch as iron breaketh in pieces and subdueth all things: and as iron that breaketh all these, shall it break in pieces and bruise." The word "bruise" is a key. That word in the Hebrew means "mark." This fourth kingdom will break into pieces all walls between nations and introduce the Mark of the Beast.

The prophecy goes on to say this world government doesn't work so well. Just as Communism doesn't work so well. The heart of people is to live free and produce. When instead they are crushed, be it Communism or World Government, the people mourn. This world government will be *"divided; ...but the kingdom shall be partly strong, and partly broken."* This means the world government as a conglomeration of Muslims, Russians and Englishmen won't work well together.

PROVERBS 29:2, "When the righteous are in authority, the people rejoice: but WHEN THE WICKED BEARETH RULE, THE PEOPLE MOURN."

SUPERPOWERS

Daniel was given a second vision in Daniel, chapter 7. This vision is of the last four superpowers that we see in the world today: a lion representing England, an eagle representing America, a bear representing Russia and a leopard representing the Muslims. This brings us to the same fourth kingdom. In case you would like to know how we arrived at the leopards representing Muslims, we did an internet search showing a map of where leopards live and overlaid it with a second map showing where Muslims live. They match. The living, mating, and fighting habits of the leopards and Muslims also match. It was an easy conclusion—not to mention Nebuchadnezzar and much of Daniel play out the last days in what are today Muslim lands.

England was formed about 1,300 years ago. This vision stretches over the last 1,300 or so years, but our interest is how the fourth world government and the fourth superpower confirm the vision and conclude at the same time. This is the overlapping picture which will give us a good idea of how much time we have.

We get a real good picture of the future by linking these two prophecies, one a 2,500-year overview of world governments and the second an overview of the last 1,300 years covering the last four superpowers.

FOURTH KINGDOM:
Meshing of the Superpowers into the Final World Government

This last or fourth kingdom is the dreadful one, which will cause great trouble. It will be headed by two leaders: a political leader the Bible calls the Beast, and a religious leader also called the Beast. This is a little confusing. For separation sake, most students of Bible prophecy refer to the political leader as the Antichrist and the religious leader as the False Prophet, but there is one point of caution in that. Remember that the Antichrist is possessed by Lucifer midway through the seven-year tribulation. His goal is NOT to rule the world! NOT TO RULE THE WORLD! His objective is to SIT on the golden-covered chair or *"throne of God"* called the Ark of the Covenant. His desire is to receive, by force if necessary, the worship of all people on earth! He wants to be worshiped. He wants the worship God freely receives! Giving people his mark, or the number of his name is simply the easiest way to keep track of those in compliance. Christians who resist taking the Mark or the number are greatly blessed.

REVELATION 15:2, "And I saw as it were a sea of glass mingled with fire: and them that had GOTTEN THE VICTORY OVER THE BEAST, AND OVER HIS IMAGE, AND OVER HIS MARK, AND OVER THE NUMBER OF HIS NAME, stand on the sea of glass, having the harps of God."

WORLD GOVERNMENT: REVELATION 13

We look in Revelation, chapter 13, to give us an idea of when this final world government arrives. Understand that it is the same *"I AM"* Who gave the Torah to Moses and gave the Book of Revelation to Jesus, Who sent His angel and gave it to John. It is the same *"I AM"* Who has the plan to cause, *"ALL them that dwell on the earth,"* to form a world government and to gather all the tares and grapes for their final destruction at Armageddon.

Revelation 13 is linked closely to Daniel 7 in that we see the same four beasts with one exception. We discover the English Lion; the Russian Bear and the Muslim Leopard are all crushed into the same fourth and final world government. The beast that is missing is the Eagle. The Eagle's wings have been plucked, which is Bible prophecy lingo for America is no longer the Superpower she was before her wings were plucked near the time of forming the world government.

Ask yourself, "What nation is standing for the rights of the people and against removing national borders and sovereignty? What nation wants to see other nations operate as sovereign nations and opposes giving all power to a central government? What nation promotes Christianity and opposes the devil?" It is America. America is the last world police officer, standing in the gap, holding back the evil of world government. When America falls, probably in the early days of WWIII, spiritual darkness will fall upon the earth more rapidly than we can possibly imagine.

> DANIEL 7:4, "The first was like a lion, and had EAGLE'S WINGS: I beheld till the WINGS THEREOF WERE PLUCKED, and it was lifted up from the earth, and made stand upon the feet as a man, and a man's heart was given to it."

The elite print in their books, publications and internet that they want to remove all borders and consolidate all currencies, laws, militaries, and religions, and give us John Lennon's Happy New World Order. "Imagine there's no countries. It isn't hard to do ... I hope someday you'll join us and the **world will be as one**. Imagine no possessions. I wonder if you can. No need for greed or hunger. A brotherhood of man. Imagine all the people sharing all the world ... You ... You may say I'm a dreamer, but I'm not the only one. I hope someday you'll join us. And the **world will live as one**." –John Lennon, *Imagine*.

The world bankers revealed their plan in secret symbols on the back of the U.S. one-dollar bill. The illuminated all-seeing eye represents their name, the "Illuminati." The 1776 in Roman numerals on the bottom row of the pyramid stands for the year the Illuminati was formed. The thirteen rows stand for the thirteen levels within their organization. The capstone on the top is the goal of Lucifer to be the "Light bearer." Of course, we know Jesus is the chief cornerstone and the foundation and the real light of the world. That is the point. Lucifer's greatest goal is to sit on the Ark of the Covenant and proclaim himself "God" and be worshiped.

> 2 THESSALONIANS 2:4, "Who opposeth and exalteth himself above all that is called God, or that is worshipped; so that HE AS GOD SITTETH IN THE TEMPLE OF GOD, SHEWING HIMSELF THAT HE IS GOD."

WORLD GOVERNMENT

Daniel was told this fourth and final world government would be the strongest of all the previous governments, and why not? It will have 2,500 years of all the accumulated wealth, wisdom and technology of a modern world. It will crush all who resist its rise and divide the seven continents into ten global regions. Each global region will have a ruler who will blaspheme God. ONE of those rulers will rise to require all people on earth to worship him. Sad to say that all will comply—except those whose name is in the Book of Life.

As he rises to power, this unique ruler will overcome three other regional rulers. Only once this world government is in place will we see all the world purged and cleansed of most Christians. It is only then that Jesus will return to set up a Kingdom which will never be destroyed.

Daniel tells us about the fourth and final world government rising.

> DANIEL 7:7-9, *"After this I saw in the night visions, and behold a FOURTH BEAST, dreadful and terrible, and strong exceedingly; and it had great iron teeth: it devoured and brake in pieces, and stamped the residue with the feet of it: and it was diverse from all the beasts that were before it; and it had ten horns* [Ten global regions]. *I considered the horns, and, behold, there came up among them another LITTLE HORN* [THE BEAST], *before whom there were three of the first horns plucked up by the roots: and, behold, in this horn were eyes like the eyes of man* [He is a man], *and a MOUTH SPEAKING GREAT THINGS. I beheld till the* [Evil] *thrones were cast down, and the Ancient of days* [Father God] *did sit, whose garment was white as snow, and the hair of his head like the pure wool: his throne was like the fiery flame, and his wheels as burning fire."*

> DANIEL 7:20, 21, *"And of the ten horns that were in his head, and of the other which came up, and before whom three fell; even of that horn that had eyes, and a mouth that SPAKE VERY GREAT THINGS, whose LOOK was more stout than his fellows. I beheld, and the same horn made WAR WITH THE SAINTS, and prevailed against them;*

Here, Revelation tells us about the same fourth and final world government rising out of the people. These verses above and below are part of the verses from which the overview is drawn.

> REVELATION 13:3-8, *"And I saw one of his heads* [Not necessarily wounded in the head, but one of these global leaders is wounded] *as it were wounded to death; and his deadly wound was healed: and all the world wondered after the beast. And they worshipped the dragon which gave power unto the beast: and they worshipped the BEAST, saying, 'Who is like unto the beast? who is able to make war with him?' And there was given unto him a mouth SPEAKING GREAT THINGS and blasphemies; and power was given unto him to continue forty and two months.* [Great things mean he speaks evil things against all that is called God] *And he opened his mouth in blasphemy against God, to blaspheme his name, and his tabernacle, and them that dwell in heaven. And it was given unto him to make WAR WITH THE SAINTS, and to OVERCOME THEM: and power was given him over all kindreds, and tongues, and nations. And ALL THAT DWELL UPON THE EARTH SHALL WORSHIP HIM, WHOSE NAMES ARE NOT WRITTEN IN THE BOOK OF LIFE OF THE LAMB SLAIN FROM THE FOUNDATION OF THE WORLD."*

WAR WITH THE SAINTS

The fall of America is certainly a *"war with the saints."* Her fall is a victory for the Beast, but the Scripture above is speaking of the world AFTER the fall of America when the world government is in place. This is a picture of that world.

The world government rises out of the ashes of the longest and bloodiest world war— World WarIII. The elite will point to the fall of America as the failure of the Bible and as a foundation to build a world on. They will say we must make a world based neither upon the Bible nor any GROUP of religions.

The Antichrist will say religious differences ARE THE PROBLEM, and we must ALL have the SAME GOD. We must form a new world, "where the world will be as one," as John Lennon said.

War with the saints here is more a war of words and bullets. The Antichrist's rise to power is accomplished in part by his overcoming of three other regional leaders. There is a bullet war, but the war of words may kill more Christians than bullets.

Ken Peters in his DVD, *I Saw the Tribulation*, and Daniel Daves in his DVD, *I Saw the Dollar Dead*, say they were shown a new kind of television screen. It will be as thin as aluminum foil and cover the entire side of skyscrapers. The world powers will put the Antichrist on all channels, 24 hours a day, around the globe. The Antichrist is the only thing you can watch on all channels with his *"mouth speaking great things and blasphemies."* He attacks everything that is good. Don't be surprised when almost everyone around you accepts it and takes the Mark!

REVELATION 13:5, "And there was given unto him a MOUTH SPEAKING GREAT THINGS AND BLASPHEMIES; and power was given unto him to continue forty and two months. And he opened his mouth in BLASPHEMY AGAINST GOD, TO BLASPHEME HIS NAME, AND HIS TABERNACLE, AND THEM THAT DWELL IN HEAVEN. And it was given unto him to make WAR WITH THE SAINTS, and to overcome them: and power was given him over all kindreds, and tongues, and nations."

The Antichrist and False Prophet deceive them that dwell on the earth by the means of those miracles. Pulling fire from the sky is only one of the ways he deceives people. The Antichrist is given, a *"mouth speaking great things"*

— The False Prophet *"exerciseth all the power of the first beast before him."* They both are working to get all people on earth to worship the first Beast (Antichrist) whose deadly wound is healed.

A more comprehensive description in another chapter lists seven early signs to spot the Beast/Antichrist.

Today, we live in one of the longest stretches of peace in world history. Following the atomic bomb and the destruction in WWII we tend to think our society of peace and prosperity will never end. The Bible says the four world governments and the last four superpowers will both be destroyed at the same time as Jesus sets up His new Kingdom, which will endure forever.

Today, the United States, whose symbol is the Eagle, sits atop a vast empire of wealth, strength and prestige. Few people stop to think this world is not going to last, as we grab our cell phones and head out the door to the next daily fun adventure.

The summary of the last four world governments and the last four superpowers leads us to the conclusion that we are running out of time and are closer to the end. Watch for the fall of the fourth superpower (America) and the rise of the fourth world government! This will be an obvious sign the end is near.

Most people reading this book will live to see the return of Jesus. This is the last generation. This is the generation which will see Jesus return.

Israel is the fig tree mentioned in several places in the Bible. The verses following say that when Israel is still a young nation we are to know that Jesus' return is near. Notice Israel has leaves, but no fruit. Israel would have to accept Jesus in order to have fruit. That will not happen in great numbers. Jesus is saying when you see Israel become a nation again, His return is near, at the doors.

On July 19, 2018, Israel became a nation! Which just happens to be her 70th year as some people count it. I wonder, could PSALM 90:10 be saying Israel will only exist as a nation in the last days for 80 years? Just asking??? I am not saying Jesus returns in 2028.

> MATTHEW 24:32-34, *"Now learn a parable of the FIG TREE; When his branch is yet tender, and putteth forth leaves, ye know that summer is nigh: So likewise ye, when ye shall see all these things, know that it is near, even at the doors. Verily I say unto you, 'THIS GENERATION SHALL NOT PASS, TILL ALL THESE THINGS BE FULFILLED.'"*

PSALM 90:10, *"The days of our years are threescore years and ten [70 years]; and if by reason of strength they be FOURSCORE YEARS [80 YEARS], yet is their strength labour and sorrow; for it is soon cut off, and WE FLY AWAY."*

- 1948: Israel became the "State of Israel"
- 1967: Jerusalem was recaptured
- 2018: THE LAND'S BIBLICAL IDENTITY RESTORED. Israel became a nation!

2018 is Israel's 70th birthday. 70 years!

What happens when Israel turns 80 years old?

On July 19, 2018, Israel became a nation! Israel has been a "State," but as of July 19, 2018, Israel became a "Nation!" This may be the sign that *"this generation shall not pass, till all these things [prophecies] be fulfilled?"* Are we about to see many of the end time prophecies begin to be fulfilled?

Here is what some say Israel becoming a Nation means:

- The land of Israel officially belongs to the Jewish people only, (God's covenant with Abraham, Isaac, and Jacob)
- Hebrew is the official language of the nation
- The Biblical calendar is now the official calendar of Israel
- Keeping the Biblical Sabbath is now a nationwide requirement
- The Biblical Feasts are officially recognized by the state and must be observed
- The government of Israel must help in gathering exiles
- Jerusalem is the undivided capital of Israel
- Jewish settlement in Israel is now officially supported by the government
- Israel shall officially work to preserve the Jewish religion
- The Star of David is the official flag
- The Second Temple's Menorah is the official state symbol
- The Hatikvah poem expressing Israelites' prophetic desire to return to Zion is the official national anthem

The "State of Israel" becomes a nation, officially known as just "Israel"

WHAT IS COMING?

From God's holy point of view, looking into our spirits, America has already fallen in terms of righteousness and has already become *"the habitation of devils and the cage of every unclean and hateful bird."* The forming of the last world government is only a few years away. The prophets say that when America falls those who hate Jesus and those who love the Antichrist will rise with boldness and anger and begin to cleanse the world of those who rebel against their grand new plan to form a perfect world society with the new leader as the new god. They will consider all who resist to be rebels against the new society of the future and kill many believers!

REVELATION 18:2, "And he cried mightily with a strong voice, saying, 'Babylon THE GREAT [Make America GREAT Again] *is fallen, is fallen, and is become the habitation of devils, and the hold of every foul spirit, and a cage of every unclean and hateful bird.'"*

MATTHEW 24:12, "And because iniquity shall abound, the love of many shall wax cold."

The evil intolerance for Christian resistors will grow until their patience runs out, and they finally decide that all who do NOT want to become part of their New World Order must be killed. The mass killings will begin, and many who were once Christians will turn and join the new order. Many will compromise by thinking, "This can't be the Antichrist. God would never expect my children to starve, rather than to join them."

Former Christians will report true believers to the New World Order, and the new Hitler/Antichrist will have perfected the art of cleansing the land. No more plumes of body ash, using inefficient ovens, but now as Prophet Maurice Sklar was shown, they will have new human disposal Kiosks disposing of rebels in large numbers. The New Society will eliminate resistors by the millions, quick and clean. No mess, no fuss. People will just disappear. Unless Jesus returns, no flesh will be saved.

"I saw multitudes of Tribulation saints refusing to renounce Jesus as LORD. They were starving, many of them, but still refused to take the stamp on their bodies so they could eat and live. There was what looked like kiosks that were in every little town. They advertised food and water, only if you went inside them and took the electronic mark. Some went in, bowed down to a holographic movie image of the Antichrist and were branded in their hands and foreheads with an electronic tattoo-like stamp. **When they came out, if they came out, they had a zombie-like look.** Their minds and souls were gone. It looked like they had a **spiritual lobotomy.** Then these immediately joined the armies of those police units and were given weapons after they were fed and drank and rested in the kiosk. **They were like robots doing the Antichrist's bidding.** I knew that they were lost forever. But, quite a few did not make it out. They were tortured mentally and physically inside the kiosk thing, but, if they still refused the mark of the beast, there was a laser that shot through their brain and heart and sliced their heads off. Then they were immediately incinerated. Nothing but ashes remained. This was the most horrifying of all. It made the Nazi death camps look like a picnic, if that is possible. Millions of people were executed in this way via computer systems automatically with such precision and efficiency that I marveled that something like this was even possible and could take place on such a large scale. The technology was more advanced than I had ever seen."
—Prophet Maurice Sklar, March 15, 2014. *https://sklarministries.com/*

HOW TO KNOW JESUS AS LORD AND SAVIOR

You might look at human existence this way. God made the heavens and the earth and formed man. He foresaw that man would fall and need a Savior—His Son, His own flesh to die to correct the fall. He made the heavens and the earth in six days. To God a day is a thousand years. He made the heavens, the earth, and all living creatures in six days and rested on the seventh day. God has given mankind six 1,000-year-days to work out their eternal existence in glory and will rest on the seventh day [Millennium].

Along the way, He has given us a book to guide us to eternal life, if we can find it, believe it, and follow it to find Christ. That guide in the English language is the King James Version Bible. The confirmation the Bible is truly from God are the prophecies within the Bible. As life is not easy, likewise, understanding the Bible is not easy, and understanding the prophecies are even more difficult. The goal of this book is to help more people understand the prophecies, and thus, find their way to put their name in the Book of Life through the shed blood of His Son, Jesus- the only way to eternal life.

ROMANS 3:23, "For all have sinned, and come short of the glory of God;"

EPHESIANS 2:8, 9, "For by grace are ye saved through faith; and that not of yourselves: it is the gift of God: Not of works, lest any man should boast."

ROMANS 10:9, "That if thou shalt confess with thy mouth the Lord Jesus, and shalt believe in thine heart that God hath raised him from the dead, thou shalt be saved. For with the heart man believeth unto righteousness; and with the mouth confession is made unto salvation."

ACTS 2:38, "Then Peter said unto them, 'Repent, and be baptized every one of you in the name of Jesus Christ for the remission of sins, and ye shall receive the gift of the Holy Ghost.'"

Simply ask Jesus to forgive you of your sins or mistakes and come into your heart and be your God. This simple prayer from your heart can be the beginning of your new life as a Christian. Follow Jesus by being baptized and join a church of other believers. You can seek out a mentor and/or Bible Study group that will help in discipling you as a new follower of Christ.

WORLD GOVERNMENT

We are not in a world government yet, but a major war like WWIII will probably move us into one at its conclusion. It is possible to have a world government form before the fall of America, but most students of prophecy believe the fall of America will occur before the rise of the final world government.

On April 15, 2018, French President Emmanuel Macron spoke to the United States Congress for over 45 minutes. His primary message was a call for world government. He is not the only leader calling for it. Many leaders say global government is the only way to have global peace. God has laid on their heart to form a world government. It is the plan of God to gather all nations who hate God to attack Jerusalem, where Jesus will return and turn them to ashes with the Morning Star, with the breath of His nostrils, with the light sword coming out of His mouth.

There are many prophecies which must be fulfilled before Jesus can return. The most blatant of them is the prophecy of world government. Jesus cannot return until there is a world government. Watch for world government to form soon.

SUMMARY: EVENTS TO WATCH FOR ...

First is the spiritual fall of America from Christian standards into the heart of evil. REVELATION 18:2— done

Israel gives the Palestinians a State, allowing Israel time to strengten their military. JOEL 3:2

The newspaper headline will read: **"Olmert Ushers in Palestinian State"** [She heard it pronounced, it sounded like "Omer," she is not sure of the spelling Omer or Olmert.]

A great catastrophe will hit America. Headline: **"Catastrophe Hits America"**

Massive amounts of crude oil will be discovered in Israel—at least twice that of the Arabs DEUTERONOMY 33:24; GENESIS 49:25-30 more.

Oil will finance the building of Israel's military. DEUTERONOMY 33:19; JEREMIAH 33:7; ISAIAH 60:5

America cries for help. Headline: **"One of America's Greatest Times of Need"**

Israel refuses to help. Headline: **"Israel Refuses Help to America"**

Israel will be attacked. Headline: **"Israel is Attacked, America Sends Troops"**

Headline: **"Chaos Reigns As Americans Protest Help to Israel"**

(Not necessarily in this order)

The fall of America will start with an internal Revolution started by the Communists ...

Then the physical fall of America occurs when Russia attacks in a surprise nuclear attack. REVELATION 18—soon

America surrenders almost immediately, removing the Christians begins shortly

WWIII rages with great bloodshed- DANIEL 7:21, 13:7; REVELATION 6:9-11, 7:14, 16:6, 17:6, 18:24, "war against the saints."

At the end of WWIII is probably when the world will set up the final world government.

Israel emerges the great victor of WWIII and gets back all her land from the Euphrates to the Nile— JEREMIAH 51:5, 19; ZECHARIAH 12:6; GENESIS 15:18

The world is filled with blood and war-torn nations

Almost all those calling themselves "by My name" will move to the very victorious prosperous land of Israel— ISAIAH 43:5-7

Israel is the last safe place for believers on earth to live —ZECHARIAH 12:3

The forming of a world government is based out of the Roman/iron/ European Empire— DANIEL 2:40

More wars rage replacing the old Bible-based order with a new secular, no-god order. (Novus Ordo Seclorum)

The Beast that ascends out of the bottomless pit will be the resurrected King Nebuchadnezzar — DANIEL 4:16.

Probably Nebuchadnezzar's seed is mingled with Lucifer, *"they shall mingle themselves with the seed of men."* DANIEL 2:43.

The Antichrist (Resurrected Nebuchadnezzar) puts down three other global-regional rulers *"before whom three fell."* DANIEL 7:20.

The Antichrist rises from a small nation and obtains the kingdom by flatteries—DANIEL 11:31.

The Antichrist comes back to life and gains international recognition— REVELATION 13:12

All the world is amazed and "wonders after the Beast." DANIEL 8:24; REVELATION 12:3, 13:13, 17:6, 8.

The Beast will probably be linked with the global computer system and has the answers to all questions. *"He had power to give life unto the image of the beast."* REVELATION 13:15.

Israel doesn't work well with the world government, but many Israelis love the Antichrist— JOHN 5:43.

In the days of this fourth world government, Jesus will return to set up His Kingdom which shall never end— DANIEL 2:44.

Chapter 6
144,000 FIRSTFRUITS

THE KEY is the word FIRSTFRUITS. The SECRET DOOR to understand Bible prophecy is linking the word FIRSTFRUITS in the Feasts, Leviticus 23:10-13, to FIRSTRFUITS in REVELATION 14:4.

> LEVITICUS 23:10, "... ye shall bring a sheaf of the FIRSTFRUITS of your [Barley] harvest unto the priest:"

> REVELATION 14:5, "... These were redeemed from among men, being the FIRSTFRUITS unto God and to the Lamb."

The word FIRSTFRUITS links the Feasts given to Moses to the Revelation given to John. By linking them we can put many prophecies in place—especially those concerning the last seven months! Many prophecies—especially in Revelation are fulfilled in connection with the feasts of the Lord given to Moses.

Refer to my *Seven-Year Tribulation Chart* as you read this.

The SEALS play over SEVEN YEARS. The TRUMPETS play over SEVEN MONTHS. The VIALS play over SEVEN DAYS. The *Seven-Year Tribulation Chart* has "call out boxes" for the first four Trumpets. The first four Trumpets occur quickly, possibly within a few weeks of Firstfruits and may be associated with the final Passover and Unleavened Bread Feasts. Meaning the first four Trumpets probably happen very quickly and within weeks of the final Firstfruits. Remember the Trumpets play over the last seven months, but that does NOT mean that one Trumpet sounds every thirty days. It may be that several Trumpets sound over a week or a month.

The 144,000 are resurrected BEFORE the locusts of the fifth trumpet. We know this because when the locusts are coming out of the smoke, they are instructed to sting ONLY those WITHOUT the seal of God. This means the 144,000 are already on the earth. This links the 144,000 and locusts as a date stamp associated with Firstfruits.

Remember the SEALS play over SEVEN YEARS. The TRUMPETS play over SEVEN MONTHS. The VIALS play over SEVEN DAYS. This understanding of the times was one of my major received revelations. A revelation is NOT information gleaned from reading Scripture. This revelation arrived by just popping into my head. It was not an audible voice, but I heard words in my spirit saying, "The Seals play over seven years. The Trumpets play over seven months, and the Vials play over seven days." I had to find scriptural proof to confirm it. I looked more closely in the Word and found the following reasons why this unique information—gift from the Lord was true.

Revelation 9:5 and 9:10 both use the word "months." The locusts sting for five MONTHS. This is further confirmation that the SEVEN TRUMPETS PLAY OVER SEVEN MONTHS.

The word "months" is found TWICE in the fifth Trumpet and is NOT found in ANY of the other Seals or Vials!

> REVELATION 9:5, "And to them it was given that they should not kill them, but that they should be tor-

mented five MONTHS: and their torment was as the torment of a scorpion, when he striketh a man."

REVELATION 9:10, "And they had tails like unto scorpions, and there were stings in their tails: and their power was to hurt men five MONTHS."

Confirmation that the VIALS play over SEVEN DAYS is found in the second and third Vials. All drinking water on earth is turned to blood because the blood of saints and prophets has been shed! This is NOT saying the water turned red because of some red algae, or has been tinted to a red color. Scripture says the water literally will be turned to blood as in the days of Pharaoh when the water turned to blood. The Lord judges those who shed the blood of saints and prophets by giving them blood to drink. How long can mankind live without drinking water? Only a few DAYS! This is part of confirming the VIALS play the last SEVEN DAYS.

REVELATION 16:3-5, "And the second angel poured out his vial upon the sea; and it became AS THE BLOOD OF A DEAD MAN: and every living soul died in the sea. And the third angel poured out his vial upon the rivers and fountains of waters; and THEY BECAME BLOOD. And I heard the angel of the waters say, 'Thou art righteous, O Lord, which art, and wast, and shalt be, because thou hast judged thus. FOR THEY HAVE SHED THE BLOOD OF SAINTS AND PROPHETS, AND THOU HAST GIVEN THEM BLOOD TO DRINK; for they are worthy.'"

REVELATION 9:3, 4, "And there came out of the smoke LOCUSTS upon the earth: and unto them was given power, as the scorpions of the earth have power. And it was commanded them that they should not hurt the grass of the earth, neither any green thing, neither any tree; but ONLY THOSE MEN WHICH HAVE NOT THE SEAL OF GOD IN THEIR FOREHEADS."

Let's look at the Lamb and the 144,000. The place of the 144,000 is one of the most important points to understand the Secret Door to Understand Bible prophecies!!

REVELATION 14:1, 4, 5, "And I looked, and, lo, a LAMB stood on the mount SION, and with him an hundred forty and four thousand, having his Father's name written in their foreheads. ... These are they which were not defiled with women; for they are virgins. These are they which follow the Lamb whithersoever he goeth. These were redeemed from among men, being the FIRSTFRUITS unto God and to the Lamb. And in their mouth was found NO GUILE: for they are without fault before the throne of God."

Here is an example of how some revelations arrived.

I was teaching this one Sunday morning at our Church. At this point many of the revelations previously given in this book were still unknown. All thirty of them came by God revealing them to my heart. Only two came in visions—the vision to write this book and the secret door of prophecy. I give Jesus all glory.

One of our congregation members said, "You know, the Firstfruits in Revelation 14 must have something to do with the Feasts. They have to!" Yes! What was I thinking?! Of course! I knew that! I had been so busy memorizing Revelation the thought had not occurred to me, so I began to STUDY THE FEASTS, especially in connection to the Firstfruits of Revelation 14. That Saturday I spent all day studying the Feasts. Praying the whole time, "Lord, give me revelations. Show me the deep and secret things.

God, give me knowledge and skill in all learning and wisdom. Help me to understand your Word."

That next Sunday morning in Adult Sunday School, I presented these new revelations and my improved prophecy chart. Before we started the discussion, I asked the congregation to just read every word on the chart, which took about 15 minutes. Then the questions began, and they all agreed the chart was correct.

I like to study the feasts the way they are written in my KJV Bible, the fourteenth day of the first month, the first day of the seventh month or Trumpets, Atonement, etc., rather than using the Jewish names like Yom Kippur. It seems to make it simpler for the western gentile mind. In the process of reading through the Feasts, I discovered the answer to a major question we had all been discussing. "What is the age of the 144,000?" And there it was! The 144,000 were one-year-old at the time of their deaths!

LEVITICUS 23:12, "And ye shall offer that day when ye wave the sheaf AN HE LAMB without blemish OF THE FIRST YEAR for a burnt offering unto the LORD."

The Barley ripens in the Spring. It is the first harvest to ripen each year hence "Firstfruits." The final barley harvest is a shadow picture of the 144,000 from each of the 12 tribes. We know that barley represents the Israelites because of this verse.

REVELATION 14:1, 4, "And I looked, and, lo, a Lamb stood on the mount Sion, and with him an hundred forty and four thousand, having his Father's name written in their foreheads ... These [144,000] were redeemed from among men, being the FIRSTFRUITS unto God and to the Lamb."

Being less than one year old at their deaths explains why they had no guile in their mouth because THEY NEVER LEARNED TO TALK. It also explains why they were not defiled with a woman and without fault before the throne of God.

For the Feast of Firstfruits, God commands Moses to *"bring a sheaf of the firstfruits"* to the priest. A *"sheaf"* is a handful, representing a small portion of the full barley harvest remaining in the field. This is the purest of pure of the children of the 12 tribes, a small sampling of the millions of the sons of Israel yet in the graves. This resurrected 144,000 will be resurrected and the first to appear on Mount Zion the first day of the final Feast of Firstfruits. This is why leaven is not allowed to be added to the barley. These 144,000 can stand before the throne of God because they are without sin. The 144,000 are a picture of the first to rise from the grave since Jesus. Jesus was the firstfruits *"of them that slept,"* the 144,000 are the firstfruits of *"the harvest."*

LEVITICUS 23:10, "... When ye be come into the land which I give unto you, and shall reap the harvest thereof, then ye shall BRING A SHEAF OF THE FIRSTFRUITS of your harvest unto the priest:"

1 CORINTHIANS 15:20, "But now is Christ risen from the dead, and become the FIRSTFRUITS OF THEM THAT SLEPT."

MATTHEW 13:39, "The enemy that sowed them is the devil;

THE HARVEST IS THE END OF THE WORLD; and the reapers are the angels."

They are probably the FIRSTBORN in the family because of this verse.

EXODUS 13:12, *"THAT THOU SHALT SET APART UNTO THE LORD ALL THAT OPENETH THE MATRIX, and every firstling that cometh of a beast which thou hast; THE MALES SHALL BE THE LORD'S."*

The feasts are a "rehearsal" or a "shadow of things to come." Everyone knows the feasts will one day play again, but when? God placed a Secret Door within the feasts to be revealed in the last days. Like Daniel was not written for Daniel's day, it was a message for the last generation, a message to the generation that would see the return of Jesus. The Secret Door allows us to see what is going to happen in the prophecies through shadow pictures in the feasts.

THE MESSAGE OF DANIEL IS FOR OUR GENERATION, telling us that as in the days of Nebuchadnezzar, once AGAIN, the Beast will set up an image and require all people to worship it, but the next image will be an image of the Beast!

Revelation was not written for John the Revelator and the people of 96 AD, but rather for the last generation. The Feasts, Daniel, Revelation and most of the rest of the prophecies were almost all written for this, the last generation to guide us through the last days!

This handful of barley is mixed with oil, but NO LEAVEN can be added. This makes one large hard cracker when cooked. The shadow picture for the last generation is:

A small group of firstborn males from the 12 tribes who died in their first year and now resurrected on the 17th day of the first month of the year Jesus returns is the FINAL FULFILLMENT OF THE FIRSTFRUITS of the barley harvest. These 144,000 represent the larger barley harvest still in the field or grave, which will be resurrected on the day of Atonement. Atonement is the day of the Great White Throne judgment in which all dead NOT in Christ stand before Jesus.

The 144,000 literally stand on Mt. Zion with Jesus about six months before Armageddon and follow the Lamb withersoever He goes. In that Jesus is called "the Lamb" is further confirmation that he has NOT yet been crowned KING OF KINGS and LORD OF LORDS. At this point He is still the "Prince of the Kings of the Earth."

As Jesus walked around for 40 days before He ascended to the Father, He MAY walk around with the 144,000 for 50 days until the Wheat harvest rises, then go to the Marriage Supper of the Lamb. After Firstfruits, Jesus walked around for 40 days, then ascended, and when He returns on Firstfruits, again he may walk around for 50 days until Pentecost, when He takes the Barley and Wheat to the Marriage.

Some have wondered if the 144,000 will still be in a one-year-old spirit-body, and if so, are they big enough to ride a horse? The 144,000 could be fully-grown men. They may have died as a one-year old and gone to be in the Bosom of Abraham, maturing in Heaven. They could have been aborted or ripped from their mothers' wombs in terrible wars. We can conclude that since they return with Jesus on white horses for Armageddon, whether large or small, they will ride horses. The Bible doesn't give us a clue to the size of their body. Some have speculated they will be fully grown. My guess is they will be fully mature. That is a guess. In that they have "no leaven" the picture is these 144,000 have no sin as opposed to the Wheat harvest which has leaven/sin, but washed in the blood of the Lamb.

SUMMARY OF FIRSTFRUITS:

The 144,000 are 12,000 males of the first year from each of the 12 tribes having died before learning to talk and have no fault before the throne of God. They are the firstfruits of the end time barley harvest. They will be the first to rise from the grave as part of the end time harvest. Remember Jesus was the first *"from them that slept"* whereas the barley harvest is the first of the "end time harvest." Remember, *"Let both grow together until the harvest."* Since we know "Firstfruits" doesn't mean "second fruits" or "third-fruits," that is an easy conclusion. No one since Jesus has received their glorified bodies from the grave before the 144,000.

SUMMARY 144,000

The 144,000 are the firstfruits barley harvest

144,000 are one-year-old males

These were redeemed from among men

These are the firstfruits unto God and the Lamb

Clothed in white garments

No guile in their mouth

Not defiled with woman

Without fault before the throne of God

Follow the Lamb withersoever He goeth

They confirm the first sliver or full dark moon HAS been sighted and that the barley is ABIB.

At this point we know "the day and hour that no man knoweth."

They are the shout, "The Bridegroom cometh, go ye out to meet him."

From this moment on, all the other prophecies concerning the last seven months can be laid in order!

They are the most important benchmark of prophecy because once we see the 144,000 we know so much more.

They are the Secret Door to understand Bible prophecy!

Once the 144,000 arrive we now know:

The DAY AND HOUR that "no man knoweth" is now known.

This is the year Jesus will return and Judgment Seat of Christ

The day and hour the Wheat Harvest is resurrected.

The day Jesus will return, Armageddon begins. [After sunset]

The day the Marriage door is shut

The day those not found written in the Book are cast into the Lake of Fire.

The day and hour of the Atonement Great White Throne

The day and hour the New Jerusalem comes down from Heaven.

Chapter 7
THE NAME ON THE FOREHEAD:

I tell this story to make the point of how important the 144,000 are as it relates to Bible prophecy.

After Church my wife had to go to our daughter's Baby Shower, so I went home. I decided to take a break from studying the Bible and relax and read a novel. While reading, the Lord spoke to my heart, "What is the name on the foreheads of the 144,000?" Pausing, I answered out loud, "I don't know." The thought never occurred to me. I never thought it was that important. To answer His question, I quoted the verse out loud to myself.

> REVELATION 14:1, *"And I looked, and, lo, a Lamb stood on the mount Sion, and with him an hundred forty and four thousand, HAVING HIS FATHER'S NAME WRITTEN IN THEIR FOREHEADS."*

I answered Him out loud saying, "That would be Yod Hay Vav Hay. Yahweh," and went back to reading my novel.

The question came again, "What is the name on the foreheads of the 144,000?"

I stopped and took the question more serious. "Okay, Lord, apparently it is important, and Yahweh is not the right answer." And I quoted the verse again out loud, *"... I looked, and, lo, a Lamb stood on the mount Sion, and with him an hundred forty and four thousand, having his Father's name written in their foreheads."* I thought, "Hmmmm ... name on the foreheads?"

I concluded, "It has to be Yahweh, or Yeshua, or Jesus, or God, or something like that. Okay, 'Jesus,' that is my answer." I said it like I was on some game show.

I went back to reading, assuming I had answered the question correctly, but no! Then the third time it was the answer which came to me! I would have never thought of this in a million years! This was wisdom from on high! "Their father's name," was the answer I was given. It was not an audible voice nor even words spoken. I was made to know the 144,000 have their "earthly father's name" on their foreheads!

You see, these are 144,000 "of the first year" males who apparently had died over the years having never learned to speak and, of course, never had a woman. In the eyes of God, they were perfect—without fault before the throne of God—without leaven! This is the Barley harvest, the Firstfruits unto God! They are special! They arrive about six months before Jesus returns in the clouds on a white horse to destroy the tares and grapes.

Try to picture the situation. We have the Two Witnesses, casting curses upon the earth and the Beast and False Prophet in Jerusalem requiring worship. All the while, 144,000 men, probably in full-grown glorified bodies in white garments, appear on Mt. Zion with the Lamb. Remember, Jesus is not King of kings yet; He is still the Lamb of God, the Prince of the Kings of the Earth. He is not on a white horse yet. These 144,000 men in white garments are following Jesus, walking all over Jerusalem! How do you explain that? For what? These are the sign, *"Behold the bridegroom cometh, GO YE OUT TO MEET HIM!"* Please notice, we are TOLD to GO OUT AND MEET HIM! If this is literal, and a person were living in Jerusalem, I assume one could go meet the Lamb of God. Remember, we are told to "go out and meet him." I realize that is far from the picture of how most people have understood the return of Jesus, but how else would you interpret Matthew 25:6?

This is not Armageddon! This is not Jesus returning on the clouds and putting his foot down on the Mount of Olives. This is Jesus the Lamb upon Mt. Zion which is about a thirty-minute walk from the Mount of Olives.

> *MATTHEW 25:6, "And at midnight there was a cry made, 'Behold, the bridegroom cometh; GO YE OUT TO MEET HIM.'"*

> *REVELATION 14:1, 4, 5, "And I looked, and, lo, a Lamb stood on the mount Sion, and with him an hundred forty and four thousand, HAVING HIS FATHER'S NAME WRITTEN IN THEIR FOREHEADS. These are they which were NOT DEFILED WITH WOMEN; FOR THEY ARE VIRGINS. These are they which follow the Lamb whithersoever he goeth. These were REDEEMED FROM AMONG MEN, BEING THE FIRSTFRUITS unto God and to the Lamb. And in their mouth was found NO GUILE: for they are WITHOUT FAULT before the throne of God."*

These are the very first humans since Jesus arose from the dead to rise from the grave and receive their glorified bodies because they are without fault before the throne of God! Others have ascended to heaven, but these are the Firstfruits to receive the new GLORIFIED BODY. We know some have arisen from the grave, but these being the Firstfruits are the first to receive the glorified body.

Are you sure, Stan? Are you sure their earthly fathers name is on their forehead? Yes, and here is how we know.

You recall David had an affair with Bathsheba, and God allowed David's seven-day old child to die. This child of David will probably be one of these 144,000 children with "David" written on his forehead!

> *2 SAMUEL 12:14, 18, "Howbeit, because by this deed thou hast given great occasion to the enemies of the LORD to blaspheme, the child also that is born unto thee SHALL SURELY DIE. And it came to pass ON THE SEVENTH DAY, THAT THE CHILD DIED ..."*

I have been asked the question: "Wouldn't it be Yahweh or Jehovah or Yeshua because the word "Father" in the KJV is capitalized?" I found a place where God wanted to say "Yahweh" and "New Jerusalem" is written on the forehead of overcomers, and it was written thus:

> *REVELATION 3:12, "Him that overcometh will I make a pillar in the temple of my God, and he shall go no more out: and I will write upon him the name of MY GOD, and the name of THE CITY OF MY GOD ..."*

When he wanted to tell us, the name written on the foreheads of some is "Jesus" it was written thus:

> *REVELATION 22:3, 4, "And there shall be no more curse: but the throne of God and of the Lamb shall be in it; and his servants shall serve him: And they shall see HIS FACE; and HIS NAME shall be in their foreheads."*

But He chose to write it this way meaning, "His EARTHLY father's name."

REVELATION 14:1, "And I looked, and, lo, a Lamb stood on the mount Sion, and with him an hundred forty and four thousand, having HIS FATHER'S NAME written in their foreheads."

Why is that significant? Can you imagine the feeling in David's heart when he sees the son he lost and his name "David" is written on his forehead?!!! But the real significance is to bring importance to the 144,000. The 144,000 is one of THE MOST IMPORTANT EVENTS of the last days. They tie the Levitical Feasts to the Book of Revelations and give us the timing of many of the prophecies! They are the Firstfruits; they are the BENCHMARK; they are the shout, "THE BRIDEGROOM COMETH." Once we see them, we have actual dates and correct order for fulfillment for many of the prophecies for the last seven months!

Chapter 8
TWO WITNESSES (Not Enoch and Elijah)

Prophecy says in the middle of Daniel's seventieth week, commonly referred to as the seven-year Tribulation, the Antichrist/Beast will sit upon the Ark of the Covenant, committing the Abomination of Desolation. The False Prophet will use great miracles to deceive the people of earth. He will order the world to make an image of the Beast. The Bible refers to this manmade being as an IMAGE because it is not made in the image of God, but rather in the image of the Beast. It is probably going to be half-Lucifer, (mingle themselves with the seed of men, Daniel 2:43), and half-human. That might explain why Daniel says he looks different than normal humans, because he is not a normal human.

> DANIEL 7:20, "And of the ten horns that were in his head, and of the other which came up, and before whom three fell; even of that horn that had eyes, and a mouth that spake very great things, whose LOOK WAS MORE STOUT THAN HIS FELLOWS."

> DANIEL 8:23, "And in the latter time of their kingdom, when the transgressors are come to the full, a king of FIERCE COUNTENANCE, and understanding dark sentences, shall stand up."

At any rate, the image of the Beast will speak and order all people on earth to worship the first beast/Antichrist. All resistors will be beheaded. The Antichrist and False Prophet will speak great words against Jesus, the Bible, and display lying signs and wonders. God meets them step for step, inch for inch, and curse for lying miracles. This last generation will see seven-fold miracles—miracles like no one in the history of man has seen! No one going back to Adam has ever seen these magnificent miracles. The New World Order leaders will try to stop the miracles, but they will not be able to succeed.

God sends two of His greatest Prophets [REVELATION 11] to walk the streets of Jerusalem, bringing His truth, and sending curses upon the evil done in Jerusalem. God uses these Two Witnesses to match the Beast and False Prophet step for step, inch for inch and miracle for miracle. This is the final play of the Elijah and the Prophets of Baal! This is the second greatest contest between God and the Devil with the return of Jesus being the greatest battle.

> REVELATION 11:3-13, "And I will give power unto my TWO WITNESSES, and they shall PROPHESY A THOUSAND TWO HUNDRED AND THREESCORE DAYS, clothed in sackcloth. These are the two olive trees, and the two candlesticks standing before the God of the earth. And if any man will hurt them, FIRE PROCEEDETH OUT OF THEIR MOUTH, AND DEVOURETH THEIR ENEMIES: and if any man will hurt them, he must in this manner be killed. These have power to shut heaven, that it rain not in the days of their prophecy: and have power over waters to turn them to blood, and to smite the earth with all plagues, as often as they will. And when they shall have finished their testimony, THE BEAST THAT ASCENDETH OUT OF THE BOTTOMLESS

PIT SHALL MAKE WAR AGAINST THEM, AND SHALL OVERCOME THEM, AND KILL THEM. And their dead bodies shall lie in the street of the great city, which spiritually is called Sodom and Egypt, where also our Lord was crucified. And they of the people and kindreds and tongues and nations shall see their dead bodies three days and an half, and shall not suffer their dead bodies to be put in graves. And they that dwell upon the earth shall rejoice over them, and make merry, and shall send gifts one to another; because these two prophets tormented them that dwelt on the earth. And AFTER THREE DAYS AND AN HALF THE SPIRIT OF LIFE FROM GOD ENTERED INTO THEM, AND THEY STOOD UPON THEIR FEET; and great fear fell upon them which saw them. And they heard a great voice from heaven saying unto them, 'COME UP HITHER.' And they ascended up to heaven in a cloud; and their enemies beheld them. And the same hour was there a great earthquake, and the tenth part of the city fell, and in the earthquake were slain of men seven thousand: and the remnant were affrighted, and gave glory to the God of heaven."*

One of the greatest questions in Bible prophecy is, **"Who are the Two Witnesses?"** In my early days as a prophecy student I made the same mistake that most Bible prophecy students make. I had lightly read:

HEBREWS 9:27, "And as it is appointed unto men ONCE TO DIE, but after this the judgment:

I had read also that one of the Two Witnesses must be Elijah, the prophet, due to this verse:

MALACHI 4:5, "Behold, I will send you Elijah the prophet before the coming of the great and dreadful day of the LORD."

My first conclusion was in order to find the identity of the Two Witnesses all I had to do was find two men in the Old Testament who didn't die. They would be the Two Witnesses! Wrong! I concluded they had to be Enoch and Elijah–right? They didn't die. A common misunderstanding. This was the first of many misunderstandings that would be corrected through personal revelations God would give me as I memorized Revelation and wrote this book. Before I began to memorize the Book of Revelation, I knew NOTHING that is in this book, NOTHING! God supplied the information and wrote this book.

Jesus said that the prophecy which said Elijah would come was fulfilled. John the Baptist fulfilled the prophecy. Don't look for Elijah. He is not coming. He has already come.

MATTHEW 11:13, 14, "For all the prophets and the law prophesied until John. And if ye will receive it, THIS IS ELIAS, WHICH WAS FOR TO COME."

LUKE 1:13, 17a, "But the angel said unto him, 'Fear not, Zacharias: for thy prayer is heard; and thy wife Elisabeth shall bear thee a son [John the Baptist], and thou shalt call his name John. And he shall go before him IN THE SPIRIT AND POWER OF ELIAS ...'"

Here is where a lot of people are thrown off course.

DEUTERONOMY 19:15b, "... at the mouth of TWO WITNESSES, OR AT THE MOUTH OF THREE WITNESSES, SHALL THE MATTER BE ESTABLISHED."

HEBREWS 9:27, "And as it is appointed unto men ONCE TO DIE, but after this the judgment:"

Concerning Hebrews 9:27, where is the second confirming verse? You see every major doctrinal point in the Bible is ALWAYS backed up by a second or third confirming statement. I had NOT gone to the trouble to see that HEBREWS 9:27 only occurs ONCE in the Bible. That would have weakened my entire theory of Enoch and Elijah being the Two Witnesses.

Is the Bible wrong? Is it saying that sometimes a person does come back to life? Is HEBREWS 9:27 wrong? Is a verse in the KJV Bible wrong? No, it is just saying it is NOT A MAJOR DOCTRINAL POINT. It doesn't stand necessarily as a rule EVERY time because it is not found in the Bible TWICE.

Is it true that people can come back to life? Yes. The Beast comes back to life! Others in the Gospels were reported to have come back to life. I had to conclude that Hebrews 9:27 is not ALWAYS a hard and fast rule! The focus is more on the surety of the judgment.

KING NEBUCHADNEZZAR ASCENDS OUT OF THE BOTTOMLESS PIT AND IS THE BEAST OF REVELATION

These verses say Nebuchadnezzar is like a stump. A stump of a tree can come back to life. A prophecy from Daniel that Nebuchadnezzar would be given a beast's heart was fulfilled in the life of Nebuchadnezzar. It could be repeated as indicated by the *"band of iron and brass,"* as he rises to become the "Beast" of Revelation and the political ruler of the world. Brass is the Grecian Empire, and Iron is the Roman Empire. They both encircle the stump and could be a hint that THE STUMP GROWS AGAIN during the Roman Empire. Nebuchadnezzar's resurrection after his first death would take place during the last world government. A resurrected Nebuchadnezzar could be the Beast that *"ascendeth out of the bottomless pit,"* also known as the Antichrist.

DANIEL 4:14-16, "He cried aloud, and said thus, 'Hew down the tree, and cut off his branches, shake off his leaves, and scatter his fruit: let the beasts get away from under it, and the fowls from his branches: Nevertheless leave the STUMP OF HIS ROOTS [Comes back to life] *in the earth, even with a band of IRON AND BRASS, in the tender grass of the field; and let it be wet with the dew of heaven, and let his portion be with the beasts in the grass of the earth: Let his heart be changed from man's, and let a beast's heart be given unto him; and let seven times pass over him.'"*

REVELATION 11:7a, 17:8a, "And when they shall have finished their testimony, THE BEAST THAT ASCENDETH OUT OF THE BOTTOMLESS PIT ... The beast that thou sawest was, and is not; and shall ascend [Comes back to life] *out of the bottomless pit, ..."*

We find the fourth Beast has teeth of iron and nails of brass, proving this stump with bands of iron and brass is speaking of the fourth and final world government when Nebuchadnezzar may be the Beast.

DANIEL 7:19, "Then I would know the truth of the FOURTH BEAST, which was diverse from all the others, exceeding dreadful, whose teeth were of IRON, and his nails of BRASS; which devoured, brake in pieces, and stamped the residue with his feet;"

Nebuchadnezzar never received the God of Daniel. He was shown amazing miracles by God. I believe God showed him many miracles in an attempt to convert him, so he would NOT become the Beast of Revelation—without success.

Nebuchadnezzar was shown four children ten times smarter than all others in his realm. He was then given a dream, showing him the four world governments of the future. Instead of receiving the God of Daniel and commanding all people in his kingdom to worship the God of Daniel, he made a golden statue and required all to worship it. God gave him a beast's heart for seven years, and when he returned, he still didn't turn to the God of Daniel! Nebuchadnezzar was shown more miracles than any other secular king in the Bible, and yet he never accepted the God of Daniel, so he could be the stump that returns as the Beast.

Four verses have "king of kings" included as the final reason. The entire KJV Bible has only six verses with "king of kings" in them. Five are below. Two speak of Nebuchadnezzar, king of Babylon, and three speak of Jesus! That is NOT a coincidence. The goal of Nebuchadnezzar (the Beast or his forerunner) is to BE WORSHIPPPED LIKE GOD. These verses give us a hint that Nebuchadnezzar COULD BE THE BEAST of Revelation.

Remember, neither David nor Solomon were called a "king of kings!" Only Nebuchadnezzar and Jesus have that title applied to them! The Beast wants to be the Messiah; hence, "Antichrist." Antichrist does not mean against Christ; it means in place of Christ!

EZEKIEL 26:7, "For thus saith the Lord GOD; 'Behold, I will bring upon Tyrus NEBUCHADREZZAR [This is the same Nebuchadnezzar just spelled differently.] king of Babylon, a KING OF KINGS, from the north, with horses, and with chariots, and with horsemen, and companies, and much people.'"

DANIEL 2:37, "Thou, [Nebuchadnezzar] O king, art a KING OF KINGS: for the God of heaven hath given thee a kingdom, power, and strength, and glory."

1 TITUS 6:15, "Which in his times he shall shew, who is the blessed and only Potentate, the KING OF KINGS, and Lord of lords;"

REVELATION 17:14, "These shall make war with the Lamb, [Jesus] and the Lamb shall overcome them: for he is Lord of lords, and KING OF KINGS: and they that are with him are called, and chosen, and faithful."

REVELATION 19:16, "And he [Jesus] hath on his vesture and on his thigh a name written, KING OF KINGS, AND LORD OF LORDS."

My final reason why Nebuchadnezzar is the Beast that ascends out of the bottomless pit. His body is wounded to death [not necessarily in the head] in the middle of the Tribulation and comes back to life. This is when Lucifer is cast down to the earth *"the great dragon was cast out, that old serpent, called the Devil, and Satan, which deceiveth the whole world: he was cast out into the earth."* Nebuchadnezzar becomes the Antichrist/Beast and is possessed by Lucifer and sits on the Ark of the Covenant committing the Abomination of desolation.

Because Ecclesiastes 1:9 says there is nothing new under the sun, the Antichrist must be a person in the past. He must ascend out of the bottomless pit. He must be a King and must have committed the Abomination of Desolation to fulfill *"that which is done is that which shall be done."* He must have been the King of Iraq/Babylon to make all the parts of the prophecy in Daniel replay.

ECCLESIASTES 1:9, "The thing that hath been, it is that which shall be; and THAT WHICH IS DONE IS THAT WHICH SHALL BE DONE: and there is no new thing under the sun."

The first Nebuchadnezzar ruled over Jerusalem, so the last Nebuchadnezzar will too.

JOHN 5:43, "I am come in my Father's name, and ye receive me not: if another shall come in his own name, him ye will receive."

The first Nebuchadnezzar/Beast/Antichrist originated in Iraq/Babylon, and the last Nebuchadnezzar will too!

The first Nebuchadnezzar decided to make a great image, and the last Nebuchadnezzar will too.

The first Nebuchadnezzar, in fact, made a great image and required God's faithful to worship it, and the last Nebuchadnezzar [the False Prophet will make an image of the beast and require worship] will too.

The first Nebuchadnezzar was given a beast's heart for seven years, and the last Nebuchadnezzar will too.

The first Nebuchadnezzar's son had his kingdom given to another, and the last Nebuchadnezzar will die and Lucifer will take over his kingdom.

Prophecy repeats.

SUMMARIZED REASONS NEBUCHADNEZZAR
may be the Beast of Revelation:

He had many miracles performed before him, yet he never accepted the God of Daniel.

Nebuchadnezzar was the stump with a band of iron and brass, meaning he will return in the days of the iron kingdom or the fourth and final world government.

Two verses call Nebuchadnezzar a "king of kings," and three verses call Jesus the "King of Kings."

Prophecies of Nebuchadnezzar in Daniel repeat again.

PROPHECY FULFILLED:

On October 3, 2018 Eddie Chumney came to my house and spent three days with me. He talked, I listened. He easily covered over 500 Bible verses.

I would get mentally exhausted and had to take a brief nap every hour hours to keep going. We went from 8:00 a.m. to 11:30 p.m. I have never studied that much in all my life!

Eddie Chumney knows the Bible better than any person I have met.

I didn't learn one thing new about the Bible. But a new spirit came upon me.

In the first hour after Eddie made the comment the third time I finally realized his purpose in coming. He kept saying, "God sent me to show you the end from the beginning. All the Bible is prophecy not just books like Daniel and Revelation! I came to show you the end from the beginning. You want to know the end. To understand the end you have to know the beginning. He was not saying to know Revelation you have to know Genesis. He was saying all the Bible is a repeating prophecy. To know the end of any specific prophecy you have to know the beginning of the prophecy.

He didn't tell me this. This is the new spirit which came upon me, the spirit to see repeating prophecies in the Bible.

Moses and Arron standing before Pharaoh is a picture of Moses and John the Revelator --the Two Witnesses standing before the Antichrist and False Prophet.

Earlier in the chapter I wrote that God would show me the end from the beginning. This is the fulfillment of that promise.

THE SECRET DOOR TO UNDERSTAND BIBLE PROPHECY

TWO WITNESSES

Here are the reasons why Moses and John the Revelator will be the Two Witnesses. What a blessing it has been to memorize the Book of Revelation. Reading out loud one evening, repeating one of the verses to memorize it, suddenly I saw something I had never seen before!

JOHN— A WITNESS

JOHN REASON 1:
"Companion in tribulation?"

REVELATION 1:9, *"I John, who also am YOUR BROTHER, and COMPANION IN TRIBULATION ..."*

I thought, "Is John saying he is going to be with us in the Tribulation—the last seven years? Is he saying he is going to be there in the Tribulation to come?" I dismissed the thought because it was contrary to what I believed at the time. I thought the Two Witnesses would be Enoch and Elijah. I kept memorizing, and moved forward. Besides, "tribulation" also means "trouble or pressure," so it is not necessarily speaking of the last seven years. It stayed in the back of my mind as a possibility for "JOHN" as being one of the Two Witnesses.

JOHN REASON 2:
John eats the sweet book and prophesies

When I reached Revelation 10:8, a second reason arrived. Taking a more serious look to see if I had misunderstood about Elijah and Enoch being the Two Witnesses, I discovered something new in the Scriptures! In these verses, John eats the little book, which was sweet as honey in his mouth. There are only two places in the Bible in which a book or roll is eaten and is as sweet as honey to the taste.

REVELATION 10:8b, 10-11, *"... Go and take the little BOOK ... And I took the little book out of the angel's hand, and ate it up; and it was in my mouth SWEET AS HONEY: and as soon as I had eaten it, my belly was bitter. And he said unto me, THOU MUST PROPHESY again before many peoples, and nations, and tongues, and kings."*

EZEKIEL 2:9-3:4 *"... a roll of a book was therein; ... it was written within and without: and there was written therein LAMENTATIONS, AND MOURNING, AND WOE. ... 'Son of man, eat that thou findest; EAT THIS ROLL, AND GO SPEAK UNTO THE HOUSE OF ISRAEL' ... it was in my mouth as HONEY FOR SWEETNESS. And he said unto me, 'Son of man, go, get thee unto the house of Israel, and SPEAK WITH MY WORDS unto them.'"*

God had Ezekiel eat the sweet roll and was immediately told to go SPEAK THE WORDS OF "LAMENTATIONS, AND MOURNING, AND WOE" to Israel. Likewise, immediately after John eats the sweet roll/book, John also is told he will prophecy before many peoples, nations and tongues. So, the sweet book is *"lamentations, mourning and woe."* The Two Witnesses speak out curses to stop the rain and turn water to blood. John eats the book of *"lamentations, mourning and woe"* and then speaks THOSE Words of God upon the earth. JOHN EATS THE BOOK WHICH GIVES HIM THE WORDS TO SAY!

Where are Enoch or Elijah found eating a sweet book of curses? Nowhere! Neither one of them is one of the Two Witnesses, nor neither one eats a book. It is John the Revelator who eats the book of lamentations, mourning and woe. Then, just as Ezekiel did, John prophesies to the nation of Israel among others.

JOHN REASON 3: Speaks to "many peoples, and nations, and tongues, and kings" is an unfulfilled prophecy.

John was told by one of the most powerful angels in the Bible that he is to go and speak to "many peoples, and nations, and tongues, and kings."

According to the book, *Foxes Book of Martyrs,* John was boiled in oil and banned to the Isle of Patmos. He never traveled the globe, prophesying to "many people, and nations, and tongues, and kings."

From the *Foxes Book of Martyrs:*

"John: The "beloved disciple," was brother to James the Great. The churches of Smyrna, Pergamos, Sardis, Philadelphia, Laodicea, and Thyatira, were founded by him. From Ephesus he was ordered to be sent to Rome, where it is affirmed he was cast into a cauldron of boiling oil. He escaped by miracle, without injury. Domitian afterwards banished him to the Isle of Patmos, where he wrote the Book of Revelation. Nerva, the successor of Domitian, recalled him. He was the only apostle who escaped a violent death."

This would be unfulfilled prophecy. The angel that made this prophecy is the angel which stood upon the earth and the sea. This angel is probably Michael, so this is no small prophecy!

JOHN REASON 4: A CONTINUATION OF THOUGHT

Only two verses later, the angel reveals the Two Witnesses! The text never changes topics from telling John that he is going to prophesy *"to many peoples, and nations, and tongues, and kings"* to *"I will give power unto my two witnesses."* While there is a chapter break, there are only TWO VERSES separating John from eating the sweet-book of lamentations, mourning and woe until power is given to the Two Witnesses!!

Furthermore, neither of the two verses change the topic or subject. *"Thou must prophecy again"* is speaking of John when it says, *"I will give power unto my two witnesses"* and is a direct prophecy. *"Thou must prophecy again,"* is speaking of John the Revelator. "I will give power unto my two witnesses," is speaking of John the Revelator and Moses. The verses are a CONTINUATION OF THOUGHT.

> REVELATION 10:11, "And he said unto me, 'Thou must prophesy again before many peoples, and nations, and tongues, and kings.'"

Skip to ...

> REVELATION 11:1, 2, "And there was given me a reed like unto a rod: and the angel stood, saying, 'Rise, and measure the temple of God, and the altar, and them that worship therein. But the court which is without the temple leave out, and measure it not; for it is given unto the Gentiles: and the holy city shall they tread under foot forty and two months.'"

> REVELATION 11:3-6, "And I WILL GIVE POWER UNTO MY TWO WITNESSES, and they shall prophesy a thousand two hundred and threescore days, clothed in sackcloth. These are the two olive trees, and the two candlesticks standing before the God of the earth. And if any man will hurt them, FIRE PROCEEDETH OUT OF THEIR MOUTH, [Morning Star] and devoureth their enemies: and if any man will hurt them, he must in this manner be killed. These have power to shut heaven, that it rain not in the days of their prophecy: and have power over waters to turn them

to blood, and to smite the earth with all plagues, as often as they will."

JOHN REASON 5:
Christians would readily listen to John

The thought came to me, "Who would most Christians respect to teach them Revelation more than John the Revelator, the one who wrote the book?" Who would most people readily believe? The answer had to be John the Revelator. These five reasons changed my mind. John must be one of the Two Witnesses—but more was to come.

I was reluctant to change my previous conclusions after studying Bible prophecy for over 40 years. I also understood that the moment we stop chasing truth with all our heart, the moment we compromise in the slightest degree, then the devil rejoices to bring us error. One of the most difficult tasks in life is to find truth. We must pursue it, forsaking all if necessary, or error will find its way into our heart and understanding.

PROVERBS 25:2,
"It is the glory of God to
conceal a thing:
but the honour of kings
is to search
out a matter.

As much as I dislike it, my studies that formed my previous conclusions were once again wrong. There is nothing wrong with being wrong, if one turns from the error. I have discovered that God is quite willing to let me hold error if I want to, and He is not necessarily obligated to help me find the truth unless I genuinely WANT it and will pursue it with all my strength.

REVELATION 3:19, "As many as
I love, I rebuke and chasten:
be zealous therefore,
and repent."

JOHN REASON 6:
John and Moses are linked through time by the Secret Door of prophecy.

They both have prophecies for the last days.

Moses had the Song of Moses and John the Book of Revelation.

Leslie was told November 23, 2007, that if I studied the Feasts, God would show me the Secret Door to Understand Bible Prophecy. This prophecy was fulfilled, confirming the word is from God. On March 23, 2018, I was shown the vision of two books linked by a Secret Door. Those two books were Moses' book of Torah and John's Book of Revelation. I saw two books side by side. I was made to know the one on the left was the Torah of Moses and the one on the right was the Revelation of John. I saw a yellow time-tunnel linking the two. The time-tunnel looked similar to a yellow stick of butter linking the two, but I knew it was a time tunnel specifically linking the word "Firstfruits" of Leviticus 23:12 to Revelation 14:4.

That Revelation was linked to the books of Moses. I count that as my sixth reason for choosing John the Revelator to be one of the Two Witnesses. Even though they were written thousands of years apart, they are linked spiritually. Moses is linked to John. Why is it we see no links between Enoch and Elijah? There is a secret spiritual door between Torah and Revelation because Moses and John are the Two Witnesses!

MOSES— A WITNESS

MOSES REASON 1:
The Tribulation Saints sing the Song of Moses

Revelation 15:2 speaks of a time near the end of the seven years. As I began to memorize this statement, another thought came to me, which by now I have concluded are the thoughts of God guiding me into writing this book. Sometimes these revelations come in the form of questions as this one did, "Why are these people standing on the sea of glass?"

REVELATION 15:2, 3, "And I saw as it were a sea of glass mingled with fire: and them that had gotten the victory over the beast, and over his image, and over his mark, and over the number of his name, STAND ON THE SEA OF GLASS, having the harps of God. And they sing the SONG OF MOSES the servant of God ..."

Why would those who had *"gotten the victory over the beast"* sing the SONG OF MOSES? I had to arrive at the conclusion that these Tribulation Saints had just battled the beast for the last 3½ years alongside Moses and John! They are standing on the sea of glass because before their death, they had just witnessed Moses and John fighting almost daily with evil in the streets of Jerusalem. Their victory was losing their life for Christ and not giving in to the Beast, his lies and mouth speaking great things! They became "Overcomers." They resisted and *"kept my works to the end."*

John the Revelator will be AN OVERCOMER, "WITNESSING" to those who dwell on the earth, a living testimony of how to be an overcomer by resisting the devil in the streets of Jerusalem near the last half of the tribulation clothed in sackcloth!

But Moses is also one of the Two Witnesses! They know and see Moses battling the Beast, which is why they play their harps and SING THE SONG OF **MOSES** (Deuteronomy 31)! Moses is there battling the Beast! They have just spent 3½ years battling with him, and this is their time of rejoicing over the Beast because they have the victory! The greatest of victories— victory over the beast! That is why they sing the Song of Moses.

MOSES REASON 2:
In Egypt, Moses Turned Water to Blood!
Moses is repeating his giftings in Egypt in modern times!
Enoch and Elijah never turned water to blood.

Many of the curses the Two Witnesses send upon the earth are the same curses Moses sent upon Pharaoh in Egypt. Moses is simply repeating the curses of God from the days before Pharaoh in Egypt! He sends the same curses in the Tribulation. We know that the Bible says the gifts and callings of God are without repentance, meaning God doesn't pull a gift back once He has given it. Moses is now repeating before the Beast the curses from before Pharaoh, a precursor of the Beast!

ECCLESIASTES 1:9, "The thing that hath been, it is that which shall be; and that which is done is that which shall be done: and there is no new thing under the sun."

Moses turned water to blood before Pharaoh:

EXODUS 7:17, "... In this thou shalt know that I am the Lord: behold, I will smite with the rod that is in mine hand upon the WATERS which are in the river, and they shall be turned to BLOOD."

Moses turns water to blood before the Beast:

REVELATION 11:6, "These have power to shut heaven, that it rain not in the days of their prophecy: and have power over WATERS to turn them to BLOOD, and to smite the earth with all plagues, as often as they will."

MOSES REASON 3:
Moses was given the Song of Moses, which plays in the last days.

My third reason is the Song of Moses itself. The Song of Moses is a prophecy given to Moses on his 120th birthday and spoken over Israel, mostly to be fulfilled in the last days. I believe the reason Moses was given the prophecy was because HE WILL BE IN ISRAEL AS IT IS FULFILLED. He will be there with his people in their darkest hour, sending out curses against evil! Fire—the Morning Star—will come from his mouth and burn up his enemies!

AUDIBLE VOICE OF GOD:

It was Saturday evening. August 8, 2015. I was preparing my sermon for the next morning. I was alone in my study. I prayed, "Lord, I don't have anything to say tomorrow for the sermon. What would you like to say to your people?" For the first time in my life I heard audible words while I was AWAKE! It was as if someone was in the room speaking to me. I have heard God speak to me in various ways, but all during the night. This time I was staring at my computer monitor, and I heard, *"This is the time of Miracles."*

In a moment I was impressed that the greatest miracles in human history will be poured out AS JUDGMENT HITS! No one since Adam has seen the miracles which are about to hit the earth! As difficulty hits, God is NOT going to leave us alone. He is going to help in our battles against evil and difficulty, step-by-step, pound-for-pound, and inch-by-inch. He will never leave us nor forsake us. The Two Witnesses will be using miracles to bring truth, just as the Beast and False Prophet use miracles to deceive.

Part of what I was impressed with is that, *"Oil will be given to Israel wondrously." (Joel 2:24).*

The same thing happened three more times.

October 3, 2015
"These are the days of Elijah."

The great, end time battle between good and evil has begun!

October 18, 2015
"These are the days of Ezekiel."

The global gathering of Israelites and Christians back to Israel is about to begin.

November 8, 2015
I heard words in the night, **"I am going to show you the end from the beginning, so you can warn my people!"**

November 1, 2015
I sat in the front row as my lovely wife was teaching that Sunday morning and heard in my spirit, **"The Song of Moses is not a song."** I knew it was not a song; it was a prophecy to Israel to help them in the last days. Now, I had to find out why God spoke this to my heart? I mean I heard literal words in my heart.

When we look at the verses before the Song of Moses, they mention the "Last Days" and Moses prophesied about the last days! That doesn't prove by itself that Moses is one of the Two Witnesses, but in light of the additional reasons, there is no doubt. Remember, this was given to Moses and delivered to Israel ON Moses' 120th birthday. Moses didn't die from old age, he died because of ONE mistake! Could it be that when Moses was given the Song of Moses he KNEW he would return in the last days when this prophecy plays? Could it be that the Song of Moses in Deuteronomy 31 links to the Song of Moses in Revelation 15:3? Once again, we see a link between Moses and John, between the Torah and Revelation!

> DEUTERONOMY 31:2a, "And he [Moses] *said unto them, 'I am an hundred and twenty years old this day;'"*

> DEUTERONOMY 34:5-7, "So Moses the servant of the LORD died there in the land of Moab ... BUT NO MAN KNOWETH OF HIS SEPULCHRE UNTO THIS DAY. And Moses was an HUNDRED AND TWENTY YEARS OLD WHEN HE DIED:"

> DEUTERONOMY 31:28, 29a, *"Gather unto me all the elders of your tribes, and your officers, that I may speak these words in their ears, and call heaven and earth to record against them. For I know that after my death ye will utterly corrupt yourselves, and turn aside from the way which I have commanded you; and evil will befall you in the LATTER DAYS ..."*

We see the Song of Moses prophesied of the LATTER DAYS. Moses gave the children of Israel a warning that they would turn aside from the commandments and evil would befall them in the LATTER DAYS. Moses knew his prophecy would be playing in the last days. Did he know he would be there? Was it the plan of God that Moses would return?

The Song of Moses summarized says:

In the latter years God will speak

Why God judged Israel

God will scatter Israel

God will remember, find, gather and bless Israel

God will use crude oil to raise Israel to be the glory of all lands!

Near the Day of the LORD

Many will turn to the Rock (Jesus)

Jesus will return to Judge. (Jesus has the keys of hell and death)

Jesus will destroy Israel's enemies (Armageddon)

Moses was given the Song of Moses because he will be in Jerusalem as one of the Two Witnesses! The Song of Moses is a prophecy that plays in the Last Days. Moses, the Song of Moses, and the Last Days! God was connecting him to the Last Days before his death!

MOSES REASON 4:
The grave of Moses was never known, and Michael and the devil fought over his body!

Do you suppose something was done with the body of Moses? Why couldn't anyone find his grave? Is this any hint that he will be one of the Two Witnesses? Perhaps the bodies of John and Moses were taken to heaven and that is the reason the devil and Michael fought over the body of Moses? Is this another hint that Moses is one of the Two Witnesses?

> DEUTERONOMY 34:5, "So MOSES the servant of the LORD

DIED there in the land of MOAB, according to the word of the LORD. And he buried him in a valley in the land of Moab, over against Beth-peor: BUT NO MAN KNOWETH OF HIS SEPULCHRE UNTO THIS DAY."

JUDE 1:9, *"Yet Michael the archangel, when contending with the devil he DISPUTED ABOUT THE BODY OF MOSES, durst not bring against him a railing accusation, but said, 'The Lord rebuke thee.'"*

MOSES REASON 5:
Moses was promised to go into the land that flows with milk and honey.

My fifth reason is an unfulfilled prophecy or promise made to Moses. Many of Moses' prophecies, spoken on his 120th birthday, the day he died, prophesied massive amounts of oil will be found in Israel in the last days! Here is the part in the Song of Moses that speaks of the coming massive oil discovery in Israel.

DEUTERONOMY 32:13-15, *"He made him RIDE ON THE HIGH PLACES OF THE EARTH [BLESSED BY OIL], that he might eat the increase of the [Crude oil fields] fields; and he made him to suck HONEY [Yellow-colored crude oil] out of the rock, and OIL OUT OF THE FLINTY ROCK;* [Flint rock is some of the best rock from which to extract crude oil.] *But Jeshurun waxed fat* [fat is crude oil], *and kicked: thou art waxen fat* [Crude oil], *thou art grown thick* [Wealth], *thou art covered with fatness* [Crude oil]; *then he forsook God which made him, and lightly esteemed the Rock of his salvation.* [The Rock of Salvation is Jesus, this is in a time when SOME of Israel receives Jesus! That is the last days.]*"*

There are 12 specific points in the prophecy in Deuteronomy 33:12-29 given by Moses to Israel that speak of oil blessings to Israel in the Last Days. This is the first prophecy given to Moses as he was standing at the burning bush.

EXODUS 3:8a, *"And I am come down to deliver them out of the hand of the Egyptians, and to bring them up out of that land unto a good land and a large, unto a land flowing with milk and honey ..."*

EXODUS 3:17, *"And I have said, 'I WILL BRING YOU up out of the affliction of Egypt ... unto a land flowing with milk and honey.'"*

EXODUS 13:5, *"And it shall be when the LORD shall BRING THEE into ... a land flowing with milk and honey..."*

LEVITICUS 20:24, *"But I have said unto you, 'Ye shall inherit their land, and I will give it UNTO YOU to possess it, a land that floweth with milk and honey...'"*

Moses was to get water from rocks at two different times. The first time he was to strike the rock. The second time Moses struck the rock when he was supposed to speak to the rock. We know God became angry with Moses because Moses messed up the prophetic picture. God was trying to say that in the Old Covenant God ruled with a rod and struck his people harshly when they broke his laws, but in the New Covenant He would speak to our heart. Moses was impatient when God was trying to show in the New Covenant through Jesus He would be patient with us and speak to our heart, rather than striking us with a stick. Moses died for this reason before entering the land that flows with milk and honey on his first incarnation.

What about his second incarnation as one of the Two Witnesses?

Moses was not able to enter the land that *"floweth with milk and honey"* the first time. These prophecies hint that Moses will EVENTUALLY walk in the land upon his return as one of the Two Witnesses.

Moses was given the Song of Moses on his 120th birthday and then died, but no one could find his grave. Michael wrestled the devil for his body. These four prophecies say that Moses will go into the land that flows with gas and oil!

My reason number 5 is **Moses was promised to go into the land that flows with milk and honey.** His Song of Moses prophesied Israel would be given massive amounts of oil in the Last Days. It seems Moses was promised he would go into the Promise Land. Perhaps as one of the Two Witnesses.

MOSES REASON 6:
The Feasts and the Torah written by Moses are part of the Secret Door of Prophecy.

The Feasts given to Moses are part of the Secret Door of Prophecy. This prophecy called the Song of Moses was given to Moses because MOSES WILL BE THERE in the last 3½ years, seeing it fulfilled! What other good reason would there be explaining why the Song of Moses would be even mentioned in Revelation—a book about the last seven years? Moses lived about 3,500 years ago. The Song of Moses is written in Revelation because Moses is one of the Two Witnesses!

The Secret Door is a time-tunnel that links the Feasts given to Moses to the Prophecies given to John the Revelator; linking the Torah to Revelation; linking the Feasts to Revelation to show the world the timing and order of the prophecies of the last seven months!

In that Revelation was linked to the books of Moses, I count that as my sixth reason for Moses.

MOSES REASON 7:
Who would the Israelites listen to, to tell them about the last days the most? – Moses.

I believe the Two Witnesses are: Moses and John the Revelator

SUMMARY:
SIX REASONS FOR JOHN

1. John says, *"I John, who also am your brother, and companion in tribulation."*

2. He ate the sweet book of "lamentations, mornings and woe," preparing to prophesy 3½ years.

3. Unfulfilled prophecy: *"... thou must prophesy again to many peoples, and nations, and tongues, and kings."*

4. *"... thou must prophesy again,"* is only two verses from, *"I will give power unto my two witnesses."*

5. John and the Book of Revelation is the New Testament part of the Secret Door.

6. Who would the Christians listen to the most to tell them about the last days? – John

SUMMARY:
SEVEN REASONS FOR MOSES

1. The Tribulation Saints sing the Song of Moses.

2. In Egypt, Moses Turned Water to Blood! Moses is repeating his giftings in Egypt in modern times!

3. Moses was given the prophecy the Song of Moses, which plays in the last days.

4. The grave of Moses was not found, and Michael and the devil fought over his body

5. Moses was promised to go into the land that flows with milk and honey.

6. The Feasts and the Torah written by Moses are the Old Testament half of the Secret Door of prophecy

7. Who would the Israelites listen to, to tell them about the last days the most? – Moses

What do Enoch and Elijah have to do with the last days? Nothing! Neither have any links to the last days, no prophecies, no songs, no sweet rolls to eat! Nothing. Moses was given the Song of Moses. John was given the Book of Revelation about the Last Days. Enoch and Elijah had nothing given to them about the Last Days.

Chapter 9
THE DAY AND THE HOUR

We have all heard it said, "No one knows the day and hour," but what does it mean? Where did the phrase come from? It is speaking of the day Jesus returns! Jesus is saying to His disciples that they can't know the day or the hour. Please notice: He did NOT say they can't know the year or the month or the season! However, it is my contention that once the 144,000 Firstfruit Witnesses arrive on Mt. Zion, we WILL then know the day and approximately the hour of the return of Jesus!

MATTHEW 24:32-36, "Now learn a parable of the fig tree; When his branch is yet tender, and putteth forth leaves, ye know that summer is nigh: So likewise ye, when ye shall see all these things, know that it is near, even at the doors. Verily I say unto you, 'This generation shall not pass, till all these things be fulfilled. HEAVEN AND EARTH SHALL PASS AWAY, but my words shall not pass away. BUT OF THAT DAY AND HOUR KNOWETH NO MAN, no, not the angels of heaven, but my Father only.'"

There is some question whether Jesus is speaking of His final return as King of kings, which we know is on Trumpets or the day the old heaven and old earth will pass away, which happens on Atonement. Since the question Jesus was answering was the day of His final return, I think that is the question He is answering. In that Trumpets is only 10 days before Atonement, it doesn't matter much. I think Trumpets is the day the old heaven and earth begin to fall apart. The process takes 10 days of shaking to level every mountain and fill in the sea, and the process is completed by Atonement, but that is just a guess. The part that is NOT a guess is that by Atonement, we have a new heaven and a new earth. We know that the Great White Throne is on Atonement, the judgment of the dead NOT in Christ, and this verse tells us the old earth and old heaven are passed away associated with the Great White Throne.

REVELATION 20:11, "And I saw a GREAT WHITE THRONE, and him that sat on it, from whose face THE EARTH AND THE HEAVEN FLED AWAY; and there was found no place for them."

Back to the discussion on the day and hour.

The way we would state this today is, "At this present time, no one knows the day and hour of Jesus' return," but about six months before Jesus returns, we CAN know the exact day and approximate hour He will arrive when we see the 144,000!

To find this secret, we must first understand "the day and hour that no man knows." The point of the 144,000 arriving on Firstfruits is the Shout, "Behold the bridegroom cometh, go ye out to meet him!" This tells us WHEN Jesus returns. He still doesn't want us to know the exact HOUR at this point. However, the 144,000 will tell us the DAY. Since we know Jesus arrives "as a thief in the night," we know He arrives as the Lion sometime after sundown on the Feast of Trumpets. The 144,000 just tells us the year, but other verses like these three tell us the

FEAST upon which He returns. Please notice each verse mentions "trump" or "trumpet" confirming Jesus the Lion returns on Trumpets. Jesus the Lamb returns on Firstfruits.

> MATTHEW 24:31, "And he shall send his angels with a great SOUND OF A TRUMPET, and they shall gather together his elect from the four winds, from one end of heaven to the other.

> 1 CORINTHIANS 15:52, "In a moment, in the twinkling of an eye, at the last TRUMP: for the trumpet shall sound, and the dead shall be raised incorruptible, and we shall be changed."

> REVELATION 10:7, "But in the days of the voice of the SEVENTH angel, when he shall begin to SOUND, [Trumpet] the mystery of God should be finished, as he hath declared to his servants the prophets."

THE DAY AND HOUR THAT NO MAN KNOWS

The first day of the Jewish new year is determined by the High Priest. Upon the first sighting of the first sliver of the new moon from Jerusalem, the High Priest examines the barley. Please note: some say it is not the first sliver, but rather a fully dark moon. The old saying is: If you have two Jews, you have three opinions. Please don't let this cause you to miss the bigger message in this book. Keep reading. If the barley is ripe, or "Abib," he declares the new year. If the barley is not ripe, they wait another full cycle of the moon. Determining when the new moon is going to appear is the easy part. But the second requirement is the barley harvest, which must be ripe in Jerusalem when the first sliver of the new moon is sighted as determined by the High Priest.

We can know the rising of the new moon, but "no man can know" if the barley is going to be ripe on the first sighting of the first sliver of the new moon. Or a fully dark moon. That is the reason they call it the "day and hour that no man knows."

Once the barley is Abib, we know we have a new year, but we DON'T know if THIS IS THE YEAR Jesus will return. But once we see the 144,000 Firstfruit Israelite boys on Mt. Zion with the Lamb, we WILL know THIS IS THE YEAR, and since we KNOW Jesus returns as KING OF KINGS on the Feast of Trumpets, we will then KNOW THE DAY Jesus will return to the Mount of Olives. We still don't know the exact hour, other than we know it is sometime after sundown.

This is another reason we KNOW the 144,000 Firstfruit Israelite boys resurrected as adults on Mt. Zion is the shout, *"Behold, the bridegroom cometh, go ye out to meet him!"*

> MATTHEW 24:36, "But of that DAY AND HOUR knoweth no man, no, not the angels of heaven, but my Father only."

> MATTHEW 25:13, "Watch therefore, for ye know neither THE DAY NOR THE HOUR wherein the Son of man cometh."

On the 14th day of the first month is the Feast of Passover. The next day begins the seven-day Feast of Unleavened Bread. On the 17th is the Feast of Firstfruits.

When we see the 144,000 from the 12 tribes—clothed in white garments, having no guile in their mouth, undefiled with women—stand upon Mount Zion, this will signal:

1. The first sliver of the new moon was sighted

2. The barley was found to be ripe or *Abib*

3. This is the year Jesus will return

4. This is the shout, "*The Bridegroom cometh.*"

The 144,000 standing on Mount Zion is the cry, "Behold, the bridegroom cometh!" We know this because the very next verse is the angel flying in the midst of heaven having the everlasting gospel. Jesus said, "This gospel of the Kingdom shall be preached unto all nations then shall the end come." The final barley harvest of the 144,000 Israelites IS the final sign, telling us this is THE YEAR JESUS RETURNS! This is the final Firstfruits, the final seven months. Jesus is to return in a little over six months, and we NOW know for sure!

MATTHEW 25:6, "And at midnight there was a cry made, 'Behold, the bridegroom cometh; GO YE OUT TO MEET HIM.'"

MATTHEW 24:14, "And THIS GOSPEL OF THE KINGDOM SHALL BE PREACHED IN ALL THE WORLD for a witness unto all nations; and THEN SHALL THE END COME."

REVELATION 14:6, 7, "And I saw another angel fly in the midst of heaven, having the EVERLASTING GOSPEL to preach unto them that dwell on the earth, and to every nation, and kindred, and tongue, and people. Saying with a loud voice, 'Fear God, and give glory to him; for THE HOUR OF HIS JUDGMENT IS COME: and worship him that made heaven, and earth, and the sea, and the fountains of waters.'"

Chapter 10
MORNING STAR

Jesus is the "Bright Morning Star," but some will qualify to receive "the Morning Star" as an additional blessing from Jesus! The Morning Star is a light sword, coming out of the mouth which destroys both soul and body. It is used by the angels to keep people away from the Tree of Life in the Garden of Eden, by the Two Witnesses, by Jesus at Armageddon, and by the Kings during the Millennium. The genuine Morning Star is much, much more powerful, and is used to defeat evil.

Here are the details:

This revelation came in the blink of an eye. I had memorized the Scriptures in Revelation about the Overcomers who "keep his works to the end." The Overcomers are given *"power over the nations,"* and they are given the Morning Star. It seemed to me this group of overcomers was similar to "police of the Millennium," who keep the laws of God with "a rod of iron," without allowing them to be bent or broken. I began to see apparently, some overcomers are given an extra power to "break people to shivers."

> REVELATION 2:26-28, *"And he that OVERCOMETH, and KEEPETH MY WORKS UNTO THE END, to him will I give POWER over the nations: And he shall rule them with a ROD OF IRON; as the vessels of a potter shall they be BROKEN TO SHIVERS: even as I received of my Father. And I will give him the MORNING STAR."*

The definition of "shivers" is, "to put under foot, to break down, to crush, to tear one's body or shatter one's strength ... to burn to ASHES."

I thought Overcomers might be given the "Morning Star," if they "keep his works to the end" to police the nations during the Millennium. Just as sheriffs have a star, overcomers have the "Morning Star" that gives them power to enforce God's law and to break violators to "shivers" who break the law! Law officers through the ages knowingly or unknowingly have worn a star. It may be that the "star" is a symbol of those who punish people who break God's law.

This was one of my first "revelations," so I was slow to recognize that I had not come by this information from the Bible, but from Him Who wrote the Bible!

This led me to search the "history of the sheriff's star badge." I discovered the "star" is the Overcomers' sign! The star is the sign of spiritual authority over evil! Law enforcement badges were used to provide a recognizable symbol of rank and authority. Many later badges were in the shape of an oval or a shield. The largest surge in the popularity of the star probably began in the western United States territories. Many sheriffs were the first, and sometimes, the only law enforcement in an area. After the elected sheriff adopted a star-badge symbol, tradition kept it going. Today, nearly all the sheriffs' offices use a star-themed badge, although they may be five, six, or seven-pointed stars.

The Morning Star is used in the Garden of Eden!

GENESIS 3:24, "So he drove out the man; and he placed at the east of the garden of Eden Cherubims, and a FLAMING SWORD which turned every way, to keep the way of the tree of life."

The overcomers, soul winners and preachers shine like "stars" in the Millennium!!! Some overcomers are given the power of the Morning Star.

DANIEL 12:3, "And they that be wise shall SHINE AS THE BRIGHTNESS OF THE FIRMAMENT; and they that TURN MANY TO RIGHTEOUSNESS AS THE STARS FOR EVER AND EVER."

The Morning Star is a "light sword," a fire which turns both flesh and soul to dust.

DEUTERONOMY 32:41a, "If I whet my glittering [lightning] SWORD, and mine hand take hold on judgment; I will render vengeance to mine enemies ..."

ISAIAH 41:2, "... he gave them as the dust to his SWORD, and as driven stubble to his bow."

ISAIAH 66:16, "For by fire and by his SWORD ... and the slain of the LORD shall be many."

JEREMIAH 12:12, "... the SWORD of the LORD shall devour from the one end of the land ..."

JEREMIAH 46:10, "... the day of the Lord ... a day of vengeance ... the SWORD shall devour ..."

EZEKIEL 32:10, "... I shall brandish my SWORD ..."

It comes out of the mouth!

REVELATION 1:16, "... out of his MOUTH went a sharp two-edged SWORD ..."

REVELATION 2:12, "These things saith he which hath the SHARP SWORD WITH TWO EDGES;"

REVELATION 2:16, "... will fight against them with the SWORD of my MOUTH."

REVELATION 19:21, "and the remnant were slain with the SWORD of him that sat upon the horse, which sword proceeded out of his MOUTH: and all the fowls were filled with their flesh."

It is breath, from the mouth, which consumes, destroys by fire. A light sword. Jesus returns using the "Morning Star" at Armageddon.

DEUTERONOMY 32:22-24, "For A FIRE IS KINDLED IN MINE ANGER, and shall BURN UNTO THE LOWEST HELL, and shall CONSUME THE EARTH WITH HER INCREASE, and SET ON FIRE THE FOUNDATIONS OF THE MOUNTAINS. ... I will spend mine ARROWS upon them. They shall be ... DEVOURED WITH BURNING HEAT."

ZECHARIAH 14:12, "And this shall be the plague wherewith the LORD will smite all the people that have fought against Jerusalem; THEIR FLESH SHALL CONSUME AWAY WHILE THEY STAND UPON THEIR FEET, AND THEIR EYES SHALL CONSUME AWAY IN THEIR HOLES, AND THEIR TONGUE SHALL CONSUME AWAY IN THEIR MOUTH."

2 SAMUEL 22:9-16, "There went up a SMOKE OUT OF HIS NOSTRILS, AND FIRE OUT OF HIS MOUTH DEVOURED: coals were kindled by it. He BOWED THE HEAVENS also, and came down; and darkness was under his feet. And HE RODE UPON A CHERUB, AND DID FLY: ... Through the brightness before him

were coals of fire kindled. The LORD thundered from heaven, and the most High UTTERED HIS VOICE. And he SENT OUT ARROWS, and scattered them; LIGHTNING, and discomfited them. And THE CHANNELS OF THE SEA APPEARED, THE FOUNDATIONS OF THE WORLD WERE DISCOVERED, at the rebuking of the LORD, AT THE BLAST OF THE BREATH OF HIS NOSTRILS."

Do all Christians get the Morning Star? No.

REVELATION 2:26-28, *"And he that OVERCOMETH, and KEEPETH MY WORKS UNTO THE END, to him will I give POWER OVER THE NATIONS: And he shall rule them with a ROD OF IRON; as the vessels of a potter shall they be broken to SHIVERS:* [Turn to ashes] *even as I received of my Father. And I will give him the MORNING STAR."*

The Morning Star comes out of the mouth and nostrils. It is light, like a "light arrow." It turns enemies of Jesus to ashes, shivers and "devours" them both body and soul. It is used to rule the nations with "a rod of iron." Further research revealed the hidden purpose behind the star. The North Star doesn't move and a "Rod of iron" does not bend! (easily) Some overcomers are also Judges, who are given the Morning Star, which is used for instant judgment. Their job will be to see the laws of God are not so much as bent.

These appear to be the qualifications: They must be beheaded for Jesus, but not at just any time in history. They MUST live in the time of the Beast. They must refuse to worship the Beast, or his image or receive his Mark or the Number of his name or lose their life resisting.

REVELATION 20:4, *"And I saw thrones, and they sat upon them, and judgment was given unto them: and I saw the souls of them that were beheaded for the witness of Jesus, and for the word of God, and which had NOT WORSHIPPED THE BEAST, NEITHER HIS IMAGE, NEITHER HAD RECEIVED HIS MARK UPON THEIR FOREHEADS, or in their hands; and they lived and reigned with Christ a thousand years."*

MALACHI 4:3. *"And ye shall tread down the wicked; for they shall be ASHES UNDER THE SOLES OF YOUR FEET ..."*

ISAIAH 10:17, 18, *"... his Holy One for a FLAME: and it shall BURN AND DEVOUR his thorns and his briers in one day; And shall consume ... BOTH SOUL AND BODY ..."*

ISAIAH 29:5, *"... strangers shall be like small dust, and ... shall be as chaff ... it shall be at AN INSTANT SUDDENLY.* [In the blink of an eye!]*"*

The Day of the LORD is one day. Specifically, one evening and morning. The Feast of Trumpets.

ISAIAH 17:14, *"And behold AT EVENINGTIDE TROUBLE; AND BEFORE THE MORNING HE IS NOT. This is the portion of them that spoil us, and the lot of them that rob us."*

"ROD OF IRON"

Those who obtain the rank of King in the Millennium rule using the Morning Star. They will reign over the nations and rule them with a rod of Iron. If any one of the people of the nations bend or break the rules, their time is over instantly. One who has the Morning Star shows up and uses the Morning Star, destroying both soul and body. The commandments of Jesus are not allowed to be broken in the Millennium as they are today.

> PSALM 2:9, *"Thou shalt break them with a ROD OF IRON; thou shalt dash them in pieces like a potter's vessel."*

> REVELATION 2:27, *"And he shall rule them with a ROD OF IRON; as the vessels of a potter shall they be broken to shivers: even as I received of my Father."*

> REVELATION 19:15, *"And out of his mouth goeth a sharp SWORD* [Morning Star], *that with it he should smite the nations: and he shall rule them with a ROD OF IRON: and he treadeth the winepress of the fierceness and wrath of Almighty God."*

TWO WITNESSES

The Morning Star is what the TWO WITNESSES use when fire proceeds out of their mouth and devours their enemies.

> REVELATION 11:3, 5, *"And I will give POWER* [Morning Star] *unto my two witnesses, and they shall prophesy a thousand two hundred and threescore days, clothed in sackcloth ... And if any man will hurt them, FIRE PROCEEDETH OUT OF THEIR MOUTH* [MORNING STAR!], *and DEVOURETH THEIR ENEMIES:* [...break them to shivers/ashes] *and if any man will hurt them, he must in this manner be killed."*

Jesus IS THE BRIGHT MORNING STAR and uses the Morning Star at Armageddon!

> 2 THESSALONIANS 1:7, 8, *"... the Lord Jesus shall be revealed from heaven with his mighty angels, In FLAMING FIRE taking vengeance on them that know not God, and that obey not the gospel of our Lord Jesus Christ:"*

MORNING STAR TURNS PEOPLE TO ASHES!

Destruction of the Antichrist's body:

> EZEKIEL 28:18, *"... I bring forth A FIRE FROM THE MIDST OF THEE, it shall DEVOUR THEE, and I will bring thee to ASHES ..."*

> REVELATION 11:5, *"And if any man will hurt them, FIRE PROCEEDETH OUT OF THEIR MOUTH, AND DEVOURETH THEIR ENEMIES: and if any man will hurt them, he must in this manner be killed."*

At Armageddon, the world's armies are destroyed by Jesus using the Morning Star and are turned to ashes:

> MALACHI 4:3, *"And ye shall tread down the wicked; for they shall be ASHES under the soles of your feet ..."*

> MATTHEW 21:44, *"And whosoever shall fall on this stone shall be broken: but on whomsoever it shall fall, it will grind him to POWDER."*

> ZEPHANIAH 1:17, 18, *"... and THEIR BLOOD SHALL BE POURED OUT AS DUST ... the whole land shall be devoured by the fire of his jealousy: for he shall make even a speedy riddance of all them that dwell in the land."*

> PSALM 50:2-5, *"Out of Zion ... A FIRE SHALL DEVOUR BEFORE HIM, AND IT SHALL BE VERY TEMPESTUOUS ROUND ABOUT HIM. He shall call to the heavens from above, and to the earth, that he may judge his people. Gather my saints together unto me; those that have made a covenant with me by sacrifice."*

THE SECRET DOOR TO UNDERSTAND BIBLE PROPHECY

SUMMARY:
THE "MORNING STAR"

The Morning Stars are Overcomers who:

"Keep His works to the end ..."

Use the light-saber from their mouth!

Overcomers/Kings/Judges will be the "Millennium Police"

Breaks nations to "shivers" like a discarded pot

Morning Star turns the nations to ashes

Overcomers will be the "Millennium Police"— judge, jury and executioner instantly!

Jesus is the bright and Morning Star. He burns up his enemies in an instant, in the blink of an eye.

It is used to rule the nations with "a rod of iron" and to force the nations to follow God's laws.

Destroys both soul and body

Users include:
Angel in Garden of Eden, the Two Witnesses, Jesus and the King/Judges

Chapter 11
NATIONS

All IN Christ stand before the Judgment Seat of Christ when Jesus returns on the day of Trumpets. The bodies of Antichrist/Beast and the False Prophet are burned, and their souls tossed into the Lake of Fire, along with those who worshipped the BEAST, his IMAGE or received his MARK or the NUMBER of his name. They are tormented day and night forever (Revelation 14:11, 20:10). The Beast, False Prophet, and those taking the Mark do not get soul-death, but rather eternal torment.

All NOT in Christ stand before the Great White Throne where Jesus judges them on the Day of Atonement. Those not in the Book of Life after Atonement are tossed into the Lake of Fire, which is the second death or soul-death, and they will be as though they had not been. Their bodies are turned to ashes or eaten by birds; their soul is destroyed (Obadiah 1:6; Revelation 19:21). Those whose names are IN the Book of Life are in the golden city clear as glass, the New Jerusalem.

That leaves one remaining group of people: Those who did NOT take the Mark, but DIDN'T ACCEPT JESUS either. The Bible calls them the NATIONS. They are referred to in the Old Testament as the "corners of the field" not harvested (Leviticus 19:9), and are given the opportunity to live for 1,000 years under strict rules.

MATTHEW 24:13, "But he that shall endure unto the end, the same shall be saved."

The Nations never accepted Jesus, so they don't report to the Judgment Seat of Christ on Trumpets. However, they are not dead, so they don't report to the Great White Throne. They are allowed to live for up to 1,000 years. Their judgment arrives when they break a law. Breaking a law after Trumpets brings instant judgment. A King-Judge shows up at the speed of thought and hits them with the Morning Star, instantly turning them into ashes, destroying both soul and body. They all ultimately break a law when Satan is released out of his prison after a thousand years and tempts them. They gather in protest around the New Jerusalem. God hits them from heaven with the Morning Star, turning them to ashes.

REVELATION 20:7-10, "And when the thousand years are expired, SATAN shall be loosed out of his PRISON, And shall go out to DECEIVE THE NATIONS which are in the four quarters of the earth, Gog, and Magog, to GATHER THEM TOGETHER TO BATTLE: the number of whom is as the sand of the sea. And they went up on the breadth of the earth, and COMPASSED THE CAMP OF THE SAINTS ABOUT, AND THE BELOVED CITY: and FIRE CAME DOWN FROM GOD OUT OF HEAVEN, AND DEVOURED THEM. And the devil that deceived them was cast into the lake of fire and brimstone, where the beast and the false prophet are, and shall be tormented day and night for ever and ever."

After the burning of the tares and crushing of the grapes all that are still standing are saved, this is the nations. In Revelation the definition of "saved" is NOT eternal life having your name in the

THE SECRET DOOR TO UNDERSTAND BIBLE PROPHECY

Book of Life, but rather being saved from the burning/wrath. Individuals in the nations are saved from the wrath of Jesus and the Morning Star. They do not get their name in the Book of Life. They do not get eternal life. They are allowed into the Millennium under strict rules.

The reason we know for certain the Nations are destroyed at the end of the Millennium is found in Daniel. It says the Kingdom will *"NOT BE LEFT TO OTHER PEOPLE,"* meaning the Nations are not allowed to live and enter the eternal Kingdom. They never accepted Jesus, so their name is not in the Book of Life. Jesus returns and destroys ALL PREVIOUS KINGDOMS and sets up a Kingdom that shall never be destroyed.

> *DANIEL 2:44, "And in the days of these kings shall the God of heaven set up a kingdom, which shall never be destroyed: and the kingdom shall NOT BE LEFT TO OTHER PEOPLE, but it shall break in pieces and CONSUME ALL THESE KINGDOMS, and it shall stand for ever."*

These are the verses which give us a description of the nations—those living in the Millennium outside the New Jerusalem. Revelation 21:8 specifically says the nations shall have their part in the Lake of Fire. They are allowed to live for up to 1,000 years, but they WILL eventually be sent to the lake of fire, they will not be given eternal life.

> *DANIEL 2:35, "Then was the iron, the clay, the brass, the silver, and the gold, broken to pieces together, and BECAME LIKE THE CHAFF OF THE SUMMER THRESHING-FLOORS; AND THE WIND CARRIED THEM AWAY, THAT NO PLACE WAS FOUND FOR THEM: and the stone that smote the image became a great mountain, and filled the whole earth.*

[Every person whose name is not in the book of life is destroyed.]"

> *REVELATION 21:8, "But the fearful, and unbelieving, and the abominable, and murderers, and whoremongers, and sorcerers, and idolaters, and all liars,* [Nations] *SHALL HAVE THEIR PART IN THE LAKE WHICH BURNETH WITH FIRE AND BRIMSTONE: WHICH IS THE SECOND DEATH."*

> *JEREMIAH 30:11, "... though I MAKE A FULL END OF ALL NATIONS ..."*

> *ISAIAH 40:15, "Behold, the NATIONS are as A DROP OF A BUCKET, and ARE COUNTED AS THE SMALL DUST of the balance ..."*

> *EPHESIANS 5:5, "For this ye know, that NO WHOREMONGER, NOR UNCLEAN PERSON, NOR COVETOUS MAN, WHO IS AN IDOLATER, hath any inheritance in the kingdom of Christ and of God."*

The nations bring gifts of fruit, vegetables and livestock. Anything the Overcomers in the New Jerusalem request is brought by the nations.

> *REVELATION 21:24, "And the NATIONS of them which are saved shall walk in the light of it: and the kings of the earth do BRING THEIR GLORY AND HONOUR INTO IT."*

> *REVELATION 21:26, 27, "And they shall BRING THE GLORY AND HONOUR OF THE NATIONS INTO IT. And there shall in no wise enter into it any thing that defileth, neither whatsoever worketh abomination, or maketh a lie: but they which are written in the Lamb's book of life."*

> *ISAIAH 61:4-7, "And THEY* [Nations] *SHALL BUILD THE OLD WASTES, they shall raise up the former desolations, and they shall REPAIR THE*

WASTE CITIES, the DESOLATIONS OF MANY GENERATIONS. And strangers shall stand and feed your flocks, and the sons of the alien shall be your PLOWMEN and your VINEDRESSERS. But ye shall be named the Priests of the LORD: men shall call you the Ministers of our God: YE SHALL EAT THE RICHES OF THE GENTILES, and in their glory shall ye boast yourselves."

From time to time the nations need healing, which they get freely from the leaves of the tree of life and/or the river of the water of life flowing from the throne of God. The nations are NOT allowed to enter the Golden City, but they can drink the water which flows out of the Throne and down the mountainside to the nations. The leaves of the tree of life are apparently plucked from the tree and taken without the city unto them. The water and the leaves give them temporary healing, but does NOT put their names in the Book of Life nor give them a glorified body.

> REVELATION 22:2, "In the midst of the street of it, and on either side of the river, was there the tree of life, which bare twelve manner of fruits, and yielded her fruit every month: and THE LEAVES OF THE TREE WERE FOR THE HEALING OF THE NATIONS."

> REVELATION 22: 14, 15,"BLESSED ARE THEY THAT DO HIS COMMANDMENTS, THAT THEY MAY HAVE RIGHT TO THE TREE OF LIFE, AND MAY ENTER IN THROUGH THE GATES INTO THE CITY. For WITHOUT are [Nations] DOGS, AND SORCERERS, AND WHOREMONGERS, AND MURDERERS, AND IDOLATERS, AND WHOSOEVER LOVETH AND MAKETH A LIE."

Overcomers are given power over the nations:

> REVELATION 2:26, "And he that overcometh, and keepeth my works unto the end, to him will I give POWER OVER THE NATIONS:"

Jesus and His Judges rule the nations, not allowing any law to be broken.

> REVELATION 12:5, "And she brought forth A MAN CHILD, WHO WAS TO RULE ALL NATIONS WITH A ROD OF IRON ..."

After 1,000 years Satan is released and deceives the nations which are destroyed, and Satan is tossed into the Lake of Fire.

> REVELATION 20:3, "And cast him into the bottomless pit, and shut him up, and set a seal upon him, that he should DECEIVE THE NATIONS NO MORE, TILL THE THOUSAND YEARS SHOULD BE FULFILLED: AND AFTER THAT HE MUST BE LOOSED A LITTLE SEASON."

> REVELATION 20:8, "And SHALL GO OUT TO DECEIVE THE NATIONS which are in the FOUR QUARTERS of the earth ... to gather them together to battle: the number of whom is as the sand of the sea."

Chapter 12
PROPHECIES IN THE FEASTS OF THE LORD

The prophecies in the Feasts of the LORD need further explanation. The Secret Door links the Feast of Firstfruits of Leviticus 23 to the Firstfruits of Revelation 14. That Secret Door helps us to understand Bible prophecies.

LEVITICUS 23:1, 2, 4, "And the LORD spake unto Moses, saying, 'Speak unto the children of Israel, and say unto them, 'Concerning the feasts [Future appointments] *of the LORD, which ye shall proclaim to be holy convocations,* [Future rehearsals] *even these are my feasts. ... These are the feasts of the LORD, even holy convocations, which ye shall proclaim in their seasons.'"*

FIRSTFRUITS

ECCLESIASTES 1:9, "THE THING THAT HATH BEEN, IT IS THAT WHICH SHALL BE; and THAT WHICH IS DONE IS THAT WHICH SHALL BE DONE: AND THERE IS NO NEW THING UNDER THE SUN."

ECCLESIASTES 3:15, "... that which hath been is now; and that which is to be hath already been; and GOD REQUIRETH THAT WHICH IS PAST."

LEVITICUS 23:10-12, "... When ye be come into the land which I give unto you, and shall reap the [barley] *harvest thereof, then ye shall bring a sheaf of the FIRSTFRUITS of your harvest unto the priest: And he shall wave the SHEAF before the LORD, to be accepted for you: on the morrow after the sabbath the priest shall wave it. And ye shall offer that day when ye wave the sheaf AN HE LAMB WITHOUT BLEMISH OF THE FIRST YEAR for a burnt offering unto the LORD."*

REVELATION 14:1, 4, 5, "And I looked, and, lo, a Lamb stood on the mount Sion, and with him an HUNDRED FORTY AND FOUR THOUSAND, having his Father's name written in their foreheads ... These are they which were not defiled with women; for they are virgins. These are they which follow the Lamb whithersoever he goeth. These were redeemed from among men, being the FIRSTFRUITS unto God and to the Lamb. And in their mouth was found NO GUILE: for they are WITHOUT FAULT before the throne of God."

Now we go into more detail, rather than a brief overview in chapter one. On the 17th day of the first month, the High Priest is commanded to take a sheaf (handful) of fine barley flour. Leviticus doesn't say the harvest is barley, but we know it is because barley is the first harvest to ripen in the spring. We also know barley represents Israelites because Revelation 14:4 says the 144,000 are *"the Firstfruits unto God and to the Lamb."*

The fields are full of barley, but only a handful is selected, symbolizing the 144,000 as a small sampling of the total Jewish harvest. The High Priest adds oil without leaven and forms a large cracker and cooks it. Leaven is a symbol for sin and these 144,000 Firstfruits have no sin. This cracker represents the 144,000 of Revelation 14, which have no sin.

The prophetic shadow picture is that there are many sons of Israel lying in graves, but only a small handful are resurrected in this Firstfruits resurrection. These 144,000 have no guile in their mouth, and likewise never had a woman. These are they who are without leaven or without sin before the throne of God. They obviously were not told about Jesus, but gain entry to the Marriage Supper of the Lamb because they are without sin or fault before the throne of God.

These 144,000 are the Firstfruits of the harvest. Jesus was the *"Firstfruits of them that slept."* The barley harvest is the first to receive their glorified body since Jesus arose. Remember the words, *"Let both grow together until the harvest."* The 144,000 are the first of the final three harvests. The three final harvests are barley, wheat and grapes. Barley on Firstfruits, Wheat on Pentecost and the grape harvest is on Trumpets.

1 CORINTHIANS 15:20, "But now is Christ risen from the dead, and become the FIRSTFRUITS OF THEM THAT SLEPT."

MATTHEW 27:51-53, "And, behold, the veil of the temple was rent in twain from the top to the bottom; and the earth did quake, and the rocks rent; And THE GRAVES WERE OPENED; AND MANY BODIES OF THE SAINTS WHICH SLEPT AROSE, AND CAME OUT OF THE GRAVES AFTER HIS RESURRECTION, and went into the holy city, and appeared unto many."

The 144,000 is the shout. We know this because in the very next verse the angel preaches the everlasting gospel, *"Fear God, and give glory to him; for the hour of his judgment is come ... "* This is one of the last events before Jesus returns.

MATTHEW 24:14, "And THIS GOSPEL OF THE KINGDOM SHALL BE PREACHED IN ALL THE WORLD FOR A WITNESS UNTO ALL NATIONS; AND THEN SHALL THE END COME."

MATTHEW 25:1-12, "Then shall the kingdom of heaven be likened unto ten virgins, which took their lamps, and went forth to meet the bridegroom ... And at MIDNIGHT THERE WAS A CRY MADE, 'BEHOLD, THE BRIDEGROOM COMETH; GO YE OUT TO MEET HIM.' [144,000 Firstfruits with Jesus on Mt. Zion] *... the bridegroom came; and THEY THAT WERE READY WENT IN ... "*

Does Jesus return twice? Once as a Lamb and once as the Lion of the Tribe of Judah? When Jesus is seen on Firstfruits with the 144,000 it clearly says, *"a LAMB stood upon Mt. Zion."* When Jesus returns as King of Kings for Armageddon, He stands upon the Mt. of Olives. Can we conclude that Jesus returns as the LAMB with the 144,000 on Mt. Zion, and the final time as the LION OF THE TRIBE OF JUDAH, the KING OF KINGS on the Mt. of Olives? Is there any other way to understand the meaning of these verses?

REVELATION 14:1, 4, "And I looked, and, lo, A LAMB STOOD ON THE MOUNT SION, and with him an hundred forty and four thousand, having his Father's name written in their foreheads. ... These are they which FOLLOW THE LAMB WHITHERSOEVER HE GOETH."

ZECHARIAH 14:4, "And his feet shall stand in that day upon the MOUNT OF OLIVES, which is before Jerusalem on the east, and the MOUNT OF OLIVES shall cleave in the midst thereof toward the east and toward the west, and there shall be a very great valley; and half of the mountain shall remove toward the north, and half of it toward the south."

POINT

Jesus returns twice, once on Mount Zion as a Lamb with the 144,000 and the final time on the Mount of Olives as King of Kings.

As further confirmation, the following verses describe the next time Jesus returns, which is on Mount Zion as the Lamb He is the SAME as when He left. He is not in His KING OF KINGS body. He has not been to the Marriage Supper of the Lamb yet; He has not been crowned KING OF KINGS yet. He is still like He was eating fish with the disciples. The Word says *"this same Jesus" "in like manner"* in a cloud.

Yes, when He returns on Trumpets to the Mount of Olives, He is King of Kings, riding a White Horse. When he returns on Firstfruits he is returning as "the Lamb."

> ACTS 1:9, *"And when he had spoken these things, while they beheld, he was taken up; and a cloud received him out of their sight. And while they looked stedfastly toward heaven as he went up, behold, two men stood by them in white apparel; Which also said, 'Ye men of Galilee, why stand ye gazing up into heaven? this SAME Jesus, which is taken up from you into heaven, SHALL SO COME IN LIKE MANNER AS YE HAVE SEEN HIM GO INTO HEAVEN.'"*

THE MARRIAGE DOOR

The Marriage Door is the door through which the Barley and Wheat pass to go to the Marriage Supper of the Lamb. It is an easy conclusion that THE MARRIAGE DOOR CLOSES ON PENTECOST. The 144,000 Firstfruits arrive on Firstfruits and 50 days later when the Wheat is resurrected they both go to the Marriage Supper.

"GO YE OUT TO MEET HIM"

Probably, the reason the Scripture says, *"Go ye out to meet him,"* is because Jesus arrived on Mt. Zion on Firstfruits and is walking around (for how long—we don't know for sure). The reason we know He walks around is because of the words, *"These are they which follow the Lamb whithersoever he goeth,"* speaking of the 144,000. If they "follow Jesus" around, that means He is walking around.

Since the Wheat Harvest arises 50 days after Jesus arrives with the 144,000, the Bible doesn't tell us exactly, but Jesus may be walking around for those 50 days from Firstfruits to Pentecost. That may be why the Bible says, *"Go ye out to meet him"* because some people literally do meet Him. This would be just as some of His disciples met Him after His crucifixion during the 40 days He walked around. Remember, they ate fish with Jesus after His death.

Jesus may walk around for more than just a day or two. It is His planet. He may be irritating the Beast! He MAY walk around for the 50 days from Firstfruits to Pentecost! The Bible is not clear how long Jesus walks on Mt. Zion, nor where else He may walk. Who is going to stop Him or say, *"What doest thou?"* As Jesus walked the earth after He arose for 40 days when He arose and went to the Father, and He MAY walk around with the 144,000 for another 50 days until the Wheat Harvest arises once again and go to the Father for the Marriage Supper of the Lamb. The Marriage Supper of the Lamb begins on the last Pentecost when the wheat harvest arises. [See chart]

> DANIEL 4:35, *"... all the inhabitants of the earth are reputed as nothing: and HE DOETH ACCORDING TO HIS WILL in the army of heaven,*

and *AMONG THE INHABITANTS OF THE EARTH: and NONE CAN STAY HIS HAND, or say unto him, 'WHAT DOEST THOU?'"*

Could it be that Jesus is allowing Himself to be seen from Firstfruits to Pentecost and letting His presence be known in order to anger the Beast as part of his plan to draw all the nations and their world army to attack Jerusalem in four months at Trumpets? Jesus is probably stirring up the tares and grapes to come and attack him! Notice the first verse does NOT say they will make war with the Lion, but rather the LAMB. When Jesus returns on Trumpets, He returns as the LION of the Tribe of Judah, the King of Kings and Lord of Lords, but here it says they make war with the *"LAMB."* Apparently, Jesus and the 144,000 are walking around more than just on Mt. Zion. Perhaps they are walking all over, exposing the bad things about the Beast and the False Prophet, drawing them to the valley of Jezreel like the moth to the flame. Then four months later after the Marriage, He returns as the Lion using the Morning Star to burn them up! Notice the kings of the world government don't make war with the Lion. They make war with the Lamb; that means this is NOT speaking of Jesus the Lion on Trumpets, but Jesus the Lamb on Firstfruits!

REVELATION 17:12-14, "And THE TEN HORNS which thou sawest are TEN KINGS ... These have one mind, and shall give their power and strength unto the beast. THESE SHALL MAKE WAR WITH THE LAMB, and the Lamb shall overcome them ..."

REVELATION 19:19, "And I saw the beast, and the kings of the earth, and their armies, gathered together TO MAKE WAR AGAINST HIM THAT SAT ON THE HORSE, and against his army."

There are those who say Jesus fulfilled the spring Feasts (Passover, Unleavened Bread, Firstfruits, and Pentecost) and will return to fulfill the last three Feasts (Trumpets, Atonement and Tabernacles). This is not true, because Jesus did not fulfill all the spring Feasts.

Think it through.

Jesus died without sin before sunset on Passover. (Passover Fulfilled)

Jesus in the heart of the earth for three days. (Unleavened Bread)

Jesus arose from the grave on Firstfruits and became the first to rise from the grave *"... of them that slept."* Two verses later it says, *"CHRIST THE FIRSTFRUITS; AFTERWARD THEY THAT ARE CHRIST'S AT HIS COMING,"* meaning the play of the Feasts STOPPED with Jesus on Firstfruits. Firstfruits starts again with Jesus and the 144,000 arriving on Firstfruits. Remember the next time Jesus touches this earth. It is NOT on the Mount of Olives for Trumpets, but on Mount Zion with the 144,000 for FIRSTFRUITS! Firstfruits is the key!

*1 CORINTHIANS 15:20-23, "But now is Christ risen from the dead, and become the **FIRSTFRUITS** of THEM THAT SLEPT. For since by man came death, by man came also the resurrection of the dead. For as in Adam all die, even so in Christ shall all be made alive. But every man in his own order: CHRIST THE **FIRSTFRUITS**; AFTERWARD THEY THAT ARE CHRIST'S AT HIS COMING."*

The 144,000 arising from the grave on Firstfruits starts up the sequence again, because they are the first of the END TIME HARVEST to rise from the grave. The 144,000 continue the sequence that Jesus began. THE FUL-

FILLMENT OF THE FEASTS SEQUENCE WAS STOPPED ON FIRSTFRUITS AND BEGINS AGAIN ON FIRSTFRUITS. It was stopped with *"Firstfruits ... from them that slept,"* and started again with *"Firstfruits ... the end time harvest."* Firstfruits is the key! Jesus walked for 40 days after Firstfruits and MAY walk for 50 days after the next Firstfruits until Pentecost and the arrival of the Wheat!

> MATTHEW 13:30, 39, *"Let both grow together until THE HARVEST: and in the time of harvest I will say to the reapers, 'Gather ye together first the tares, and bind them in bundles to burn them: but gather the wheat into my barn. ... The enemy that sowed them is the devil; THE HARVEST IS THE END OF THE WORLD ..."*

Jesus had NOTHING TO DO WITH PENTECOST at that time. He wasn't on earth for the feasts following His death (Pentecost, Trumpets, Atonement or Tabernacles). Prophetic time stopped with Firstfruits and will begin again on Firstfruits. The last Feast Jesus experienced on earth was Firstfruits, and it is the first Feast He will see when He returns as the Lamb with the 144,000 on Mt. Zion!

Jesus ascended after walking around for forty days, and he MAY walk around on Mt. Zion for the 50 days between Firstfruits and Pentecost. That would mean he was walking around when He left, and He would walk around when He returns! He left walking and returned walking. He left after Firstfruits and returned on Firstfruits. He left as the Lamb of God on Firstfruits and RETURNS AS THE LAMB OF GOD ON FIRSTFRUITS! After 40 days of walking, He went to the Father, and it may be that after 50 days of walking, He once again arises to the Father for the Marriage. Prophetic time stood still for some 2,000 years, and Jesus returns to, "Pick it up from Firstfruits where He left off." Sinless Jesus arose on Firstfruits, and the sinless 144,000 arise on Firstfruits to conclude the fulfillment of the Feasts!

MARRIAGE SUPPER OF THE LAMB

I must give thanks to Jesus before I go further with this book. Jesus gave us the information in this book. I want to be there with you casting my crowns at His feet saying,

> *"Thou art worthy, O Lord, to receive glory and honour and power: for thou hast created all things, and for thy pleasure they are and were created!"*

I was given 30 revelations and two visions in the process of memorizing Revelation, which provided the information in this book. Before I started memorizing Revelation, I knew NOTHING in this book!

Sometimes these "revelations" came in an instant by the Holy Spirit. Sometimes they came by receiving deeper information WITHIN Scripture. ALL revelation information is confirmed in the Scriptures. Only a few revelations were deeper knowledge within the Scriptures. These revelations came in less than the blink of an eye. What I received in the blink of an eye sometimes can take as much as 20 minutes to explain.

I always pray before I refresh or memorize Scripture, "Lord, show me the deep and secret things in Your Word. Give me revelations and help me to better understand, memorize, and always remember Your Word."

One evening my wife was in the other room preparing her teaching for Sunday. I was "running my lines," meaning, I was either reciting or reading aloud the Book of Revelation to keep it fresh in my mind. In an instant I received my 25th revelation. I had already memorized the entire Book of Revelation, but I had not seen this. At the time I was NOT working on the part of the book speaking of the Marriage. I got the revelation and immediately went to my wife and said, "Honey, I just got another revelation! This one is really big. I will only give you one guess, because there is no use in wasting your time because you will never guess this one! Five minutes ago, I would not have known it, and I dare say, there are only a handful of people alive who know the answer to this one!"

The first question was: **When is Jesus anointed?**

This blank look came to her face. The same thing happens to everyone else I have asked this question. I didn't say, "When, 'was' Jesus anointed, the question was, "When 'is' He anointed?" He doesn't have this anointing yet.

She began putting forth guesses like everyone else, including me before this revelation: "At His birth? In the river Jordan? At His ascension?" I was not ready to give the answer yet.

One of the best teaching techniques designed to get us thinking is asking questions. It helps us to think it through.

I asked a second question. **"What is He anointed as?"**

… again, a blank stare …

Then a third question. **"We anoint people with oil, what will Jesus be anointed with?"**

Likewise, as with many other people I have asked … no answer.

I put these questions out in an email to my Fastrack team, and after two weeks, only four people got more than half of them correct. None got all of them.

I then asked, **"What three items does He receive at this anointing? Who is in attendance? What does He do once He is anointed?"**

I began to give the answers and explain the revelation when a "goose-bump-anointing" came on me. God uses many ways to communicate to us. This has happened with me less than 25 times. Most of those were confirmations I needed for this book. A "goose-bump-anointing" for me is a strong confirmation that what I am saying or doing is RIGHT! It is like the Holy Spirit is saying, "YES!" with an exclamation mark!

I am about to show you in Scripture and explain the Greatest Event in Human History. Yes, we all know the birth and crucifixion of Jesus are great events from our perspective, but in the eyes of the Father and the Son, His Coronation (the crowning of Jesus as KING OF KINGS and LORD OF LORDS) is the culmination, climax, and the objective since before the creation of Adam! This is the day when the Lamb of God, Prince of the Kings of the earth, is crowned as KING OF KINGS and LORD OF LORDS. This is the day for which His Bride has made herself ready for the Marriage of the Lamb! This is the day when the Lamb of God becomes the Lion of the Tribe of Judah and King of Kings. This is the day when His *"sons and daughters"* become His *"Kings and Priests!"* This is the objective of all of creation: to give Jesus His Bride and Wife.

The birth, death, burial and resurrection are important and glorious, but the apex is the Marriage of the Lamb! The culmination is the crowning of Jesus as King of Kings and us as His Kings and Priests to serve Him in spirit and truth without sin for all eternity!

Now the answers:

When is Jesus anointed? Jesus is anointed at the Marriage Supper of the Lamb.

What is He anointed as? He is anointed as KING OF KINGS and LORD OF LORDS!

We anoint people with oil. What is He anointed with? He is anointed with His own blood sacrificed 2,000 years ago. He is given a Vesture dipped in His blood. Remember the blood of Jesus is the most powerful purifying thing in all creation.

You may recall when Mary went to the garden tomb looking for Jesus. She thought she was speaking to a gardener and asked the location of the body of Jesus. Jesus called her name and immediately she responded, "Rabboni" and Jesus said, *"Touch me not; for I am not yet ascended to my Father."* Yet, later He told Thomas, *"Reach hither thy finger, and behold my hands; and reach hither thy hand and thrust it into my side."* So, we must conclude that Jesus ascended twice. Once shortly after the visit with Mary and again 40 days later. One can conclude that Jesus went to fulfill the Levitical Laws (Leviticus 16:14) to sprinkle His blood on the mercy seat eastward, and He must have also put His blood on His vesture (White wedding garment) laid aside for His future wedding day! Because we see AFTER the wedding He is wearing a "Vesture dipped in blood." Some think it was all soaked in blood as in wholly dipped in blood. Others think it was just sprinkled with blood. Personally, I think it is mostly white with a red spot, "dipped in His blood." God knows…

JOHN 20:16, 17a, "Jesus saith unto her, 'Mary.' She turned herself, and saith unto him, 'Rabboni;' which is to say, Master. Jesus saith unto her, 'TOUCH ME NOT; FOR I AM NOT YET ASCENDED TO MY FATHER: …'"

JOHN 20:27, "Then saith he to Thomas, 'REACH HITHER THY FINGER, AND BEHOLD MY HANDS; AND REACH HITHER THY HAND, AND THRUST IT INTO MY SIDE: and be not faithless, but believing.'"

What three items does He receive at the anointing? Many crowns, a vesture dipped in His blood with "King of Kings and Lord of Lords" written on it and a white horse.

REVELATION 19:13, "And HE WAS CLOTHED WITH A VESTURE DIPPED IN BLOOD: and his name is called The Word of God."

REVELATION 19:11-16, "And I saw heaven opened, and behold a WHITE HORSE; and he that sat upon him was called Faithful and True, and in righteousness he doth judge and make war. His eyes were as a flame of fire, and on his head were MANY CROWNS; and he had a name written, that no man knew, but he himself … And he hath on his vesture and on his thigh a name written, KING OF KINGS, AND LORD OF LORDS."

Who is in attendance? All of heaven, the four and twenty elders, the four beasts, the heavenly hosts and the Barley Harvest and the Wheat Harvest. Not all are called to the Marriage.

REVELATION 19:9, "… BLESSED ARE THEY WHICH ARE CALLED UNTO THE MARRIAGE SUPPER OF THE LAMB …"

REVELATION 20:6, "Blessed and holy is he that hath part in the FIRST RESURRECTION: on such the second death hath no power, but they shall be priests of God and of Christ, and shall reign with him a thousand years."

What does He do once anointed? Jesus takes His bride, the Lamb's wife, and rides to destroy the enemies of Jesus and His bride at Armageddon.

REVELATION 19:14-21, "And the ARMIES WHICH WERE IN HEAVEN followed him upon WHITE HORSES, clothed in fine linen, white and clean. And OUT OF HIS MOUTH GOETH A SHARP SWORD, THAT WITH IT HE SHOULD SMITE THE NATIONS: and he shall rule them with a rod of iron: and HE TREADETH THE WINEPRESS OF THE FIERCENESS AND WRATH OF ALMIGHTY GOD ... And the remnant were SLAIN WITH THE SWORD of him that sat upon the horse, which SWORD PROCEEDED OUT OF HIS MOUTH: and all the fowls were filled with their flesh."

The Wedding Ceremony

The Marriage Supper of the Lamb takes place on Pentecost. Daniel 7:13 speaks of the Marriage of the Lamb. *"Son of man"* is referring to Jesus. The *"Ancient of days"* is the Father. *"They brought him near"* is the Marriage at which time the Father crowns Him King of Kings and Lord of Lords.

DANIEL 7:13, 14, "I saw in the night visions, and, behold, one like the Son of man [Jesus] came with the clouds of heaven, and came to the Ancient of days [Father], and THEY BROUGHT HIM NEAR [Marriage of the Lamb] BEFORE HIM. AND THERE WAS GIVEN HIM DOMINION, AND GLORY, AND A KINGDOM, that all people, nations, and languages, should serve him: his dominion is an everlasting dominion, which shall not pass away, and his kingdom that which shall not be destroyed."

The most complete description of the Marriage Supper of the Lamb is found in Revelation 19. The Marriage Supper is the Greatest Event in Human History! It is the ultimate objective of the creation of God from before the world was created. God wanted to have people live eternally with Him that *"sitteth on the throne and unto the Lamb."*

This verse describes the Barley and Wheat when we see Jesus for the first time. We are rejoicing and worshiping Jesus at our first gathering as the Bride of Christ in Heaven at the Marriage of the Lamb. This happens on Pentecost.

REVELATION 19:1, 5, "And after these things I heard A GREAT VOICE OF MUCH PEOPLE IN HEAVEN, saying, 'Alleluia; Salvation, and glory, and honour, and power, unto the Lord our God:' And a voice came out of the THRONE, saying, 'PRAISE OUR GOD, ALL YE HIS SERVANTS, and ye that fear him, both small and great.'"

All the BRIDE OF CHRIST says is, "Yes, let the Marriage begin, we are ready to be wed!" The *"great multitude"* is the Barley and Wheat. The words *"Alleluia: for the Lord God omnipotent reigneth"* represents the Bride saying, "I Do. I accept this groom to be my husband, and I will be His wife, and we shall be one."

REVELATION 19:6, 7, "And I heard as it were the voice of A GREAT MULTITUDE, and as the voice of many waters, and as the voice of mighty thunderings, saying, 'ALLELUIA: FOR THE LORD GOD OMNIPOTENT REIGNETH.' Let us be glad and rejoice, and give honour to him: for the MARRIAGE OF THE LAMB IS COME, and his WIFE HATH MADE HERSELF READY."

The Bride and Groom don't exchange rings, but rather white wedding garments. The Groom gives the bride white wedding garments. The Father gives the Son a Vesture dipped in blood for His wedding. Throughout the Bible, the servants of God wear FINE LINEN and only fine linen. It is specifically forbidden to wear wool, as it is unclean being from an animal which has sweat. As in Revelation 18, the fine linen is a sign this is the Saints of God, chosen to be at the Marriage.

> REVELATION 19:8, "And to her was granted that she should be ARRAYED in FINE LINEN, CLEAN AND WHITE: for the fine linen is the righteousness of saints."

The Barley and Wheat are gathered for the Marriage at Pentecost (see chart). The 144,000 and Only the dead IN Christ are invited. Only those who were resurrected at this point are allowed admittance.

> REVELATION 19:9, "And he saith unto me, 'Write, Blessed are they which are called unto the marriage supper of the Lamb ...'"

> REVELATION 20:5, 6, "... This is the first resurrection. Blessed and holy is he that hath part in the first resurrection: on such the second death hath no power, but they shall be priests of God and of Christ, and shall reign with him a thousand years."

Some will wonder about those IN Christ who die between Pentecost and Trumpets when Jesus returns. Provision is made for them. They still get all their rewards, but they don't get to attend the Marriage because they are still alive.

> REVELATION 14:13, "And I heard a voice from heaven saying unto me, 'Write, Blessed are the dead which die in the Lord from henceforth: Yea,' saith the Spirit, that they may rest from their labours; and their works do follow them."

The Prince of the Kings of the earth has NOW been transformed from "Lamb" to "Lion," from "Prince of the kings of the earth" to KING OF KINGS and LORD OF LORDS. Notice in Revelation 1:5 He is called, "...the prince of the kings of the earth" meaning He has not yet been promoted and crowned yet. When a baby is born who is in linage to become a King, he is referred to as a "Prince," but it is not until he is crowned that he becomes a King. Likewise, in Revelation 1:5, Jesus is a "Prince," but here He is crowned KING OF KINGS and LORD OF LORDS! It is the Father, the Ancient of Days Who gives Him the crowns. In these verses it is a picture of the Barley and Wheat at the Marriage Supper watching Jesus receive His rewards from the Father.

> REVELATION 19:11, "And I saw heaven opened, and behold a white horse; and he that sat upon him was called Faithful and True, and in righteousness he doth judge and make war. His eyes were as a flame of fire, and on his head were MANY CROWNS; and he had a name written, that no man knew, but he himself. And he was clothed with a VESTURE DIPPED IN BLOOD: and his name is called The Word of God."

Here are the Barley and Wheat Harvests, worthy to be the Bride of Christ, in our new glorified bodies, wearing white wedding garments, riding white horses, and accompanying Jesus to the great winepress of the wrath of God!

> REVELATION 19:14, 15, "And the armies which were in heaven followed him upon WHITE HORSES, clothed in FINE LINEN, white and clean. And out of his mouth goeth A SHARP SWORD, that with it he SHOULD SMITE THE NATIONS: and he shall rule them with a rod of iron: and he

treadeth the winepress of the fierceness and wrath of Almighty God. And he hath on his VESTURE and on his THIGH a name written, KING OF KINGS, AND LORD OF LORDS."

After the Marriage Supper, about four months later, Jesus returns with His bride to clean the earth making a place for His house for His new bride. This is Armageddon where Jesus uses the Morning Star to destroy His enemies who hate Him!

> REVELATION 19:19-21, "And I saw the beast, and the kings of the earth, and their armies, gathered together to MAKE WAR AGAINST HIM THAT SAT ON THE HORSE, and against his army ... And THE REMNANT WERE SLAIN WITH THE SWORD OF HIM THAT SAT UPON THE HORSE, WHICH SWORD PROCEEDED OUT OF HIS MOUTH: and all the fowls were filled with their flesh."

The Bride does not participate in Armageddon but only watches. The Bride will be carried over the threshold to the New Jerusalem on Tabernacles. The Groom and two Angels do all the killing.

SUMMARY:
MARRIAGE SUPPER OF THE LAMB

Jesus appears on Firstfruits on Mt. Zion with the 144,000. The Barley Harvest is the shout, *"Behold the Bridegroom cometh."* Fifty days later, on Pentecost, the Wheat Harvest is resurrected, and both go to the Marriage Supper of the Lamb.

About four months after Pentecost the Barley and Wheat return with Jesus on the 1st day of the 7th month for the Feast of Trumpets and Armageddon.

The Marriage of the Lamb to His Bride is the apex of all creation. Jesus will receive His Bride!

Those dying in the Lord from Pentecost to Trumpets still receive a blessing. They *"rest from their labors and their works do follow them."*

The Angel sounds the Seventh and final trumpet for the day of Trumpets. Remember, a trumpet sounding is a call for war! Trumpets is THE DAY OF THE LORD, the final evening and morning. The final war is between *"him that sitteth on the horse"* and *"the Beast and the Kings of the earth and their armies."* Jesus comes as a shocker: *"Behold I come as a thief in the night."* He uses the Morning Star which He received of His Father (Revelation 2:27). This appears as, *"arrows of lightning ... The LORD shall be seen over them, and his arrow shall go forth as the lightning: and the Lord GOD shall blow the trumpet ..."* (Zechariah 9:14). *"As the lightning cometh out of the east, and shineth even unto the west; so shall also the coming of the Son of man be"* (Matthew 24:27).

After the burning of the tares and the slicing/crushing of the grapes, there will be great voices in heaven saying, *"The kingdoms of this world are become the kingdoms of our Lord, and of his Christ"* (Revelation 11:15). *"...he shall send his angels with a great sound of a trumpet, and they shall gather together his elect from the four winds, from one end of heaven to the other"* (Matthew 24:31).

Jesus returns with His rewards (*"my reward is with me"*) and all Barley and Wheat. All IN Christ, dead or alive, stand before the Judgment Seat of Christ to receive their rewards for those things done in their body. It appears the worst that happens for some is their works are burned up, but they are still in the Lamb's Book of Life. This is not saying there is a guarantee of "once saved, always saved." That is the decision of Jesus. Jesus has the

THE SECRET DOOR TO UNDERSTAND BIBLE PROPHECY

keys of hell and death. Read Ezekiel 3:20. This is where we receive all our rewards and glorified bodies.

1 CORINTHIANS 3:12-15, "Now if any man build upon this foundation gold, silver, precious stones, wood, hay, stubble; EVERY MAN'S WORK SHALL BE MADE MANIFEST: for the day shall declare it, because it shall be revealed by fire; and THE FIRE SHALL TRY EVERY MAN'S WORK of what sort it is. If any man's work abide which he hath built thereupon, he shall receive a reward. IF ANY MAN'S WORK SHALL BE BURNED, HE SHALL SUFFER LOSS: BUT HE HIMSELF SHALL BE SAVED; yet so as by fire."

Ten days later on Atonement, all dead NOT IN CHRIST report to the GREAT WHITE THRONE. The Judgment is set. The books are opened. Both good and bad souls are judged.

Five days later on Tabernacles, all whose name is in the Book of Life are allowed entry into the camp of the Saints, the beloved city, the holy city, New Jerusalem, coming down from God out of heaven, prepared as a bride adorned for her husband ... the city is made of pure gold, not yellow, but clear as glass. It has the glory of God: and her light is so bright the light of the Lamb lights the entire earth! The sun never relights. Jesus literally is the light of the world.

I am repeating myself, but most say this is so much new information the repetition is helpful.

PENTECOST

LEVITICUS 23:15-22, "And ye shall count unto you from the morrow [Firstfruits] after the sabbath, from the day that ye brought the sheaf of the wave offering; seven sabbaths shall be complete: Even unto the morrow after the seventh sabbath shall ye number FIFTY DAYS; ... Ye shall bring out of your habitations TWO WAVE LOAVES OF TWO TENTH DEALS; THEY SHALL BE OF FINE FLOUR; they shall be BAKEN WITH LEAVEN; they are the FIRSTFRUITS unto the LORD ... And the priest shall wave them with the bread of the firstfruits [Wheat] for a wave offering before the LORD ... And when ye reap the harvest of your land, THOU SHALT NOT MAKE CLEAN RIDDANCE OF THE CORNERS OF THY FIELD when thou reapest, neither shalt thou gather any gleaning of thy harvest: thou shalt leave them unto the poor, and to the stranger:"

REVELATION 19:9, "... Blessed are they which are called unto the marriage supper of the Lamb..."

Pentecost is exactly 50 days after the spring barley firstfruits harvest. This is the day, 50 days after Jesus arose from the grave that the Holy Spirit arrived, and the Church spoke in tongues, and 3,000 souls were added to the Church.

On the day of Pentecost, the High Priest is commanded to take *"two tenth deals; ... of fine flour"* and bake it with leaven. A tenth deal is about six pints of wheat flour (about one cubic foot or a little over 2 liters). He mixes these two tenth deals separately, adding oil and leaven. Leaven symbolizes sin. This makes two loaves of wheat bread about the size of two small watermelons. This represents two groups of people, the Israelites and Non-Israelites. Those who have sinned make it to heaven only because they have been washed in the blood of the Lamb of God. The High Priest waves these two loaves before the LORD.

REVELATION 7:14, "And I said unto him, 'Sir, thou knowest.' And he said to me, 'THESE ARE THEY WHICH CAME OUT OF GREAT TRIBULATION, AND HAVE WASHED THEIR ROBES, AND MADE THEM WHITE IN THE BLOOD OF THE LAMB.'

The symbolism as it relates to prophecy is this: The two loaves are a shadow picture of the Israelites and Non-Israelites washed in the blood. This full resurrection has many times more people in this harvest as compared to one "sheaf" of barley. They were allowed entrance to the Marriage Supper, even though they have leaven because they "washed their robes in the blood of the lamb." These were unlike the 144,000 of the Firstfruits who were, *"without fault before the throne of God."*

The WHEAT harvest is NOT without fault; yet, they have been chosen to go to the Marriage Supper. This group is made clean because they are washed in the blood of Jesus. They come out of "Great Tribulation," NOT because they lived during the tribulation, but because they are RESURRECTED DURING the Great Tribulation. This group includes those going back to the days of Jesus. Those IN Christ have been washed in the Blood of the Lamb.

This harvest has much **more** wheat flour, meaning many **more** people will be in this Wheat Harvest. We know this is the Wheat Harvest because this is the **second** harvest. The Barley is the spring harvest, the first harvest. The wheat is the second harvest, and the last harvest of the year is the grape harvest. The Barley is the Israelites, the Wheat is those washed in the blood of Jesus. The Grape harvest is the harvest which has the blood rising to the horse bridles during Armageddon.

The Barley Harvest is only a handful of barley flour without leaven, representing the 144,000. But this Wheat Harvest is much larger, signifying two groups, and many more will be in this second Pentecost harvest.

The Barley is a specific number, only 144,000. But the Wheat Harvest is *"...a great multitude, which no man could number, of all nations, and kindreds, and people, and tongues."*

When the High Priest makes two loaves of fine wheat flour with oil and leaven, the prophetic picture is that these two groups of Israelites and Non-Israelites, washed in the Blood of the Lamb, are now clean and approved to enter the Marriage of the Lamb. The leaven represents sin; and yet, they have been called to the Marriage Supper of the Lamb. How did they get in? They are washed in the Blood of the Lamb of God. The Marriage Supper begins on this final feast of Pentecost. They get to see Jesus crowned King of Kings and Lord of Lords!

REVELATION 7:9, 13, 14, "After this I beheld, and, lo, A GREAT MULTITUDE, WHICH NO MAN COULD NUMBER, OF ALL NATIONS, AND KINDREDS, AND PEOPLE, AND TONGUES, STOOD BEFORE THE THRONE, AND BEFORE THE LAMB, clothed with white robes, and palms in their hands; ... And one of the elders answered, saying unto me, 'What are these which are arrayed in white robes? and whence came they?' And I said unto him, 'Sir, thou knowest.' And he said to me, 'THESE ARE THEY WHICH CAME OUT OF GREAT TRIBULATION, and have washed their robes, and made them white in the blood of the Lamb.'"

Those who die in the LORD between the Wheat harvest on Pentecost and the Grape Harvest four months later on Trumpets are still blessed. This promise is made immediately after the Barley and Wheat Harvests are taken to the Marriage Supper of the Lamb. If they are alive on Pentecost they miss the Marriage Supper, but they keep their rewards. If they are IN Christ dead or alive after the burning and crushing, they receive their rewards on Trumpets.

REVELATION 14:13, "And I heard a voice from heaven saying unto me, 'Write, BLESSED ARE THE DEAD WHICH DIE IN THE LORD FROM HENCEFORTH: Yea,' saith the Spirit, that they may rest from their labours; and THEIR WORKS DO FOLLOW THEM."

The everlasting Gospel was preached to all who dwell upon the earth IMMEDIATELY AFTER THE BARLEY HARVEST OF FIRSTFRUITS. The Wheat harvest is gathered. Four months later is the final harvest, the Day of the Lord, the Feast of Trumpets, when ALL IN CHRIST stand before the Judgment Seat of Christ and Jesus judges.

SUMMARY:
PENTECOST,
WHEAT HARVEST

The Barley Harvest of 144,000 are resurrected and appear on Mt. Zion with Jesus about six months before Armageddon. Jesus is still the Lamb of God, the Prince of the Kings of the Earth. He is not anointed King of Kings until the Marriage Supper on Pentecost.

The Wheat Harvest of two loaves, symbolizing the two groups, both Israelites and Non-Israelites resurrect on Pentecost, and both the Barley and Wheat go to the Marriage Supper of the Lamb.

About four months later, the world first sees Jesus as King of Kings on the Feast of Trumpets after sunset when the Barley and Wheat harvests return with Him on white horses to watch the burning of the tares and crushing of the grapes and gathering of the remaining Wheat IN Christ!

Chapter 13
MARRIAGE SUPPER OF THE LAMB

HOW DO WE KNOW THE MARRIAGE SUPPER OF THE LAMB IS ON PENTECOST?

This chapter answers a question some may have. If you have not had a lot of traditional teaching about the Feasts you might not need proof the Marriage is on Pentecost. If you don't need that proof feel free to skip this segment.

REASON 1
THE FIRST MARRIAGE OCCURRED ON PENTECOST

The third month is the same month in which Pentecost occurs. In Exodus 19, when the children of Israel first arrived at Mt. Sinai, God offered to marry them saying:

> EXODUS 19:1-8, "In the third month, when the children of Israel were gone forth out of the land of Egypt, the same day came they into the wilderness of Sinai. ... and were come to the desert of Sinai, ... and there Israel camped before the mount. And Moses went up unto God, ... tell the children of Israel; ... 'I bare you on eagles' wings, and brought you unto myself. ... if ye will obey my voice indeed, and keep my covenant, then ye shall be a peculiar treasure [Marriage] unto me above all people:' ... And all the people answered together, and said, 'All that the LORD hath spoken we will do. [I do!]'"

Just as in our marriage ceremony today we hear, "Do you take this man to be your lawfully wedded husband?" And the bride responds, "I do." The children of Israel were "married" to God in the third month. I loosely call this a marriage, but in reality it is a betrothal or a promise to one day be married. That day of marriage will be the Marriage Supper of the Lamb. The ONLY feast occurring in the third month is Pentecost! Once again, the Bible repeats. On this last Pentecost, those washed in the blood of Christ, both Jew and non-Jew, will be wed at the Marriage Supper of the Lamb!

This proves the Marriage is NOT on Trumpets, NOT on Tabernacles and certainly NOT at the end of the Millennium!

REASON 2
PENTECOST IS A NEW TESTAMENT CHURCH—WHEAT EVENT

The word Pentecost only appears in the Bible three times. It does NOT appear in the Old Testament. Pentecost in the Old Testament was called the Feast of Weeks. Pentecost is a Feast mostly for the Gentiles and those reading and believing in the New Testament, specifically for those washed in the Blood of the Lamb. Just as Firstfruits is ONLY Israelites, Pentecost is primarily Christians. The Marriage Supper will have 144,000 from the twelve tribes of Israel, but Non-Israelites will make up the majority of those multitudes in attendance.

REASON 3
THE "GREAT MULTITUDE" IS THE WHEAT/CHURCH AND RISES 50 DAYS AFTER THE BARLEY ARISES

In Revelation 7, the first eight verses specifically list the 12 tribes from which the 144,000 are resurrected to be the Firstfruits. Afterward, in verse 9, the topic shifts to the Wheat. The Barley 144,000 arises on Firstfruits, but this group, *"no man could number, of all nations, and kindreds, and people, and tongues,"* made up mostly of Gentiles, arises on the next Feast, Pentecost. *"Blessed are they which are called unto the marriage supper of the Lamb."* Not every person in the Book of Life is called to the Marriage, only those who were ready.

REVELATION 7:9, 10, "After this I beheld, and, lo, A GREAT MULTITUDE, which no man could number, of all nations, and kindreds, and people, and tongues, stood before the THRONE, and before the Lamb, clothed with white robes, and palms in their hands; And cried with a loud voice, saying, 'Salvation to our God which sitteth upon the THRONE, and unto the Lamb.'"

REVELATION 8:1, 2, 6, "And when he had opened the seventh seal ... And I saw the seven angels which stood before God; and to them were given SEVEN TRUMPETS. ... And THE SEVEN ANGELS WHICH HAD THE SEVEN TRUMPETS PREPARED THEMSELVES TO SOUND."

Immediately after the 144,000 are listed, we see the Wheat that, *"no man could number, of all nations, and kindreds, and people, and tongues."* They *"stand before the throne."* They are in heaven "before the throne" on Pentecost. Beginning on Firstfruits, the 144,000 walk around on Mt. Zion with the Lamb, awaiting the Wheat to ripen. Those washed in the blood of the Lamb are resurrected 50 days later to the throne with the Barley. They BOTH ascend to the throne on Pentecost for the Marriage.

REASON 4

THE WHEAT ARE BEFORE THE THRONE BEFORE THE TRUMPETS HAVE COMPLETED

Remember, I was told that the Seven Seals play over seven years, the seven Trumpets play over seven months and the seven Vials play over seven days. The seven Trumpets would have all played before we see the great multitude if the Marriage were on Trumpets. If the Marriage were on Tabernacles, we would have seen the seven Trumpets complete sounding before the Wheat is even in heaven. Since the great multitude is seen BEFORE both the Trumpets and Tabernacles, the Marriage could only occur on the Feast of Pentecost. There is no other option.

NOT everything in Revelation is chronological, but some things are. It is not easy to discern the correct placement; however, the placement of the Marriage at the Feast of Pentecost is the correct one. **We see the "great multitude" of Wheat appear BEFORE the seven Trumpets have completed playing.** Since the seven Trumpets play over seven months, that puts this great multitude at the throne BEFORE Trumpets/Armageddon.

I think the first, second, third and fourth Trumpets play in quick succession, probably within two weeks of Passover. I think they are all the result of an object, one-third the size of the sun, striking the sun. The *"great multitude"* will be *"before the throne"* at a time closer to Pentecost, making it will be impossible for the Marriage to be on Trumpets or Tabernacles.

REASON 5
REVELATION 19 IS NOT SAYING THE MARRIAGE TAKES PLACE ON TRUMPETS

Revelation 19 APPEARS to put the Marriage on Trumpets, but that is a misplacement of events.

At first, the Bible speaks of the Barley and Wheat rejoicing in Heaven.

REVELATION 19:1, 2, "And after these things I heard a great voice of MUCH PEOPLE IN HEAVEN, saying, 'ALLELUIA; SALVATION, AND GLORY, AND HONOUR, AND POWER, UNTO THE LORD OUR GOD: For true and righteous are his judgments: for he hath judged the great whore ...'"

We see the *"GREAT MULTITUDE"* in heaven is NOT in chronological order as sometimes happens in Revelation. The Marriage happens BEFORE ARMAGEDDON. The picture of "the great multitude of Barley and Wheat" jumps back to Pentecost at the Marriage Supper of the Lamb. We know this because of the words, *"the Lord God omnipotent reigneth."* Jesus becomes King of Kings at the Marriage Supper. Many of the great multitude were put to death by the tares and grapes. The great multitudes will ride on white horses with Jesus to the Armageddon slaughter of the enemies of Christ.

REVELATION 19:5, "And a voice came out of the throne, saying, 'Praise our God, ALL YE HIS SERVANTS, and ye that fear him, both small and great.' And I heard as it were the voice of a GREAT MULTITUDE, and as the voice of many waters, and as the voice of mighty thunderings, saying, 'Alleluia: for the Lord God omnipotent reigneth.'"

REVELATION 19:7, 9, "LET US BE GLAD AND REJOICE, and give honour to him: for the MARRIAGE OF THE LAMB IS COME, and his wife hath made herself ready. ... Blessed are they which are called unto the marriage supper of the Lamb."

This is a picture of the Marriage where Jesus is crowned with many crowns, and given a Vesture dipped in blood with *"King of Kings and Lord of Lords"* written on it.

REVELATION 19:11-16, "And I saw heaven opened, and behold a white horse; and he that sat upon him was called Faithful and True, and in righteousness he doth judge and make war. His eyes were as a flame of fire, and on his head were MANY CROWNS; and he had a name written, that no man knew, but he himself. And HE WAS CLOTHED WITH A VESTURE DIPPED IN BLOOD: and his name is called The Word of God. And the ARMIES WHICH WERE IN HEAVEN [barley and wheat] FOLLOWED HIM UPON WHITE HORSES, clothed in fine linen, white and clean. And out of his mouth goeth a SHARP SWORD, that with it he should SMITE THE NATIONS: and he shall rule them with a ROD OF IRON: and he treadeth the winepress of the fierceness and wrath of Almighty God. And he hath on his vesture and on his thigh a name written, KING OF KINGS, AND LORD OF LORDS."

Now he burns the tares at Armageddon.

REVELATION 19:17-21, "And I saw an angel standing in the sun; and he cried with a loud voice, saying to all the fowls that fly in the midst of heaven, 'Come and gather yourselves together unto the supper of the great God;' ... And the remnant were slain with the SWORD of him that sat upon the horse, which SWORD PROCEEDED OUT OF HIS MOUTH: and all the fowls were filled with their flesh."

THE SECRET DOOR TO UNDERSTAND BIBLE PROPHECY

This is the order of events:

PENTECOST:

The Barley and Wheat rejoice before the throne.

The Marriage takes place.

Jesus is crowned, given a Vesture and many crowns and a white horse.

TRUMPETS:

We accompany Jesus on white horses to Armageddon

We watch as the tares and grapes are destroyed.

It is the same order found in Revelation 19. Just understand the Marriage occurred on Pentecost not Trumpets or Tabernacles.

REASON 6
WHY THE MARRIAGE CAN'T BE ON TRUMPETS:

The Marriage Supper of the Lamb is a day of CELEBRATION. This verse speaks of the Barley and Wheat standing before the throne in worship at the Marriage.

> REVELATION 19:7, "LET US BE GLAD AND REJOICE, and give honour to him: for the marriage of the Lamb is come ..."

The following verses describe TRUMPETS, and they DON'T SOUND LIKE VERSES OF A DAY OF CELEBRATION; they sound like A DAY OF WAR! Trumpets is a day of war. That is why the Trumpets sound on the day of Trumpets. Trumpets are a call to war! The Marriage is a day of celebration!

> AMOS 5:18, "WOE UNTO YOU THAT DESIRE THE DAY OF THE LORD! to what end is it for you? THE DAY OF THE LORD IS DARKNESS, AND NOT LIGHT."

> ISAIAH 9:19, "THROUGH THE WRATH OF THE LORD OF HOSTS IS THE LAND DARKENED, AND THE PEOPLE SHALL BE AS THE FUEL OF THE FIRE: no man shall spare his brother."

> EZEKIEL 32:7, 8, 10. "I WILL COVER THE HEAVEN, AND MAKE THE STARS THEREOF DARK; I WILL COVER THE SUN WITH A CLOUD, AND THE MOON SHALL NOT GIVE HER LIGHT. All the bright lights of heaven will I make dark over thee, and set darkness upon thy land, ... WHEN I SHALL BRANDISH MY SWORD BEFORE THEM ..."

> ZEPHANIAH 1:15, "That day is A DAY OF WRATH, a day of TROUBLE and DISTRESS, A DAY OF WASTENESS AND DESOLATION, A DAY OF DARKNESS AND GLOOMINESS, A DAY OF CLOUDS AND THICK DARKNESS,"

REASON 7
WHY THE MARRIAGE CAN'T BE ON TABERNACLES

The Bible says there is NO TEMPLE in the New Jerusalem. Heaven has a Temple, but there is NO TEMPLE in the New Jerusalem. The following three verses are NOT pictures of Tabernacles. The Marriage Supper of the Lamb CAN'T take place on Tabernacles.

> REVELATION 21:22, "And I SAW NO TEMPLE THEREIN: for the Lord God Almighty and the Lamb are the temple of it."

> REVELATION 7:14, 15, "And I said unto him, 'Sir, thou knowest.' And he said to me, 'These are they which came out of great tribulation, and have WASHED THEIR ROBES, and made them white in THE BLOOD

OF THE LAMB.' *Therefore are they before the throne of God, and serve him day and night in his TEMPLE ..."*

REVELATION 20:11, *"And I saw a GREAT WHITE THRONE, and him that sat on it, FROM WHOSE FACE THE EARTH AND THE HEAVEN FLED AWAY; AND THERE WAS FOUND NO PLACE FOR THEM."*

The Wheat (washed in the blood) are IN THE TEMPLE, so the Marriage CANNOT be on Tabernacles. Tabernacles is the day the New Jerusalem comes down from heaven, and it has no TEMPLE. I might also add that it is NOT speaking of Trumpets either. Trumpets is not a day to gather in the TEMPLE, it is a day of war—not celebration! The old heaven and the old earth are passed away on Atonement at the Great White Throne, so the Marriage CAN'T be on Tabernacles.

These next two verses mention the BRIDE and the New Jerusalem, which may confuse some people, but none of these are saying the Marriage Supper takes place ON Tabernacles. They picture us SEEING the New Jerusalem come down from heaven on Tabernacles. We have been in our glorified bodies since Pentecost and ARE the Bride of Christ. Yes, the New Jerusalem is also the Bride of Christ. Just as the Church is not a building it is a congregation of people; a Synagogue is a building and not the congregation of Israel. Likewise, the "Bride of Christ" is the Congregation washed in the blood of Christ.

Remember, Jesus returns on Mt. Zion as a Lamb one more time on FIRSTFRUITS. Jesus changes from being the Prince of the kings of the earth to King of Kings at the Marriage Supper on PENTECOST. Four months later, Jesus returns as the Lion of the Tribe of Judah on TRUMPETS as the King of Kings.

Jesus can't be Married and become King of Kings ON Armageddon (on Trumpets), nor fifteen days later ON Tabernacles. He MUST BE King of Kings and Lord of Lords before Trumpets—before He returns to burn the tares.

THE GREAT WHITE THRONE ON ATONEMENT

The New Jerusalem, the Tabernacle of God comes down out of heaven from God on TABERNACLES.

If the Marriage Supper were on any other Holy Day, it would leave Pentecost with only one event occurring on that Feast—Just the ascension of the Barley and Wheat to Heaven.

If the Marriage did not occur on Pentecost it would leave the barley and wheat standing on Mt. Zion with nothing to do.

REVELATION 21:2, *"And I John saw the holy city, new Jerusalem, coming down from God out of heaven, PREPARED AS A BRIDE adorned for her husband."*

REVELATION 21:9, *"And there came unto me one of the seven angels which had the seven vials full of the seven last plagues, and talked with me, saying, 'Come hither, I will shew thee THE BRIDE, THE LAMB'S WIFE.'"*

The order MUST be:

1. Pentecost/Marriage
2. Trumpets/Day of the Lord/ Judgment Seat of Christ
3. Atonement/Great White Throne
4. Tabernacles/New Jerusalem

The New Jerusalem arrives on Tabernacles, so we can "tabernacle with Him." The New Jerusalem is the fulfillment of JOHN 14:2, *"In my Father's house are many mansions ... I go to prepare a place for you."*

THE SECRET DOOR TO UNDERSTAND BIBLE PROPHECY

Here we see the Wheat, those washed in the blood of the Lamb, *"serve him day and night in his TEMPLE."* Once again, this can't be Tabernacles because there is NO TEMPLE in the New Jerusalem.

REVELATION 7:14-8:6, "And I said unto him, 'Sir, thou knowest.' And he said to me, 'These are they [Wheat] which came out of great tribulation, and have WASHED THEIR ROBES, AND MADE THEM WHITE IN THE BLOOD OF THE LAMB.' Therefore are they BEFORE THE THRONE of God, and serve him day and night in his TEMPLE: and he that sitteth on the throne shall dwell among them ..."

REVELATION 8:2, 6, "And I saw the seven angels which stood before God; and to them were given SEVEN TRUMPETS. ... And the seven angels which had THE SEVEN TRUMPETS PREPARED THESELVES TO SOUND."

REASON 8
THERE ARE THREE RESURRECTIONS

The FIRST RESURRECTION is the Barley on Firstfruits and the Wheat on Pentecost, which go to the Marriage Supper of the Lamb together. They are the FIRST RESURRECTION because they are ASSURED THEY ARE IN THE BOOK OF LIFE as they are at the Marriage. THEY ARE ASSURED SALVATION and have the authority to reign over the Nations with a rod of iron for 1,000 years. Which is another confirmation the Nations only live a maximum of 1,000 years, which is why those who reign over them only reign for 1,000 years. After 1,000 years there is no one to reign over.

REVELATION 20:6, "BLESSED AND HOLY is he that hath part in the FIRST RESURRECTION: ON SUCH THE SECOND DEATH HATH NO POWER, but they shall be priests of God and of Christ, and shall reign with him A THOUSAND YEARS."

MATTHEW 22:11-13, "And when the king came in to see the guests, he saw there A MAN WHICH HAD NOT ON A WEDDING GARMENT: And he saith unto him, 'FRIEND, how camest thou in hither not having a wedding garment?' And he was SPEECHLESS. Then said the king to the servants, 'Bind him hand and foot, and take him away, and CAST HIM INTO OUTER DARKNESS, THERE SHALL BE WEEPING AND GNASHING OF TEETH.'"

I find no verse saying those invited to the Marriage Supper are cast into the fire, but some weep and gnash teeth if they have no garment.

The SECOND RESURRECTION are those IN CHRIST NOT CALLED TO THE MARRIAGE. These are they who are called to the Judgment Seat of Christ. Both good and bad are judged, and some are *"cut down and cast into the fire,"* hearing: *"I know you not."* Some may not make it in. I am not their judge and won't say specifically, because Jesus has the keys of hell and death. It is His decision. I will say the best resurrection is to the Marriage Supper on Pentecost, second would be the Judgment Seat of Christ on Trumpets, third the Great White Throne on Atonement.

The THIRD RESURRECTION are those NOT IN CHRIST and called to the Great White Throne. Most who report to this judgment do NOT make it in because they have no advocate. They have no covering for their sin and must give an account of every idle word with no sins washed away!

1 JOHN 2:1, "My little children, these things write I unto you, that ye sin not.

And if any man sin, WE HAVE AN ADVOCATE WITH THE FATHER, JESUS CHRIST the righteous:"

REVELATION 20:15, "And whosoever was not found written in the book of life was cast into the lake of fire."

REASON 9

The Marriage Supper takes place on Pentecost because Revelation 20:6 says there must be one resurrection in which all that are resurrected make it into the Book of Life. It is certainly NOT the Judgment Seat of Christ on Trumpets, nor the Great White Throne on Atonement. It is the Marriage Supper on Pentecost! Remember, the first resurrection is both the Barley and Wheat on Pentecost.

REVELATION 20:6, "BLESSED AND HOLY is he that hath part in the FIRST RESURRECTION: ON SUCH THE SECOND DEATH HATH NO POWER, but they shall be priests of God and of Christ, and shall reign with him A THOUSAND YEARS."

REASON 10

When Jesus returns as the King of Kings, as a Lion and sets His foot down on the Mount of Olives, it is on Trumpets, a day of war described below.

ZECHARIAH 14:4, "And his feet shall stand in that day upon THE MOUNT OF OLIVES, ... and the mount of Olives shall cleave in the midst thereof toward the east and toward the west ... And it shall come to pass in that day, that the light shall not be clear, nor dark: [because the sun went out on the fifth Vial and has been out for three days] ... And this shall be the plague wherewith the LORD will smite all the people that have fought against Jerusalem; Their FLESH SHALL CONSUME AWAY WHILE THEY STAND UPON THEIR FEET, AND THEIR EYES SHALL CONSUME AWAY IN THEIR HOLES, AND THEIR TONGUE SHALL CONSUME AWAY IN THEIR MOUTH."

Whereas the Marriage Supper of the "Lamb" tells us that the Marriage is when Jesus is a "LAMB" not a LION, when he is still the Prince of the Kings of the earth, not the King of Kings. The very name Marriage Supper of the "LAMB" tells us it CAN'T BE ON TRUMPETS nor on Atonement, nor on Tabernacles because He is still a "LAMB." It is not called the Marriage Supper of the "Lion."

He turns from Lamb to Lion at the Marriage Supper.

He turns from a Prince to a King at the Marriage Supper.

The name Marriage Supper of the "LAMB" can't be on Trumpets, Atonement nor Tabernacles because Jesus is a Lion not a Lamb on Trumpets! Trumpets is before Atonement and Tabernacles. Revelation 14:4 says the 144,000 are the Firstfruits. This leaves the only Feast that the Marriage Supper of the Lamb could be on is Pentecost!

Firstfruits- Jesus is a Lamb upon Mt. Zion, Revelation 14:1

Pentecost- Jesus changes from Lamb to a Lion at the Marriage Supper of the Lamb

Trumpets- Jesus is the Lion of the tribe of Judah (Not a Lamb)

Atonement- Jesus is the Lion of the tribe of Judah (Not a Lamb)

Tabernacles- Jesus is the Lion of the tribe of Judah (Not a Lamb)

SUMMARY: TEN REASONS
Why the Marriage Supper of the Lamb is on Pentecost

1. The first Marriage occurred in the third month at Mt. Sinai. The only feast in the third month is Pentecost.

THE SECRET DOOR TO UNDERSTAND BIBLE PROPHECY

2. The Marriage Supper of the Lamb is mostly a New Testament Church: Wheat washed in the Blood of the Lamb event.

3. The "great multitude" appears immediately after the 144,000, hinting the Marriage takes place on Pentecost.

4. The Wheat stand before the throne BEFORE the Trumpets have completed.

5. Revelation 19 is not saying the Marriage takes place on Trumpets.

6. Revelation 21:2, 9; 22:17 are NOT putting the Marriage on Tabernacles, only saying we will be there.

7. The Marriage is a day of celebration eliminating Trumpets a day of war!

8. The Marriage can't be on Tabernacles, because the New Jerusalem has no temple.

9. Those going to the Marriage Supper are the FIRST RESURRECTION and are all in the Book of Life.

The name the Marriage Supper of the "LAMB" tells us it must take place on Pentecost. Jesus is a Lion on Trumpets, Atonement and Tabernacles.

TRUMPETS
JUDGMENT SEAT OF CHRIST: JESUS JUDGES THOSE IN CHRIST DEAD OR ALIVE

EXODUS 19:11-13, "And be ready against the third day: for the third day THE LORD WILL COME DOWN IN THE SIGHT OF ALL THE PEOPLE upon Mount Sinai. And thou shalt set bounds unto the people round about, saying, 'Take heed to yourselves, that ye go not up into the mount, or touch the border of it: WHOSOEVER TOUCHETH THE MOUNT SHALL BE SURELY PUT TO DEATH:' ... when the trumpet soundeth long, they shall come up to the mount."

LEVITICUS 23:24, "Speak unto the children of Israel, saying, 'In the seventh month, in the first day of the month, shall ye have a sabbath, a memorial of BLOWING OF TRUMPETS, an holy convocation.'"

NUMBERS 10:9, "And if ye GO TO WAR in your land against the enemy that oppresseth you, then YE SHALL BLOW AN ALARM WITH THE TRUMPETS; and ye shall be remembered before the LORD your God, and ye shall be saved from your enemies."

On the day of Trumpets, the children of Israel were commanded to blow a trumpet. The trumpet sounding is a call to war. Trumpets will sound on the day Jesus returns. It will be a day of war between evil and holiness. It will be a day of war between Satan, the Beast and the False Prophet and Jesus and His two angels with sharp sickles. It will be a day Jesus wins.

REVELATION 19:19-21, "And I saw the BEAST, and the KINGS OF THE EARTH, and THEIR ARMIES, GATHERED together TO MAKE WAR AGAINST HIM THAT SAT ON THE HORSE, and against his army. And the beast was taken, and with him the false prophet that wrought miracles before him, with which he deceived them that had received the mark of the beast, and them that worshipped his image. These both were cast alive into a lake of fire burning with brimstone. And THE REMNANT WERE SLAIN WITH THE SWORD OF HIM THAT SAT UPON THE HORSE, WHICH SWORD PROCEEDED OUT OF HIS MOUTH: AND ALL THE FOWLS WERE FILLED WITH THEIR FLESH."

Jesus returns in thick clouds with the sound of a trumpet and the Morning Star.

EXODUS 19:14, 16, "And Moses went down from the mount unto the people, and sanctified the people; and they washed their clothes. ... there were thunders and lightnings, and a THICK CLOUD upon the mount, and the VOICE OF THE TRUMPET EXCEEDING LOUD; so that all the people that was in the camp trembled."

MATTHEW 24:30, 31, "... they shall see the SON OF MAN COMING IN THE CLOUDS of heaven with power and great glory. And he shall send his angels WITH A GREAT SOUND OF A TRUMPET, and they shall gather together his elect from the four winds, from one end of heaven to the other."

The earth shook on the first Trumpets. Likewise, it will shake on the last Trumpets. Other verses say Jesus arises to shake terribly the earth with the voice of the Archangel, and here, God speaks once again.

EXODUS 19:18, 19, "And mount Sinai was altogether on a smoke, because the LORD descended upon it in fire: and the smoke thereof ascended as the smoke of a furnace, and THE WHOLE MOUNT QUAKED GREATLY. And when the voice of the trumpet sounded long, and waxed louder and louder, Moses spake, and GOD ANSWERED HIM BY A VOICE."

ISAIAH 2:19, "And they shall go into the holes of the rocks, and into the caves of the earth, for fear of the LORD, and for the glory of his majesty, when he ARISETH TO SHAKE TERRIBLY THE EARTH."

God calls Moses to the top of the mountain to meet Him. God came to prove them as Jesus comes to prove or judge all IN Christ to meet Jesus in the air on Trumpets. On both the first and last Trumpets there is the blowing of Trumpets!

EXODUS 19:20, 20:20, 21, "And the LORD came down upon mount Sinai, on the top of the mount: and THE LORD CALLED MOSES UP TO THE TOP OF THE MOUNT; and Moses went up ... And Moses said unto the people, 'Fear not: for GOD IS COME TO PROVE YOU, and that his fear may be before your faces, that ye sin not.' And the people stood afar off, and Moses drew near unto the THICK DARKNESS WHERE GOD WAS."

1 CORINTHIANS 15:51, 52, "Behold, I shew you a mystery; We shall not all sleep, but we shall all be changed, In a moment, in the twinkling of an eye, at the LAST TRUMP: for THE TRUMPET SHALL SOUND, AND THE DEAD SHALL BE RAISED INCORRUPTIBLE, AND WE SHALL BE CHANGED."

Many of the same events of Exodus 19 repeat on the final Feast of Trumpets. Trumpets is the Day of the Lord, the day of Armageddon. The tares are burned, the grapes are crushed, and all IN Christ receive their rewards. This is the day the judgment is set for them. No one else gets saved. No one else falls away. We receive our judgment for those things done in our body, good or bad. This is the final day of sin on earth, the judgment for those in Christ. The Marriage door is shut on Pentecost and the final door to salvation through Jesus is shut on Trumpets.

Jesus returns after sunset, uses the Morning Star to burn up the tares. Two Angels with sharp sickles slice/crush the grapes. The Barley and Wheat return with Him on white horses clothed in white garments. The last trump awakening blast calls all dead or alive in Christ to the Judgment Seat of Christ. All receive their rewards good or bad.

JOHN 10:27-30, "My sheep hear my voice, and I know them, and they follow me: And I give unto them eternal life; and they shall never perish, NEITHER

SHALL ANY MAN PLUCK THEM OUT OF MY HAND. My Father, which gave them me, is greater than all; and NO MAN IS ABLE TO PLUCK THEM OUT OF MY FATHER'S HAND. I AND MY FATHER ARE ONE."

We can jump out of His hand by our CHOICE to receive the MARK, worship the BEAST, his IMAGE or receive the NUMBER of his name. We are the only person who can put our name in the Book of Life or take it out. It is our choice to accept and follow Christ.

REVELATION 14:9-12, "And the third angel followed them, saying with a loud voice, [This is the most serious warning to the Church in Revelation] 'If any man WORSHIP THE BEAST AND HIS IMAGE, AND RECEIVE HIS MARK IN HIS FOREHEAD, OR IN HIS HAND, The same shall drink of the wine of the wrath of God, which is poured out without mixture into the cup of his indignation; and HE SHALL BE TORMENTED WITH FIRE AND BRIMSTONE in the presence of the holy angels, and in the presence of the Lamb: And the smoke of THEIR TORMENT ASCENDETH UP FOR EVER AND EVER: AND THEY HAVE NO REST DAY NOR NIGHT, who worship the beast and his image, and whosoever receiveth the mark of his name. Here is the PATIENCE OF THE SAINTS: here are they that keep the commandments of God, and the faith of Jesus.'"

Let me be clear about this warning. Revelation 14:9-12 is saying: even if you have received Jesus, even if you have won people to Jesus, even if you are an Apostle, Prophet, Pastor, Teacher or Evangelist, but if you worship the beast and/or his image, and/or receive his mark in your forehead or your hand, you are tossed into the Lake of fire. You don't get soul death. You are tormented forever with the Beast, the False Prophet and Lucifer! It is the worst of the worst punishment, torment that never ends!

You CAN'T repent of it. You can cut your hand off, but once you have received the Mark, you can't remove it from your spirit. It will bring you everlasting spiritual torment. It is worshiping the Arch enemy of Jesus. It is the spiritual denial of Jesus. Notice that any one of four acts brings the curse. Either worshiping the BEAST, his IMAGE, receiving his MARK or … the NUMBER of his name will bring destruction. One is not worse than the other. Any of the four is permanent torment with Lucifer, the Beast and False Prophet!!!! There will be no soul death for you!

REVELATION 15:2, "And I saw as it were a sea of glass mingled with fire: and them that had gotten the victory over the BEAST, and over his IMAGE, and over his MARK, and over the NUMBER OF HIS NAME, stand on the sea of glass, having the harps of God."

Don't make this mistake whatever comes your way! Please notice it comes with a specific warning for the saints! The word "patience" in Revelation means: "Don't quit. Don't fall away. Don't submit to the Beast." When the Bible says, *"Here is the patience of the saints: here are they that keep the commandments of God, and the faith of Jesus,"* this is a stern warning that this WILL cause you TO LOSE YOUR SALVATION. DON'T DO IT! Near the end, almost all people on earth will be worshiping the beast and/or his image, and/or receiving his mark in their forehead, or hand. Don't be a "joiner" be an "Overcomer!"

In the Bible, grapes are not highly regarded. Al Neal spoke at the Prophecy Club and made a DVD in August of 1998 entitled *New World Order Mind Control*. He said that it was his opinion that the fruit that Adam and Eve ate was not an apple, but rather a grape. If you think about it, there is no story in the Bible reflecting negatively on an apple, but there are many referring to grapes and wine and the destruction they have brought! He may be right. (DVD disks are available at **www.ProphecyClub.com** or watch instantly at **www.WatchProphecyClub.com**).

Trumpets is also the time for crushing grapes, which I believe is different from the burning of the tares. The Bible says the tares are burned. Linking other Scriptures together, we know Jesus burns them with the Morning Star (Revelation 2:26-28). Jesus uses the Morning Star to turn the tares to ashes under the souls of our feet. However, the grapes are crushed, and wine representing the blood of His enemies comes out. The Bible says that blood flows out of the winepress up to the horse bridles for about 200 miles!

Ezekiel 39 tells us that after the beasts and birds eat the flesh. It takes seven months to bury the bones of those killed in the Armageddon war.

EZEKIEL 39:4, "Thou shalt fall upon the mountains of Israel, thou, and all thy bands, and the people that is with thee: I will give thee unto the RAVENOUS BIRDS OF EVERY SORT, AND TO THE BEASTS OF THE FIELD TO BE DEVOURED."

EZEKIEL 39:11-20, "... there shall they bury Gog and all his multitude... And SEVEN MONTHS SHALL THE HOUSE OF ISRAEL BE BURYING OF THEM, that they may cleanse the land. ... And they shall sever out men of continual employment, passing through the land to bury ... those that remain upon the face of the earth, to cleanse it: after the end of seven months shall they search. Thus saith the Lord GOD; 'SPEAK UNTO EVERY FEATHERED FOWL, AND TO EVERY BEAST OF THE FIELD ... that ye may eat flesh, and drink blood. Ye shall EAT THE FLESH OF THE MIGHTY, AND DRINK THE BLOOD OF THE PRINCES OF THE EARTH ... Thus ye shall be filled at my table with ... mighty men ... of war,' saith the Lord GOD."

REVELATION 19:17, 18, "And I saw an angel standing in the sun; and he cried with a loud voice, saying to ALL THE FOWLS THAT FLY IN THE MIDST OF HEAVEN, 'Come and gather yourselves together unto the supper of the great God; That ye may EAT THE FLESH OF KINGS, and the flesh of captains, and the flesh of mighty men, and the flesh of horses, and of them that sit on them, and THE FLESH OF ALL MEN, both free and bond, both small and great."

This means that since Jesus BURNS the tares to ashes, where does the blood come from? The Bible says that there are two angels with sickles that also participate in the devastation. I believe these two angels kill literally with a sharp sickle, causing the blood to rise to horse bridles!! These two angels slash with a sickle releasing their blood. All this takes place in one evening and morning.

*REVELATION 14:14-20, "And I looked, and behold a white cloud, and upon the cloud one sat like unto the Son of man, having on his head a golden crown, and in his hand a SHARP **SICKLE**. And another angel came out of the temple, crying with a loud voice to him that sat on the cloud, 'Thrust in thy **SICKLE**, and reap: for the time is come for thee to reap; for the harvest of the earth is ripe.' And he that sat on the cloud thrust in his sickle on the earth; and the earth was reaped. And another angel came out of the temple which is in heaven, he ALSO HAVING A SHARP*

SICKLE. *And ANOTHER ANGEL came out from the altar, which had power over fire; and cried with a loud cry to him that had the sharp sickle, saying, 'Thrust in thy sharp sickle, and GATHER THE CLUSTERS OF THE VINE OF THE EARTH; FOR HER GRAPES ARE FULLY RIPE.' AND THE ANGEL THRUST IN HIS* **SICKLE** *INTO THE EARTH, AND GATHERED THE VINE OF THE EARTH, AND CAST IT INTO THE GREAT WINEPRESS OF THE WRATH OF GOD. AND THE WINEPRESS WAS TRODDEN WITHOUT THE CITY, AND BLOOD CAME OUT OF THE WINEPRESS, EVEN UNTO THE HORSE BRIDLES, BY THE SPACE OF A THOUSAND AND SIX HUNDRED FURLONGS."*.

Chapter 14
TRUMPET - ATONEMENT - TABERNACLES

Many Christians have been taught that Christians stand before the Judgment Seat of Christ only to receive blessings at the 6,000-year mark; then, at the end of the Millennium, the bad stand before the Father at the Great White Throne for judgment. They have heard that Jesus judges at the Judgment Seat of Christ and God the Father judges at the Great White Throne.

Jesus is the judge at both the Judgment Seat of Christ and the Great White Throne.

What does it mean when Jesus says He has the keys of hell and death? It means Jesus decides who lives and who dies and who goes to heaven and who goes to hell. That is being the judge— the judge at both the Judgment Seat of Christ and the Great White Throne.

> JOHN 5:22, "For the Father judgeth no man, but hath committed all judgment unto the Son:"

> REVELATION 1:18, "I am he that liveth, and was dead; and, behold, I am alive for evermore, Amen; AND HAVE THE KEYS OF HELL AND OF DEATH."

> 2 TIMOTHY 4:8, "Henceforth there is laid up for me a crown of righteousness, which THE LORD, THE RIGHTEOUS JUDGE, shall give me at that day: and not to me only, but unto all them also that love his appearing."

JUDGMENT SEAT OF CHRIST: JESUS JUDGES THOSE IN CHRIST DEAD OR ALIVE

The order of events on the DAY OF THE LORD include: (1) Jesus burns the tares, (2) the angels crush the grapes (3) those IN Christ are judged at the JUDGMENT SEAT OF CHRIST, and (4) all IN Christ (dead or alive) must appear before the Judgment Seat of Christ. Both of these verses are speaking to Christians.

> ROMANS 14:10, "But why dost thou judge thy brother? or why dost thou set at nought thy brother? for we shall all stand before the JUDGMENT SEAT OF CHRIST."

> 2 CORINTHIANS 5:10, "For we must all appear before the JUDGMENT SEAT OF CHRIST; that every one may receive the things done in his body, according to that he hath done, whether it be good or bad."

Trumpets is the day ALL IN CHRIST are judged at the JUDGMENT SEAT OF CHRIST. One verse says some have their works burned up, but still make it in. All these verses speak of the day Jesus returns on Trumpets. Those attending the Marriage get their Wedding garment and a white horse. They receive the rest of their rewards (along with everyone else) on Trumpets.

> REVELATION 22:12, "And, behold, I COME QUICKLY [TRUMPETS]; AND MY REWARD IS WITH ME, to give every man according as his work shall be."

> MATTHEW 16:27, "For the Son of man shall come in the glory of his Father with his angels; [Trumpets] and then he shall reward every man according to his works."

> REVELATION 3:11, "Behold, I COME QUICKLY: [Trumpets]

hold that fast which thou hast, that no man take THY CROWN."

1 CORINTHIANS 3:14, 15, "If any man's WORK ABIDE which he hath built thereupon, HE SHALL RECEIVE A REWARD. If any man's WORK SHALL BE BURNED, [Trumpets] *he shall suffer loss: but HE HIMSELF SHALL BE SAVED; YET SO AS BY FIRE."*

These scriptures describe the fourth world government thrones being cast down, the Beast slain and cast into the Lake of Fire, and Jesus returning in the clouds of heaven. He uses the Morning Star to turn the tares to ashes and the Judgment is set for THOSE IN CHRIST.

DANIEL 7:9-13, "I beheld till the THRONES WERE CAST DOWN, [Jesus returning on Trumpets] *... A FIERY STREAM issued and came forth from before him:* [Jesus using the Morning Star on tares] *thousand thousands ministered unto him, and ten thousand times ten thousand STOOD before him: the JUDGMENT WAS SET, and the BOOKS WERE OPENED.* [Trumpets] *... I beheld even till the BEAST WAS SLAIN, and his body destroyed, and given to the burning flame.* [Which happens on Trumpets] *... the rest of the beasts, they had their dominion taken away: yet their lives were prolonged for a season and time.* [Nations] *... I saw in the night visions, and, behold, one like the Son of man came with the clouds of heaven ...* [Jesus returns on Trumpets]*."*

The Israelites recognize the blowing of trumpets as a call for war! In this case, it is a call for all the nations of the world to gather around Jerusalem to destroy it. Jesus returns and destroys His enemies and saves His people Israel in the most famous battle of all time! This is the day the Israelites see their Messiah save them from their enemies! (Read Jeremiah 4.)

The trumpet is blowing, calling for war! The Beast armies are gathering to make war with the Lamb. This world army is the strongest, best-equipped, and most advanced in history, but they are no match for Him Who sits on the horse. This New World Order army, the culmination of 6,000 years of building the most advanced war machine in the history of man is destroyed by Jesus in one evening.

JOEL 2:1-11, "BLOW YE THE TRUMPET IN ZION, and sound an alarm in my holy mountain: let all the inhabitants of the land tremble: for THE DAY OF THE LORD COMETH, for it is nigh at hand; A day of darkness and of gloominess, a day of CLOUDS and of thick darkness, as the morning spread upon the mountains: a great people and a strong; THERE HATH NOT BEEN EVER THE LIKE, neither shall be any more after it, even to the years of many generations. A fire devoureth before them; [The New World Order Armies] *and behind them a flame burneth: the land is as the garden of Eden before them, and behind them a desolate wilderness; yea, and nothing shall escape them. The appearance of them is as the appearance of horses; and as horsemen, so shall they run. Like the noise of chariots on the tops of mountains shall they leap, like the noise of a flame of fire that devoureth the stubble, as a strong people set in battle array. Before their face the people shall be much pained: ALL FACES SHALL GATHER BLACKNESS.* [Skin blasted with seven times hotter sun?] *They shall run like mighty men; they shall climb the wall like men of war; and they shall march every one on his ways, and they shall not break their ranks:* [Genetically altered-strengthened soldiers?] *Neither shall one thrust another; they shall walk every one* in his path: and when they fall upon the sword, they shall not be wounded. [Instant healing] *They shall run to and fro in the city; they shall run upon the wall, they shall climb up upon the houses; they shall enter in at the windows like a thief. The earth shall quake before them; the heavens shall tremble: the sun and the moon shall be dark, and the stars shall withdraw their shining: And the LORD shall UTTER HIS VOICE before his army: ... for the DAY OF THE LORD is great and very terrible; and who can abide it?"*

The Christians recognize this as the day Jesus returns in the clouds. Most of the dead in Christ arose on Pentecost in the Wheat harvest, but about four months later on Trumpets, all those remaining IN Christ (dead or alive) are gathered for the Judgment Seat of Christ. Likewise, the Barley and Wheat appear, but they already KNOW they are saved. *"Blessed and holy is he that hath part in the first resurrection:* [marriage] *on such the second death hath no power."*

Jesus has returned in the clouds at this point and sends His angels out to gather the living Christians, *"we which are alive and remain."* Remember *"... we shall all stand before the judgment seat of Christ."*

Those with wedding garments have their sins covered so their nakedness does not appear. Their sins are removed as far as the east is unto the west. Those without wedding garments have their sins revealed. Nothing is hidden that is not manifested, except for those covered with white fine linen garments. Admission is by the blood of the Lamb. The garment of fine linen that we wear is the righteous works of that person. When Henry Gruver was in heaven, he said when he approached someone, their fine linen garment began to speak of the righteous works of the wearer!

(www.watchprophecyclub.com, 6 Hours in Heaven).

It was not that they could see his private parts, but rather they could see his sin like the man at the wedding who had no garment. The garment is the righteous works that cover the sinful works. Without a garment, our sins are shown as if our body is a television screen showing our sins, *"open and manifest"* and *"shouted from the roof tops."* We are admitted to the marriage and our sinful works are covered with the garment of praise as our garment speaks forth our righteous works.

REVELATION 16:15, "Behold, I come as a thief. Blessed is he that watcheth, and keepeth his garments, lest he walk NAKED, AND THEY SEE HIS SHAME.

MATTHEW 24:30, 31, "And then shall appear the sign [Trumpets sounding] *of the Son of man in heaven: and then shall all the tribes of the earth mourn, and they shall see the Son of man coming in the clouds of heaven with power and great glory. And he shall send his angels with a great sound of a TRUMPET,* [Feast of Trumpets] *and they shall GATHER TOGETHER HIS ELECT* [In Christ] *from the four winds, from one end of heaven to the other."*

PSALM 103:12, "AS FAR AS THE EAST IS FROM THE WEST, so far hath he removed our transgressions from us."

MATTHEW 13:8, "BUT OTHER FELL INTO GOOD GROUND, AND BROUGHT FORTH FRUIT, SOME AN HUNDREDFOLD, SOME SIXTYFOLD, SOME THIRTYFOLD."

MARK 4:28, 29, "For the earth bringeth forth fruit of herself; first the blade, then the ear, after that the full corn in the ear. But WHEN THE FRUIT IS BROUGHT FORTH,

IMMEDIATELY HE PUTTETH IN THE SICKLE, BECAUSE THE HARVEST IS COME."

MATTHEW 13:35, "... I WILL UTTER THINGS WHICH HAVE BEEN KEPT SECRET FROM THE FOUNDATION OF THE WORLD."

MARK 4:22, "For THERE IS NOTHING HID, WHICH SHALL NOT BE MANIFESTED; NEITHER WAS ANY THING KEPT SECRET, but that it should come abroad."

JOHN 3:21, "But he that doeth truth cometh to the light, that his DEEDS MAY BE MADE MANIFEST, that they are wrought in God."

REVELATION 3:18, "I counsel thee to buy of me gold TRIED IN THE FIRE, [Morning Star] that thou mayest be rich; and white raiment, THAT THOU MAYEST BE CLOTHED, and that THE SHAME OF THY NAKEDNESS DO NOT APPEAR ..."

REVELATION 16:15, "... BLESSED IS HE THAT WATCHETH, AND KEEPETH HIS GARMENTS, LEST HE WALK NAKED, AND THEY SEE HIS SHAME."

The trumpets begin to sound loud and long, growing louder and longer as in the days of Moses on Mt. Sinai, gathering the tares for *"the great battle of God Almighty."* Here we see the Euphrates River dried to make passage as the devils gather the tares and grapes for their destruction.

LEVITICUS 23:24, "... In the SEVENTH MONTH, IN THE FIRST DAY OF THE MONTH, SHALL YE HAVE A SABBATH, A MEMORIAL OF BLOWING OF TRUMPETS ..."

REVELATION 16:12-16, "And the sixth angel poured out his vial upon the great river Euphrates; and the water thereof was dried up, that the way of the KINGS OF THE EAST MIGHT BE PREPARED. And I saw three unclean spirits like frogs come out of the mouth of the dragon, and out of the mouth of the beast, and out of the mouth of the false prophet. For they are the spirits of devils, working miracles, which go forth unto the kings of the earth and of the whole world, to GATHER THEM TO THE BATTLE OF THAT GREAT DAY OF GOD ALMIGHTY. BEHOLD, I COME AS A THIEF. Blessed is he that watcheth, and keepeth his garments, lest he walk naked, and they see his shame. [Jesus has NOT returned for the saints yet. He still warns them he is coming, and this is literally the day before Armageddon on the day of Trumpets.] And he gathered them together into a place called in the tongue Armageddon."

Here we see after the burning the angels collect those IN Christ dead or alive *"in the air"* for the Judgment Seat of Christ. We KNOW this is Trumpets because both verses tell us the Trumpets are blowing!

1 CORINTHIANS 15:52, "In a moment, in the twinkling of an eye, AT THE LAST TRUMP: [Feast of Trumpets] for the TRUMPET shall sound, and the dead shall be raised incorruptible, and we shall be changed."

1 THESSALONIANS 4:16, 17, "For the Lord himself shall descend from heaven with a shout, with the voice of the archangel, and with the TRUMP of God: and THE DEAD IN CHRIST SHALL RISE FIRST: [Pentecost] Then WE WHICH ARE ALIVE AND REMAIN shall be caught up together with them in the clouds, [Trumpets] to meet the Lord in the air: and so shall we ever be with the Lord. [Tabernacles]."

Here, an Angel calls for a clean-up after all evil has been destroyed.

REVELATION 19:14-19, *"And the armies which were in heaven followed him [Jesus] upon white horses, clothed in fine linen, white and clean.* [The barley and wheat are with him.] *And OUT OF HIS MOUTH GOETH A SHARP SWORD,* [Morning Star] *that with it he should smite the nations: and he shall rule them with a rod of iron: and he treadeth the winepress* [Grape harvest the wine is their blood.] *of the fierceness and wrath of Almighty God. And he hath on his vesture and on his thigh a name written, KING OF KINGS, AND LORD OF LORDS. And I saw an angel standing in the sun; and he cried with a loud voice, saying to all the fowls that fly in the midst of heaven, Come and gather yourselves together unto the supper of the great God; That ye may EAT THE FLESH OF KINGS, and the flesh of captains, and the flesh of mighty men, and the flesh of horses, and of them that sit on them, and the FLESH OF ALL MEN, both free and bond, both small and great. And I saw the beast, and the kings of the earth, and their armies, gathered together to make war against him that sat on the horse, and against his army."*

When the battle is about to begin, the first thing that happens is the bodies of the beast and false prophet are destroyed, but their souls will be tormented for ever and ever. The greatest battle on earth is concluded in one evening and morning. (Isaiah 17:14).

REVELATION 19:20, 21, *"And the beast was taken, and with him the false prophet that wrought miracles before him, with which he deceived them that had received the mark of the beast, and them that worshipped his image. These both were CAST ALIVE INTO A LAKE OF FIRE BURNING WITH BRIMSTONE. ... And the remnant were SLAIN WITH THE SWORD of him that sat upon the horse, which SWORD PROCEEDED OUT OF HIS MOUTH: and all the FOWLS WERE FILLED WITH THEIR FLESH."*

This is a description of the world after Jesus has destroyed the old earth. Not much is left, but we are not affected since we have new glorified bodies, white fine linen garments, crowns and live in the golden city. We never work again, hunger or thirst again. We never grow old or sin or hurt or cry again. We get to see Jesus, face to face, and can fly through time and space at the speed of thought!

JEREMIAH 4:19-29, *"... the sound of the TRUMPET, THE ALARM OF WAR. ... for the whole land is spoiled: ... I beheld the earth, and, lo, it was without form, and void; and the heavens, and they had no light. I beheld the mountains, and... lo, they trembled, and all the HILLS MOVED LIGHTLY. I beheld, and, lo, there was NO MAN,* [Men are underground] *and all the BIRDS OF THE HEAVENS WERE FLED. I beheld, and, lo, the FRUITFUL PLACE WAS A WILDERNESS, and all the cities thereof were broken down at the presence of the LORD, and by his fierce anger. ... THE WHOLE LAND SHALL BE DESOLATE; YET WILL I NOT MAKE A FULL END.* [The nations]... *and the heavens above be black ... every city shall be forsaken, and not a man dwell therein."*

By the time all seven seals, seven trumpets and seven vials have played, most people on earth are dead—and that is okay and part of God's plan. Three days before Trumpets all drinkable water on earth (See Seals, Trumpets, Vials chart) is undrinkable and has been turned to blood. The sun has gone out and the temperature on earth is dropping quickly as the temperature in space is -455 degrees! The moisture in the atmosphere has frozen, causing great hail stones about 75 pounds each. No human can live on the face of the earth. The Bible does not directly say, but probably all the animals on earth are killed by the hailstones. It is possible that as all the living creatures in the sea die it may also be that all the animals die and many if not most birds die. We know not all birds die because it takes seven months for the birds of the air to clean the land after Armageddon. EZEKIEL 39:4 and REVELATION 19:17, 18.

The living have moved underground. One of the interesting things about the Day of the Lord is how often the Bible talks about idols. Apparently, many people make images or IDOLS of the Beast and worship them. Idols are mentioned often in the prophecies of the Tribulation.

ISAIAH 2:19-21, "And they shall go into the HOLES OF THE ROCKS, AND INTO THE CAVES OF THE EARTH, for fear of the LORD, and for the glory of his majesty, when he ariseth to SHAKE terribly the earth. In that day a man shall cast his IDOLS of silver, and his IDOLS of gold, which THEY MADE each one for himself to worship, to the moles and to the bats; To go into the clefts of the rocks, and into the tops of the ragged rocks, for fear of the LORD, and for the glory of his majesty, when he ariseth to shake terribly the earth."

Only one-third of the people on earth will survive the seven-year tribulation.

ZECHARIAH 13:9, "And I WILL BRING THE THIRD PART THROUGH THE FIRE, and will refine them as silver is refined, and will try them as gold is tried: they shall call on my name, and I will hear them: I will say, It is my people: and they shall say, The LORD is my God."

Israel will be the victor in all wars in the future, even Armageddon, because Jesus returns to assure it!

ZECHARIAH 12:3, 4, "And in that day will I make Jerusalem a burdensome stone for all people: all that burden themselves with it shall be cut in pieces, [Sharp sickle] *THOUGH ALL THE PEOPLE OF THE EARTH BE GATHERED TOGETHER AGAINST IT ..."*

The beast, false prophet, the kings of the earth and their armies are gathered to make war against Jesus as King of Kings and Lord of Lords and are destroyed in a moment. This is the DAY of the LORD, and He shall save His people out of it. The Beast and False Prophet are slain, and their bodies given to the burning flame. After the tares have been burned to ashes (Matthew 13:30) and grapes slashed in pieces, then He gathers the remaining of those in Christ into the barn. Trumpets is the judgment by fire. The fire is the Morning Star.

ISAIAH 17:14, "And behold AT EVENINGTIDE TROUBLE; AND BEFORE THE MORNING HE IS NOT. This is the portion of them that spoil us, and the lot of them that rob us."

ZECHARIAH 9:14, "And the LORD shall be seen over them, and HIS ARROW SHALL GO FORTH AS THE LIGHTNING: [Morning Star] *and the Lord GOD shall blow the trumpet ..."*

MATTHEW 24:27, 29-31, "For as the LIGHTNING COMETH OUT OF THE EAST, AND SHINETH EVEN UNTO THE WEST; [Morning Star] *so shall also the coming of the Son of man be. Immediately after the tribulation of those days shall the sun be darkened, and the moon shall not* give her light, and the stars shall fall from heaven, and the powers of the heavens shall be shaken: ... and they shall see the Son of man coming in the clouds of heaven with power and great glory. And he shall send his angels with a great sound of a trumpet, [The feast of Trumpets] and THEY SHALL GATHER TOGETHER HIS ELECT FROM THE FOUR WINDS, from one end of heaven to the other. [At which time they attend the Judgment Seat of Christ, then off to the New Jerusalem.]"

Tares are burned, and then the Wheat receive glorified bodies.

MATTHEW 13:39-43, "The enemy that sowed them [tares] is the devil; the harvest is the end of the world; and the reapers are the angels. As therefore the tares are gathered and burned in the FIRE; so shall it be in the end of this world. The Son of man shall send forth his angels, and they shall gather out of his kingdom all things that offend, and them which do iniquity; And shall cast them into a furnace of FIRE: there shall be wailing and gnashing of teeth. Then shall the RIGHTEOUS SHINE FORTH AS THE SUN in the kingdom of their Father ..."

These are IN Christ, the true vine:

JOHN 15:5, 6, "I am the vine, ye are the branches: He that abideth in me, and I in him, the same bringeth forth much fruit: for without me ye can do nothing. IF A MAN ABIDE NOT IN ME, HE IS CAST FORTH AS A BRANCH, AND IS WITHERED; AND MEN GATHER THEM, AND CAST THEM INTO THE FIRE, AND THEY ARE BURNED."

These are tried by fire, during Trumpets, not Atonement.

1 PETER 1:7-12, "That the trial of your faith, being much more precious than of gold that perisheth, though it be TRIED WITH FIRE, might be found unto praise and honour and glory at the APPEARING OF JESUS CHRIST:"

Trumpets is judgment by fire. Atonement is judgment by books. Notice, all these verses are pertaining to Trumpets. They all speak of FIRE. When we get to Atonement next, you will see they are judged by books.

2 PETER 3:7-12, "But the heavens and the earth, which are now, by the same word are kept in store, reserved unto FIRE against the day of judgment and perdition of ungodly men. ... But the day of the Lord will come as a thief in the night; in the which the heavens shall pass away with a great noise, and the elements shall MELT WITH FERVENT HEAT, the earth also and the works that are therein shall be BURNED UP. Seeing then that all these things shall be dissolved, what manner of persons ought ye to be in all holy conversation and godliness, Looking for and hasting unto the coming of the day of God, wherein the HEAVENS BEING ON FIRE SHALL BE DISSOLVED, AND THE ELEMENTS SHALL MELT WITH FERVENT HEAT?"

Trumpets is Jesus returning like a refiner's fire. Those left standing after the burning are saved, as in saved from the wrath of God.

MALACHI 3:2, 3, "But who may abide the day of his coming? and who shall STAND when he appeareth? for he is like a REFINER'S FIRE, and like fullers' soap: And HE SHALL SIT AS A REFINER AND PURIFIER OF SILVER ..."

Fire, sword many slain.

ISAIAH 66:15, 16, "For, behold, the LORD will come with FIRE, and with his chariots like a whirlwind, to render his anger with FURY, and his rebuke

THE SECRET DOOR TO UNDERSTAND BIBLE PROPHECY

with flames of FIRE. For by FIRE AND BY HIS SWORD will the LORD plead with all flesh: and THE SLAIN OF THE LORD SHALL BE MANY."

All the world sees His Morning Star destroy His enemies as the hills melt like wax.

PSALM 97:2, "Clouds and darkness are round about him: righteousness and judgment are the habitation of his throne. A FIRE goeth before him, and BURNETH UP HIS ENEMIES round about. His LIGHTNINGS ENLIGHTENED THE WORLD: the earth saw, and TREMBLED. The HILLS MELTED LIKE WAX AT THE PRESENCE OF THE LORD, at the presence of the Lord of the whole earth. The heavens declare his righteousness, and ALL THE PEOPLE SEE HIS GLORY."

The Morning Star destroys both soul and body. When the Morning Star hits them, they fall to the ground in a pile of ashes and bones like a person fainting.

ISAIAH 10:16-18, "Therefore shall the Lord, the Lord of hosts, send among his fat ones leanness; and under his glory HE SHALL KINDLE A BURNING LIKE THE BURNING OF A FIRE. And the light of Israel shall be for a fire, and his Holy One for a FLAME: and it shall BURN and DEVOUR HIS THORNS AND HIS BRIERS IN ONE DAY; And shall consume the glory of his forest, and of his fruitful field, BOTH SOUL AND BODY: and they shall be as when a standardbearer fainteth."

All day long, the day of Trumpets, Fire, Wrath, Shaking, Mountains removed, fire and brimstone.

EZEKIEL 38:19-23, "For in my jealousy and in the fire of my wrath have I spoken, Surely in that day there shall be a great shaking in the land of Israel; So that the fishes of the sea, and the fowls of the heaven, and the beasts of the field, and all creeping things that creep upon the earth, and ALL THE MEN THAT ARE UPON THE FACE OF THE EARTH, SHALL SHAKE AT MY PRESENCE, and the MOUNTAINS SHALL BE THROWN DOWN, and the STEEP PLACES SHALL FALL, and EVERY WALL SHALL FALL TO THE GROUND. And I will call for A SWORD against him throughout all my mountains ... I will rain upon him, ... an overflowing rain, and great hailstones, fire, and brimstone. Thus will I magnify myself, and sanctify myself; and I WILL BE KNOWN IN THE EYES OF MANY NATIONS, AND THEY SHALL KNOW THAT I AM THE LORD."

Trumpets is judgment by fire. Atonement is judgment by books.

Trumpets is a test to see who remains STANDING and what rewards are left after the burning?

NAHUM 1:5-10, "The mountains quake at him, and the hills melt, and the earth is burned at his presence, yea, the world, and all that dwell therein. WHO CAN STAND before his indignation? and who can abide in the fierceness of his anger? his fury is poured out like fire, and the rocks are thrown down by him. The LORD is good, a strong hold in the day of trouble; and he knoweth them that trust in him. But with an overrunning flood he will make an utter end of the place thereof ... For while they be folden together as thorns, and while they are drunken as drunkards, they shall be devoured as stubble fully dry."

LUKE 21:36, "Watch ye therefore, and pray always, that ye may be accounted worthy to escape [The burning] all these things that shall come to pass, and to STAND BEFORE THE SON OF MAN."

2 THESSALONIANS 1:7, *"And to you who are troubled rest with us, when the Lord Jesus shall be revealed from heaven with his mighty angels, In FLAMING FIRE TAKING VENGEANCE on them that KNOW NOT GOD, and that obey not the gospel of our Lord Jesus Christ:"*

TRUMPETS SUMMARY
JUDGMENT SEAT OF CHRIST: JESUS JUDGES ALL IN CHRIST, DEAD OR ALIVE

"It is done" is stated from the throne.

The Feast of Trumpets is a one-day feast.

The four angels bound in the Euphrates were released to slay 1/3 of men.

The water of the Euphrates is dried up, allowing the kings of the east to reach the Valley of Jehoshaphat.

The three unclean spirits, like frogs, are released to gather the whole world to Armageddon.

The Beast and False Prophet gather their world armies to fight against Jesus at Jerusalem.

In one day the tares are burned to ashes.

The grapes are slashed/crushed, and the blood rises to horse bridles.

Blow ye the trumpet in Zion ... for the day of the LORD cometh, for it is nigh at hand;

A day of darkness and of gloominess, a day of clouds and of thick darkness.

The Trumpet call to war sounds long and loud, calling all the tares and grapes.

This is the **DAY OF THE LORD**, one evening and morning. "... I come as a thief in the night."

The wrath of Jesus has come.

The nations are angry.

Jesus returns at evening with the Barley and Wheat harvests on white horses.

Jesus uses the Morning Star light sword out of his mouth.

As lightning out of the east shines to the west, the bright Morning Star burns the tares.

The Barley and Wheat observe the victory, but do not participate.

The only three participants are Jesus and the two angels with sickles.

The angel on the cloud is told: *"Thrust in thy sickle and reap: ... for the harvest of the earth is ripe."*

The angel with the sharp sickle is told: *"Thrust in thy sharp sickle and gather the clusters of the vine of the earth; for her grapes are fully ripe ... the winepress was trodden without the city."*

In the eveningtide they are and by morning all tares are burned, and grapes crushed.

After the burning Jesus sends his angels out to gather all IN Christ dead or alive. *"... shall be caught up together with them in the clouds, to meet the Lord in the air."*

The Beast and False Prophet are tossed into the Lake of Fire burning their bodies but not their souls.

The Beast and False Prophet are tormented for ever and ever and joined by the devil a thousand years later.

Fowls and beasts take seven months eating the dead bodies of the grapes, cleansing the land. *"... .and shouldest destroy them which destroy the earth."*

"... there was a great earthquake; and the sun became black as sackcloth of hair ..."

"... *a great earthquake, and the tenth part of the city fell, and in the earthquake were slain of men seven thousand ...*"

"... *there was a great earthquake, such as was not since men were upon the earth, so mighty an earthquake ...*"

Great hail, every stone about the weight of a talent (75 lbs.). Earth is frozen, those alive live underground.

"*Every ... man, hid themselves in the dens and in the rocks of the mountains; And said to the mountains and rocks, fall on us, and hide us from the face of him that sitteth on the throne, and from the wrath of the Lamb:*"

The great day of the awakening blast.

There is time no longer for the LIVING, eternity begins for those in the Book of Life.

Those in Christ dead or alive stand before the JUDGMENT SEAT OF CHRIST.

Those with good works get Wedding garments. Those without works—their nakedness/shame is seen and are cast into the fire.

We get to see a replay of all IN Christ. Those with garments have their shame covered.

All rewards are given for those IN Christ.

REV 11:15 And the seventh angel sounded; and there were great voices in heaven, saying, The kingdoms of this world are become the kingdoms of our Lord, and of his Christ; and he shall reign for ever and ever.

Everything done in secret is open and made manifest.

Everything hidden is shouted from the roof tops.

Trumpets is judgment by fire. Atonement is judgment by books.

Trumpets is a test to see who remains STANDING, as well as to see what rewards are left after the burning?

ATONEMENT

LEVITICUS 23:27-29, "... on the TENTH DAY of this SEVENTH MONTH there shall be A DAY OF ATONEMENT: ... and YE SHALL AFFLICT YOUR SOULS ... for it is a day of atonement, to make an atonement for you before the LORD your God. For WHATSOEVER SOUL IT BE THAT SHALL NOT BE AFFLICTED IN THAT SAME DAY, HE SHALL BE CUT OFF FROM AMONG HIS PEOPLE."

Trumpets is the judgment by the Morning Star **FIRE**. Those remaining standing those works remaining after the fire of the Morning Star are standing before the LORD!

LUKE 21:36, "Watch ye therefore, and pray always, that ye may be accounted worthy to escape all these things [the fire of the Morning Star] *that shall come to pass, and to STAND BEFORE THE SON OF MAN."*

Atonement is a different judgment. Atonement is the judgment of **WORKS by BOOKS**. Those not in the Book of Life are cast away. It is not judgment by fire, but the conclusion for most appearing at this judgment will be soul-death in the Lake of Fire.

MATTHEW 7:13, "Enter ye in at the strait gate: for wide is the gate, and broad is the way, that leadeth to destruction, and MANY THERE BE WHICH GO IN THEREAT: Because strait is the gate, and narrow is the way, which leadeth unto life, and few there be that find it."

Atonement is the day when people are commanded to "afflict" themselves. A form of "self-punishment" for sins committed. It is a day to repay sin with affliction, a day of balancing sin with pain in which *"whatsoever a man soweth, that shall he also reap."* The prophetic message is: if we can correct ourselves, perhaps on the Day of Judgment, the correction from Jesus won't be as harsh.

This is the day when all sin is accounted for in those NOT in Christ. All sin imbalance is now balanced with punishment; a day to "afflict themselves." This is the Day of Judgment, the day the book of the DEAD is opened, and the day the judgment is set.

There is one Book of Life but there are many BOOKS of WORKS. The first look is to see if the name is in the Book of Life, the second look is to see what rewards the DEAD receive, bad or good. Then *"whosoever was not found written in the book of life was cast into the lake of fire."*

This is very important to remember. Some get confused and think the new heaven and new earth arrive at the end of the Millennium, but these clearly put the new heaven and new earth arriving upon Atonement—Great White Throne.

REVELATION 20:11-15, "And I saw a GREAT WHITE THRONE, [Judgment of the DEAD] *and him that sat on it,* [JESUS] *from whose face the earth and the heaven fled away;* [Old heaven and earth are destroyed.] *and there was found no place for them.* [The new earth is forming, and our mansions arrive on Tabernacles in five days.] *And I SAW THE DEAD, small and great, stand before God; and the BOOKS were opened: and another BOOK was opened, which is the BOOK of life: and the DEAD were judged out of those things which were written in the BOOKS, according to their WORKS.* [Every soul back to Adam.] *And the sea gave up the DEAD which were in it; and death and hell delivered up the DEAD which were in them: and they were judged every man according to their WORKS. And death and hell were cast into the lake of fire. This is the second death. And whosoever was not found written in the BOOK of life was cast into the lake of fire."*

This is the day that the dead NOT in Christ beginning with Adam stand before the GREAT WHITE THRONE where Jesus is the judge. No one else is saved, no one else falls away. The judgment is set. Those who are filthy or clean stay that way forever more.

DANIEL 12:2, "And many of them that SLEEP IN THE DUST of the earth shall awake, some to EVERLASTING LIFE, and SOME TO SHAME and everlasting contempt."

LUKE 12:42-48, "And the Lord said, 'Who then is that faithful and wise steward, whom his lord shall make ruler over his household, to give them their portion of meat in due season? Blessed is that servant, whom his lord when he cometh shall find so doing.' Of a truth I say unto you, 'that he will make him ruler over all that he hath. But and if that servant say in his heart, 'My lord delayeth his coming; and shall begin to beat the menservants and maidens, and to eat and drink, and to be drunken; The lord of that servant will come in a day when he looketh not for him, and at an hour when he is not aware, and WILL CUT HIM IN SUNDER, AND WILL APPOINT HIM HIS PORTION WITH THE UNBELIEVERS. And THAT SERVANT, WHICH KNEW HIS LORD'S WILL, AND PREPARED NOT HIMSELF, NEITHER DID ACCORDING TO HIS WILL, SHALL BE BEATEN WITH MANY STRIPES. BUT HE THAT KNEW NOT, AND DID COMMIT THINGS WORTHY OF STRIPES, SHALL BE BEATEN WITH FEW

STRIPES. *For unto whomsoever much is given, of him shall be much required: and to whom men have committed much, of him they will ask the more.'"*

On the Day of Atonement, everyone NOT in Christ, both good and bad is afflicted, and some are cut off and cast into the Lake of Fire. This is the day *"will I destroy from among his people."* People whose names are not written in the Book of Life are cast into the Lake of Fire.

MATTHEW 13:47-50, *"Again, the kingdom of heaven is like unto a net, that was cast into the sea, and gathered of every kind: Which, when it was full, they drew to shore, and sat down, and GATHERED THE GOOD INTO VESSELS, BUT CAST THE BAD AWAY. So shall it be AT THE END OF THE WORLD: the angels shall come forth, and SEVER THE WICKED FROM AMONG THE JUST, And shall CAST THEM INTO THE FURNACE OF FIRE: there shall be wailing and gnashing of teeth."*

REVELATION 11:18, *"And the nations were angry, and thy wrath is come, and the TIME OF THE DEAD, THAT THEY SHOULD BE JUDGED, and that thou shouldest GIVE REWARD unto thy servants the prophets,* [Good] *and to the saints, and them that fear thy name, SMALL AND GREAT; and shouldest destroy them which destroy the earth.* [Bad]*"*

Trumpets is judgment by fire, whereas Atonement is judgment by WORKS, the opening of the BOOKS. Notice the last verse is fire after judgment. In Trumpets the fire IS the judgment. In Atonement books or looking at one's life brings the fire afterwards.

MATTHEW 13:47-50, *"Again, the kingdom of heaven is like unto a net, that was cast into the SEA, AND GATHERED OF EVERY KIND: Which, when it was full, they drew to shore, and sat down, and gathered the GOOD into vessels, but cast the BAD away. So shall it be at the end of the world: the angels shall come forth, and sever the wicked from among the just, And shall cast them into the furnace of FIRE: there shall be wailing and gnashing of teeth."*

These next verses are trees with no fruit. This is like the virgins with no oil in their lamps. These are on the left at the Great White Throne. Some with good works get saved; some with no good works are cast into the Lake of Fire. Notice, this is not judgment by fire, but by WORKS; not by the Morning Star, but by BOOKS. This is speaking of Atonement, the Great White Throne, with Jesus judging.

MATTHEW 25:31-46, *"When the Son of man shall come in his glory, and all the holy angels with him, then shall he sit upon the throne of his glory: And before him shall be gathered all NATIONS:* [Not wheat, or trees nor servants these are NOT in Christ] *and he shall separate them one from another, as a shepherd divideth his sheep from the goats: And he shall set the sheep on his right hand, but the goats on the left. Then shall the King say unto them on his right hand, 'Come, ye blessed of my Father, inherit the kingdom prepared for you from the foundation of the world:'* [notice there is no mention of the blood of Christ, their judgment is works, the works which are written in the books.] *'For I was an hungred, and ye gave me meat: I was thirsty, and ye gave me drink: I was a stranger, and ye took me in: Naked, and ye clothed me: I was sick, and ye visited me: I was in prison, and ye came unto me.' Then shall the righteous answer him, saying, 'Lord, when saw we thee an hungred, and fed thee? or thirsty, and gave thee drink? When saw we thee a* stranger, and took thee in? or naked, and clothed thee? Or when saw we thee sick, or in prison, and came unto thee?' And the King shall answer and say unto them, 'Verily I say unto you, Inasmuch as ye have DONE it unto one of the least of these my brethren, ye have DONE IT UNTO ME.' Then shall he say also unto them on the left hand, 'Depart from me, ye cursed, into everlasting fire, prepared for the devil and his angels: For I was an hungred, and ye gave me no meat: I was thirsty, and ye gave me no drink: I was a stranger, and ye took me not in: naked, and ye clothed me not: sick, and in prison, and ye visited me not.' Then shall they also answer him, saying, 'Lord, when saw we thee an hungred, or athirst, or a stranger, or naked, or sick, or in prison, and did not minister unto thee?' Then shall he answer them, saying, 'Verily I say unto you, Inasmuch as ye did it NOT to one of the least of these, ye did it NOT TO ME.' And these shall go away into everlasting punishment: but the righteous into life eternal."

EARTH SHAKES:The old heaven and earth pass away. Jesus makes a New Heaven and a New Earth on Atonement.

ISAIAH 13:13, "... I WILL SHAKE THE HEAVENS, and the EARTH SHALL REMOVE OUT OF HER PLACE ..."

ISAIAH 24:1, 18-23, "Behold, the LORD maketh the earth empty, and maketh it waste, and turneth it upside down, and scattereth abroad the inhabitants thereof. ... the windows from on high are open, and the FOUNDATIONS OF THE EARTH DO SHAKE. The earth is UTTERLY BROKEN DOWN, the earth is CLEAN DISSOLVED, THE EARTH IS MOVED EXCEEDINGLY. The earth shall reel to and fro like a drunkard, ... and it shall fall, and not rise again. ... they shall be gathered together, as prisoners are gathered in the pit, ... the moon shall be confounded, and the sun ashamed, when the LORD of hosts shall reign in mount Zion ..."

JOEL 3:16, "... the heavens and the earth shall SHAKE: but the LORD will be the hope of his people, and the strength of the children of Israel."

When Jesus returns, He shakes the earth and all mountains fall and all valleys are filled in like taking a pan of loose sand and shaking it till it becomes smooth and level.

ISAIAH 40:4, "Every VALLEY shall be EXALTED, and every MOUNTAIN and hill shall be made LOW: and the CROOKED shall be made STRAIGHT, and the ROUGH PLACES PLAIN:"

ISAIAH 2:19, "And they shall go into the HOLES OF THE ROCKS, and into the CAVES OF THE EARTH, for fear of the LORD, and for the glory of his majesty, when he ariseth to SHAKE TERRIBLY THE EARTH."

As a result, the sea fills in and everything in the sea dies.

REVELATION 21:1, "And I saw a new heaven and a new earth: for the first heaven and the first earth were passed away; and there was NO MORE SEA."

JOB 14:11, "As THE WATERS FAIL FROM THE SEA, and the flood decayeth and DRIETH UP:"

PSALM 46:2, "Therefore will not we fear, though the earth be removed, and though THE MOUNTAINS BE CARRIED INTO THE MIDST OF THE SEA;"

ISAIAH 19:5, "And the waters shall fail from the sea, and THE RIVER SHALL BE WASTED AND DRIED UP."

THE SECRET DOOR TO UNDERSTAND BIBLE PROPHECY

ISAIAH 50:2, "... at my rebuke I DRY UP THE SEA, ... their fish stinketh, because there is NO WATER, and DIETH FOR THIRST."

This verse gives us an idea of what "shakes the earth" might be like. The mountains have fallen, the valleys filled in so much so that you can walk across what used to be the Egyptian Sea in sandals and not get your feet wet!

ISAIAH 11:15, "And the LORD shall utterly destroy the tongue of the Egyptian sea; and with his mighty wind shall he shake his hand over the river, and shall smite it in the seven streams, and make MEN GO OVER DRYSHOD."

ATONEMENT SUMMARY
GREAT WHITE THRONE: JESUS JUDGES ALL DEAD *NOT* IN CHRIST

The Day of Atonement is one evening and morning.

The Book of Life and the books of works are opened.

The DEAD, small and great, stand before God.

The Judgment for the DEAD is set, no one else gets saved or falls away.

He that is unjust is unjust still; he that is holy is holy still.

All sins are revealed, except those covered by the garment.

Those not judged on Trumpets now stand before Jesus (except the nations).

There is time no longer, eternity begins for those in the Book of Life.

REV 11:15 And the seventh angel sounded; and there were great voices in heaven, saying, The kingdoms of this world are become the kingdoms of our Lord, and of his Christ; and he shall reign for ever and ever.

Everything done in secret is open and made manifest.

Everything hidden is shouted from the roof tops.

All secrets are revealed, except those covered by a white garment. 6,000 years of sins are revealed.

Jesus is the Righteous Judge who has the keys of death and hell.

Jesus sits in judgment, not the Father. *"For the Father judgeth no man, but hath committed all judgment unto the Son" (John 5:22).*

All souls created NOT in Jesus stand before Jesus for the Great White Throne Judgment.

"... shouldest give reward unto thy servants the prophets, and to the saints, and them that fear thy name ..."

"... nations were angry, and thy wrath is come, and the time of the dead, that they should be judged ..."

The bad are cast away, and the good will be gathered on Tabernacles into the New Jerusalem.

Those whose names are in the Book of Life receive their just reward.

Those whose names are NOT in the Book of Life receive their just punishment.

Death and hell are cast into the Lake of Fire. This is the second death.

No one else is judged then killed.

Whosoever is not found written in the Book of Life is cast into the Lake of Fire, which is the second death.

Jesus arises and *"shakes terribly the earth."*

Earth is transformed to a round, smooth ball, no valleys and only one hill for the New Jerusalem.

No more sea, rivers or sunshine. Jesus literally is the light of the world.

The Nations never accepted Jesus, so they don't report to the Judgment Seat of Christ.

They are not dead, so they don't report to the Great White Throne.

The Nations are allowed to "enter into my rest" for 1,000 years, unless they break a law.

The Nations' judgment arrives upon them breaking a law after Trumpets.

They are judged to die upon breaking a law or (at the latest) at the end of the Millennium.

They are instructed that they will be ruled with a *"rod of iron."*

If any law is broken both body and soul is immediately destroyed by a Morning Star Judge.

Those nations surviving to the end of the Millennium will be destroyed when Satan is loosed.

"The nations ...the kingdom shall not be left to other people ..." (Daniel 2:44).

TABERNACLES

LEVITICUS 23:34, "... The fifteenth day of this seventh month shall be the FEAST OF TABERNACLES for seven days ..."

REVELATION 21:1-3, "And I saw a NEW HEAVEN AND A NEW EARTH: for the first heaven and the first earth were passed away; and there was no more sea. And I John saw THE HOLY CITY, NEW JERUSALEM, COMING DOWN FROM GOD OUT OF HEAVEN, prepared as a bride adorned for her husband. And I heard a great voice out of heaven saying, 'Behold, THE TABERNACLE OF GOD IS WITH MEN, and he will dwell with them, and they shall be his people, and God himself shall be with them, and be their God.'"

The command to Moses was to live in booths. The final fulfillment of Tabernacles is for those whose name is in the Book of Life to live in the golden city, New Jerusalem.

God gave these Feasts as prophecies to be revealed in the last days. His wonderful plan is to bless those worthy to live eternally with Jesus in the new golden city, clear as crystal, having a wall great and high with twelve <u>foundations</u> with the names of the 12 Apostles of the Lamb engraved in them, and 12 <u>gates</u> made of pearl with the names of the 12 Tribes of Israel engraved on them!

JOHN 14:2, 3, "In my Father's house are many MANSIONS: if it were not so, I would have told you. I GO TO PREPARE A PLACE FOR YOU. And if I go and prepare a place for you, I will come again, and receive you unto myself; that WHERE I AM, THERE YE MAY BE ALSO."

REVELATION 21:12, 14, "And had a wall great and high, and had TWELVE GATES, and at the gates twelve angels, and names written thereon, which are the names of the TWELVE TRIBES OF THE CHILDREN OF ISRAEL: ... And the WALL OF THE CITY HAD TWELVE FOUNDATIONS, and in them the NAMES OF THE TWELVE APOSTLES OF THE LAMB."

Those worthy to enter in through the gates can eat of fruit from the Tree of Life!

REVELATION 2:7, "... To him that overcometh WILL I GIVE TO EAT OF THE TREE OF LIFE, which is in the midst of the paradise of God."

REVELATION 22:14, "Blessed are they that do his commandments, that THEY MAY HAVE RIGHT TO THE TREE OF LIFE,

THE SECRET DOOR TO UNDERSTAND BIBLE PROPHECY

AND MAY ENTER IN THROUGH THE GATES INTO THE CITY."

Tabernacles is the gathering of the good into vessels. This is the harvest of all fruit after the bad is cast away in the two judgment cycles, Trumpets and Atonement. The good is now gathered into the barn/New Jerusalem.

On the first day of Tabernacles these are the groups of people:

GROUPS DESTROYED:

A. All living TARES and GRAPES have now been burned or crushed at Armageddon. Trumpets.

B. The DEAD whose name is NOT FOUND IN THE BOOK OF LIFE have been cast into the Lake of Fire, and for them, it is the second death or soul-death. Atonement.

C. SATAN IS BOUND FOR 1,000 YEARS in the bottomless pit and can't deceive the nations until the 1,000 years are fulfilled.

D. The BEAST AND THE FALSE PROPHET are also in the Lake of Fire, but for them it is NOT soul-death. They are tormented day and night forever. Satan joins them after the 1,000 years are fulfilled.

E. Those who took the MARK OF THE BEAST are also in the Lake of Fire, but they do NOT GET SOUL-DEATH, but join the Beast and False Prophet and are TORMENTED DAY AND NIGHT FOREVER.

GROUPS REMAINING:

1. Those surviving the judgment by the Morning Star fire and left standing receive rewards. [Luke 21:36] Trumpets.

2. Those, with their NAME IN THE BOOK OF LIFE, receive their rewards and glorified bodies. Atonement.

3. The NATIONS are allowed the opportunity to live for another 1,000 years until they are also burned by fire from God out of heaven, unless they break a law and are destroyed instantly–hence "ruled with a rod of iron." The rest of the dead lived not again until the 1,000 years are finished. No judgment at the end. Their judgment came on Trumpets, but effected at the first sin or at the end of the Millennium.

NOTE:

No soul-death for the Beast, False Prophet or those receiving the Mark, and after the Millennium—Satan.

Those whose names not in the Book of Life are destroyed in the Lake of Fire, both body and soul. *"...they shall be as though they had not been" (Obadiah 1:16).*

Those whose names are in the Book of Life will go into the New Jerusalem on Tabernacles.

Those who earned "King," "Priest," or "Judge" have already received the honor.

Those who have earned the Morning Star receive it.

"...they that be wise shall shine as the brightness of the firmament ..." (Daniel 12:3).

"...they that turn many to righteousness [shall shine] *as the stars for ever and ever."*

Up to seven crowns are awarded and received.

All who will be given a white garment have received it.

The Barley and Wheat Harvests have received the rest of their rewards.

The "Nations" or the "corners of the field" cannot enter the New Jerusalem.

The nations may drink of the water

of life and use the leaves of the Tree of Life, but it is only a temporary healing.

The water and leaves of the Tree of Life do NOT give them eternal life or a glorified body.

At the end of the 1,000 years, Satan is loosed and deceives the nations.

The nations gather from the four corners of the earth to battle.

They encircle the golden Holy City, and The Morning Star turns them all to ashes.

The verse to prove it is Daniel 2:44, *"the kingdom shall not be left to other people."*

The New Jerusalem is the holy city made of pure gold, clear as crystal or glass. It only has one throne, which Jesus and the Father both occupy. There is another set of thrones upon which the Kings sit. It has only one street, one tree, one river and no windows or doors! We have spirit bodies and move at the speed of thought and need no doors or windows.

TABERNACLES: Summary

The Holy City, New Jerusalem, is lowered onto the one and only mountain on earth.

The New Jerusalem sits just south of where Jerusalem sits today.

It is about 1,500 miles square made of solid, transparent gold, clear as glass.

It has one throne for the Father and Son.

It has one street, one river and one tree in the middle of it and no temple.

It is surrounded by a high wall about 216 feet high.

It has 12 gates each made of a single pearl.

Each gate has an angel guarding the gate keeping the nations out.

The Priests live in the presence of Jesus and see His face, and His name is in their foreheads.

The 24 Elders sit on seats, not thrones. The four Beasts have no seats.

The Kings sit on thrones having the Morning Star and Judgment.

Jesus judges the people; the Kings judge the angels and nations.

The Judges/Kings are those who resisted the Mark, Image and were beheaded in the time of the Beast.

Jesus shall break in pieces and consume all the first four world governments.

This is the kingdom God will set up which shall never be destroyed.

THE FEASTS SUMMARY
FIRSTFRUITS BARLEY HARVEST:
17th day of the 1st Month:

The firstfruits Barley harvest is the 144,000 chosen from the 12 tribes with no guile in their mouth and are without fault before the throne of God. They have their earthly fathers name written on their foreheads, sing a new song, and *"follow the Lamb withersoever he goeth"* beginning on Mt. Zion.

PENTECOST: WHEAT HARVEST:
EXACTLY 50 DAYS LATER

The second firstfruits is the Wheat harvest which occurs exactly 50 days after the Barley harvest on Pentecost. These are two groups, part non-Jew and part 12 tribes. They had their sins washed away in the blood of the Lamb and they are a great multitude which no man could number which stand before the throne and the Lamb clothed in White robes and palms in their hands.

The Marriage door is shut, and the Barley and Wheat harvests go to the Marriage Supper of the Lamb where they receive a wedding garment and a white horse to return with Jesus for Armageddon. *"Blessed and holy are they which are called to the marriage supper of the Lamb on such the second death hath no power."*

TRUMPETS—JUDGMENT SEAT OF CHRIST: JESUS JUDGES THOSE IN CHRIST DEAD OR ALIVE

TRUMPETS is the call to war, the battle of Armageddon. The last trumpet of Armageddon is the awakening blast which awakens the rest of those IN Christ not called to the Marriage Supper of the Lamb. The angels of Jesus gather *"we which are alive and remain"* to the Judgment Seat of Christ to receive our rewards from Jesus. No one else gets saved. No one else falls away. The Kingdoms of this world become the Kingdoms of our LORD and His Christ.

All living in Christ after the burning of the tares and crushing of grapes report to the Judgment Seat of Christ on Trumpets, but they are already assured their name is in the Book of Life in that they are left standing after the burning (except the Nations.)

NATIONS: The Nations never accepted Jesus, so they don't report to the Judgment Seat of Christ, but didn't take the Mark, so they were not burned up. They have not died, so they don't report to the Great White Throne, but receive their judgment upon their first sin after Trumpets or at the end of the Millennium. The Nations receive their rules to live by at the Judgment Seat of Christ. If you break a rule you receive instant judgment and will not be allowed entry into eternity. The nations are *"the rest of the dead lived not again until the thousand years are finished." "The corners not harvested."*

ATONEMENT— GREAT WHITE THRONE: JESUS JUDGES THE DEAD

The judgment is set. The books of works and the book of life are opened, and all souls are judged out of the books according to their works. Whosoever is not found in the book of life is cast into the Lake of Fire which is soul death.

TABERNACLES: 15th day 7th Month

Tabernacles is five days after Atonement. This is the day we are shown to our mansions and allowed to eat of the tree of life and drink of the river of water of life clear as crystal flowing from the throne of God and the Lamb. We see the city made of pure gold, clear as crystal. We see all of our friends, but the past life is no longer remembered nor comes to mind. The Nations serve us and bring us gifts. We see Jesus face-to-face and have already received our eternal rewards.

ISAIAH 65:17-20, "For, behold, I create new heavens and a new earth: and THE FORMER SHALL NOT BE REMEMBERED, NOR COME INTO MIND. There shall be no more thence an infant of days, nor an old man that hath not filled his days: for the child shall die an hundred years old; [Nations] *but the sinner being an hundred years old shall be accursed.* [The nations still die, but those with their name in the book of life live forever.]*"*

The Nations are not allowed to enter the New Jerusalem. The pure river of water of life flows out of the New Jerusalem, and the Nations can drink the water which runs down the side of the mountain into the valley below.

JOEL 3:18, "And it shall come to pass in that day, that the mountains shall drop down new wine, and the hills shall flow with milk, and all the rivers of Judah shall flow with waters, and A FOUNTAIN SHALL COME FORTH OUT OF THE HOUSE OF THE LORD, AND SHALL WATER THE VALLEY OF SHITTIM."

SUMMARY OF POINTS

The Seals play over 7 years, Trumpets play over 7 months, Vials play over the last 7 days.

The 144,000 are resurrected as the Firstfruits of the Barley Harvest on the 17th day of the 1st month.

The 144,000 are one-year old boys which never sinned or learned to talk, resurrected as adults.

Their earthly fathers' name is on their forehead.

The Barley Harvest of 144,000 are sealed before locusts arrive.

All water on earth is undrinkable 96 hours before "It is done."

The sun goes novae and burns out/dark with 72 hours remaining.

Only the Barley - 144,000 and Wheat - Christian Harvests go to the Marriage Supper of the Lamb on Pentecost.

There are 3 resurrections of the dead: Barley, Wheat, all souls NOT IN Christ on Atonement.

Resurrections: The 144,000 on Firstfruits, the Wheat on Pentecost, the remaining Wheat on Trumpets, and all dead souls on Atonement.

The 7th Trumpet sounds on the final feast of Trumpets.

Jesus is Coronated at Marriage Supper ON PENTECOST and receives His Vesture dipped in His own blood, labeled KING OF KINGS and LORD OF LORDS, receives many crowns and leads the armies of Angels, Barley and Wheat harvests to Armageddon

The Judgment Seat of Christ takes place on Trumpets, where Jesus is the judge, all souls IN CHRIST report, and it is a judgment by fire.

The Great White Throne takes place on Atonement where Jesus is the Judge, and the dead souls NOT IN CHRIST are judged by books according to their works.

The New Jerusalem arrives on Tabernacles. Those who have survived the three judgments of the Marriage Supper, Trumpets and Atonement are gathered into our mansions.

All "nations" are destroyed by the "fire from God out of heaven" (Morning Star) at the end of the Millennium or at their first sin.

The 7 Vials are the last 7 days before Armageddon.

Revelation 16:15 is the day before Armageddon and is proof Jesus has not returned for the living in Christ yet.

The lamp of Leviticus 24:1 portrays our glorified bodies

BOUGHS, LAMPS, BREAD

BOUGHS:

LEVITICUS 23:39-42, "Also in the fifteenth day of the seventh month, when ye have gathered in the fruit of the land, ye shall keep a feast unto the LORD seven days: on the first day shall be a sabbath, and on the eighth day shall be a sabbath. ... **take boughs of goodly trees, branches of palm trees, and the boughs of thick trees, and willows of the brook** *... AND YE SHALL REJOICE BEFORE THE LORD YOUR GOD seven days ... Ye shall dwell in booths seven days ..."*

MATTHEW 21:6-9, "... the disciples went ... brought the ass ...

and they set him thereon. And a very **great multitude** spread their garments in the way; others CUT DOWN BRANCHES FROM THE TREES, and strawed them in the way. And the multitudes that went before, and that followed, cried, saying, 'HOSANNA TO THE SON OF DAVID: BLESSED IS HE THAT COMETH IN THE NAME OF THE LORD; HOSANNA IN THE HIGHEST.'"

Israelites cut down branches on the day that Jesus rode a colt into Jerusalem. [Mark 11:7]. They thought Jesus was their Messiah, returning to vanquish their enemy, the Roman army, and set up His Kingdom, but the time was not yet. They took down branches thinking their victory had arrived. All have received our rewards in the Feasts of either Trumpets or Atonement when Jesus returns and the New Jerusalem arrives. Branches will be cut down to receive Jesus as KING OF KINGS AND LORD OF LORDS (Matthew 21:6-9). This time it will be for the final fulfillment. The Nations shall cut down boughs and rejoice, because Jesus has now truly become KING OF KINGS AND LORD OF LORDS.

This is most likely when we will cast our crowns at the feet of Jesus saying, *"Thou art worthy, O Lord, to receive glory and honour and power: for thou hast created all things, and for thy pleasure they are and were created."*

REVELATION 4:10, 11, "The four and twenty elders fall down before him that sat on the throne, and worship him that liveth for ever and ever, and CAST THEIR CROWNS before the throne, saying, 'THOU ART WORTHY, O LORD, TO RECEIVE GLORY AND HONOUR AND POWER: FOR THOU HAST CREAT-ED ALL THINGS, AND FOR THY PLEASURE THEY ARE AND WERE CREATED.'"

LAMPS

The final fulfilment of Lamps will take place when we receive our glorified bodies. Out of our bellies will flow the light of life, the glory of God, or rivers of living water!

JOHN 7:38, "... out of his belly shall flow rivers of living water."

LEVITICUS 24:2-4, "Command the children of Israel, that they bring unto thee pure oil olive beaten FOR THE LIGHT, to cause the lamps to burn continually. Without the vail of the testimony, IN THE TABERNACLE of the congregation ... BEFORE THE LORD CONTINUALLY: it shall be a statute FOR EVER ... HE SHALL ORDER THE LAMPS UPON THE PURE CANDLESTICK BEFORE THE LORD CONTINUALLY."

When Jesus returns, He arises to shake terribly the earth. Every mountain and high place lowers, and every valley is filled in and there is no more sea. The New Jerusalem will sit atop the one and only mountain on earth, located just south of where Jerusalem sits today. The New Jerusalem will glow from the glory of God because the Lamb is the light thereof and gives the whole world light, which is why Jesus said, *"I am the light of the world,"* because Jesus is the light given to us and our new home that lights the world— literally, as the sun is out and will never relight.

Those whose names are in the Book of Life will glow. Some will glow brighter than others.

JOHN 8:12, "Then spake Jesus ... saying, 'I AM THE LIGHT OF THE WORLD: he that followeth me shall not walk in darkness, but shall have THE LIGHT OF LIFE.'"

MATTHEW 6:22, "... THY WHOLE BODY SHALL BE FULL OF LIGHT."

MATTHEW 5:14, "Ye are the light of the world. A CITY THAT IS SET ON AN HILL CANNOT BE HID."

JOHN 12:36, "While ye have light, BELIEVE IN THE LIGHT, THAT YE MAY BE THE CHILDREN OF LIGHT. ..."

JOHN 12:46, "I am come a LIGHT INTO THE WORLD, that whosoever believeth on me should not abide in darkness."

EPHESIANS 5:14, "Wherefore he saith, 'Awake thou that sleepest, and ARISE FROM THE DEAD, AND CHRIST SHALL GIVE THEE LIGHT.'"

REVELATION 21:23-25, "And the city had NO NEED OF THE SUN, NEITHER OF THE MOON, to shine in it: for THE GLORY OF GOD DID LIGHTEN IT, and the Lamb is the light thereof. And the NATIONS of them which are saved SHALL WALK IN THE LIGHT OF IT: and the kings of the earth do bring their glory and honour into it. And the gates of it shall not be shut at all by day: for there shall be no night there."

His Kings and Priests receive their new glorified body which burns like coals in a fireplace for ever and ever. We *"shall shine as the brightness of the firmament; and they that turn many to righteousness as the stars for ever and ever."*

"Without the vail of the testimony," is a prophecy of us seeing the face of the King of Kings!

REVELATION 22:4, "And THEY SHALL SEE HIS FACE; and his name shall be in their foreheads."

JOHN 1:4, "In him was life; and THE LIFE WAS THE LIGHT OF MEN."

JOHN 8:12, "Then spake Jesus again unto them, saying, 'I am the light of the world: he that followeth me shall not walk in darkness, but SHALL HAVE THE LIGHT OF LIFE.'"

DANIEL 10:6, "His body also was like the beryl, and HIS FACE AS THE APPEARANCE OF LIGHTNING, AND HIS EYES AS LAMPS OF FIRE, AND HIS ARMS AND HIS FEET LIKE IN COLOUR TO POLISHED BRASS ..."

DANIEL 12:3, "And they that be wise shall SHINE AS THE BRIGHTNESS OF THE FIRMAMENT; and they that turn many to righteousness AS THE STARS FOR EVER AND EVER."

LEVITICUS 24:2, 4, "Command the children of Israel, that they bring unto thee pure oil olive beaten for the LIGHT, TO CAUSE THE LAMPS TO BURN CONTINUALLY. ... He shall order the lamps upon the pure candlestick before the LORD CONTINUALLY."

BREAD FOR THE TABERNACLE:

LEVITICUS 24:5-7, "And thou shalt take fine flour, and bake twelve cakes thereof: two tenth deals shall be in one cake. And thou shalt set them in TWO ROWS, SIX ON A ROW, upon the pure table before the LORD. And thou shalt put pure frankincense [A picture of the blood of Jesus] upon each row, that it may be on the bread for a memorial, even an offering made by fire unto the LORD."

This is a picture of the Israelites and Gentiles, the Barley and Wheat in the New Jerusalem being sprinkled with the "light of life" from Jesus. The two rows of fine flour seem to picture the Israelites and the Non-Israelites dining with Jesus.

Chapter 15
THE JUGDMENT SEAT OF CHRIST and the GREAT WHITE THRONE

THE GREATEST MISUNDERSTANDING OF REVELATION

The first misunderstanding is WHEN these two judgments—the Judgment Seat of Christ and the Great White Throne—take place. Some think the Great White Throne takes place before the Millennium; others think it happens at the end of the Millennium.

One must question, what is the purpose of the Feasts? Why did God give them to Moses in the first place? He didn't just want to inconvenience His people and put them to a lot of trouble for some 3,500 years for nothing. What was the purpose?

FIRST REASON BOTH JUDGMENTS OCCUR BEFORE THE MILLENNIUM

Every Feast keeper will tell you that the Feasts are a shadow of things to come, a rehearsal of things to come. We get that, but what is the point? What are we rehearsing for? Here is the first big surprise:

The Feasts were given to Moses to guide His people through the last seven months, and to point them to Jesus their Messiah. Once the Children of Israel understand the secret door links the Feasts to Revelation, God wants them to see that the same God Who spoke to Moses also spoke to John. The same God Who wrote the Torah also wrote Revelation. We pray the Children of Israel will agree with the points of the Secret Door when they examine these in depth.

Yahweh wrote both books, and Jesus truly is the Messiah. **The purpose of the Feasts is to point the Israelites to Jesus, their Messiah.**

The Messiah will be revealed to the earth as the Lamb on Firstfruits, and there will be no question Jesus is about to return as King of Kings and Lord of Lord on Trumpets. Once Jesus has returned and destroyed His enemies, why would God ask us (who are living with Him in His house) to continue the Feasts to point them to Jesus? What purpose would keeping the Feasts serve when we are living in the New Jerusalem with Jesus? None. Tabernacles is the only exception. THE NATIONS ARE THE ONLY PEOPLE REQUIRED TO OBSERVE THE FEAST OF TABERNACLES each year during their 1,000 years of living.

ZECHARIAH 14:16, 17, "And it shall come to pass, that EVERY ONE THAT IS LEFT OF ALL THE NATIONS which came AGAINST JERUSALEM shall even go up FROM YEAR TO YEAR TO WORSHIP THE KING, the LORD of hosts, and to KEEP THE FEAST OF TABERNACLES. And it shall be, that whoso will not come up of all the families of the earth unto Jerusalem to worship the King, the LORD of hosts, even upon them shall be NO RAIN."

ALL major prophetic events happen on the Feasts, and all the Feasts except Tabernacles stop upon Jesus' return. There is no future Feast to judge the Nations at the end of the Millennium. Those who die during the Millennium are the *"rest of the dead lived not again until the thousand years were finished.*" Their treatment was assigned at the Judgment Seat of Christ. They were judged to die by the end of the Millennium.

In the American court system when a person is judged to die, it may take over ten years before the person is executed. Likewise, the nations are judged on Trumpets, but they don't die on Trumpets. They are judged to die upon their first sin, be that the day after Trumpets or the last day of the Millennium when fire from God out of heaven devours them. If they sin before the end of the Millennium a Morning Star King appears and hits them with the Morning Star, destroying both body and soul. This is their judgment. There is NO judgment past Atonement. The nations are judged to die upon their first sin; hence, *"ruled with a rod of iron."*

SECOND REASON
BOTH JUDGMENTS OCCUR
BEFORE THE MILLENNIUM

The Feasts are NEVER kept in the Millennium by those who live in the New Jerusalem. Zechariah 14:16 clearly says the Nations are the ones required to "GO UP" and worship on Tabernacles. Why does the Bible say they are to "GO UP" and worship? Because the New Jerusalem sits atop the one and only mountain on the earth! The Nations are not allowed entry, but they are required to observe Tabernacles, meaning the other Feasts are NO LONGER OBSERVED.

REVELATION 21:10, "And he carried me away in the spirit to a GREAT AND HIGH MOUNTAIN, and shewed me that great city, THE HOLY JERUSALEM, descending out of heaven from God,"

We know now that the Book of Revelation is NOT chronological. It DOES skip around, and the verse before does not necessarily mean the next verse is the next event. Such is true with the following.

REVELATION 20:7-10, "And when the THOUSAND YEARS ARE EXPIRED, Satan shall be LOOSED OUT OF HIS PRISON, And shall go out to DECEIVE THE NATIONS which are in the four quarters of the earth, Gog, and Magog, TO GATHER THEM TOGETHER TO BATTLE: the number of whom is as the sand of the sea. And they went up on the breadth of the earth, and COMPASSED THE CAMP OF THE SAINTS ABOUT, and the beloved city: and FIRE CAME DOWN FROM GOD OUT OF HEAVEN, AND DEVOURED THEM. And the devil that deceived them was cast into the lake of fire and brimstone, where the beast and the false prophet are, and shall be tormented day and night for ever and ever. [End of Millennium]"

Now, the Bible jumps back 1,000 years in time to the last Feast of Atonement before the Millennium. There is only ONE verse in the Bible with GREAT WHITE THRONE in it, and this is the verse, and it is speaking of all dead NOT in Christ who report to the Great White Throne on the Feast of Atonement. Notice on Atonement there is no judgment by fire, but rather judgment by works written in books. Those not in the book of life are cast into the fire. The Great White Throne is judgment BY BOOKS, those not in the books are cast into the fire, but the judgment is BY BOOKS.

REVELATION 20:11-15, "And I saw a GREAT WHITE THRONE, and him that sat on it, from whose face the earth AND THE HEAVEN FLED AWAY; AND THERE WAS FOUND NO PLACE FOR THEM. And I saw the DEAD, small and great, stand before God; and the BOOKS WERE OPENED: and another

BOOK was opened, which is the BOOK of life: and the DEAD were judged out of those things which were written in the BOOKS, according to their works. And the sea gave up the dead which were in it; and death and hell delivered up the dead which were in them: and they were judged every man according to their works. And death and hell were cast into the lake of fire. This is the second death. And whosoever was not found written in the BOOK of life was cast into the lake of fire."

Please notice the words *"GREAT WHITE THRONE, and him that sat on it, from whose face THE EARTH and THE HEAVEN fled away; and there was found no place for them."* This verse is saying that the old heaven and the old earth are removed on Atonement. If they were removed at the end of the Millennium that would mean when Jesus returns on Trumpets His reward would NOT be with Him, and we would not live in His Father's house like He said we would. That puts the New Heaven and New Earth at the beginning of the Millennium, specifically on Tabernacles.

If the old heaven and old earth did not pass away on the last Atonement and the New Heaven and New Earth did not arrive on Tabernacles that would mean that we wander around for 1,000 years, living out on a scorched earth among sinful Nations trying to build a place to live out of ashes, waiting for the New Jerusalem and our mansions to come down. Jesus clearly said, *"My reward is with me."* What major event would take place five days after Atonement on Tabernacles? The whole point of Tabernacles is for us, His Bride to live or to "Tabernacle" with Him.

Thinking that the New Jerusalem doesn't arrive before the Millennium is to say that Jesus is going to give us white robes and ask us to live on a scorched earth with sinners for 1,000 years! No way!

JOHN 14:2, 3, "In MY FATHER'S HOUSE [New Jerusalem] *are many mansions: if it were not so, I would have told you. I go to prepare a place for you. And if I go and prepare a place for you, I WILL COME AGAIN, and receive you unto myself; that WHERE I AM, THERE YE MAY BE ALSO."*

Doesn't this say that when Jesus returns we get to live with Him in His Father's house, our new mansions, the New Jerusalem?

Since the Feasts are no longer observed, and we have seen that God attaches the events of the Last Days to His Feasts, what Feast would the GREAT WHITE THRONE FALL ON AT THE END OF THE MILLENNIUM? There is not one, because the Great White Throne takes place on the last Feast of Atonement, 10 days after Jesus returned on Trumpets.

In conclusion, the New Jerusalem arrives <u>before</u> the Millennium for the Feast of Tabernacles.

THIRD REASON
BOTH JUDGMENTS OCCUR
BEFORE THE MILLENNIUM

We have to define what "wrath" is as it is used in Revelation. Wrath is the Morning Star, which Jesus uses to burn the tares on the day of Trumpets.

We must know that the seventh trumpet is the final trumpet, which sounds on the day of Trumpets.

We must know that the time of the dead to be judged is on Atonement, which is 10 days after Trumpets.

We must know that the bad is cast away and rewards are given to the good on both Trumpets and Atonement.

These verses tell us that the seventh trumpet sounds when His wrath is come and the DEAD is judged. These verses prove the Judgment Seat of Christ and the Great White Throne are both pre-Millennial. There is NO judgment after the Great White Throne. If the nations are resurrected at the end of the Millennium, it is only to destroy them. There is no further judgment.

> REVELATION 11:15-18, "And the SEVENTH ANGEL SOUNDED; and there were great voices in heaven, saying, 'The kingdoms of this world are become the kingdoms of our Lord, and of his Christ; and he shall reign for ever and ever.' ... And the nations were angry, and thy WRATH IS COME, and the TIME OF THE DEAD, THAT THEY SHOULD BE JUDGED, and that thou shouldest give reward unto thy servants the prophets, and to the saints, and them that fear thy name, small and great; and shouldest destroy them which destroy the earth."

> REVELATION 20:12-14, "And I saw the DEAD, small and great, STAND BEFORE GOD; and the books were opened: and another book was opened, which is the book of life: and THE DEAD WERE JUDGED out of those things which were written in the books, according to their works. And the sea gave up the dead which were in it; and death and hell delivered up the dead which were in them: and they were judged every man according to their works. And death and hell were cast into the lake of fire. This is the second death."

Now let us examine <u>the greatest misunderstanding in Revelation.</u>

Let's start with the typical MISUNDERSTANDING. Remember that Revelation is NOT CONSECUTIVE. It jumps, and it is up to us to search and find the truth. (Proverbs 25:2). If one simply reads Revelation, chapter 20, and understands it consecutively, this will be the understanding one arrives at. It is important to study it in light of other verses.

The Bible APPEARS to say that when Jesus returns near the 6,000th year that the Christians appear before the Judgment Seat of Christ—not to determine if we are saved or not, but to determine our rewards.

The Bible APPEARS to say at the **end** of the Millennium, the 7,000th year, the sinners stand before the Great White Throne where the Father judges them and casts them into the Lake of Fire.

Now that we have the Secret Door of prophecy we can better understand.

NATIONS

The confusion is caused by the TREATMENT of the nations.

Trumpets: Judgment Seat of Christ: All those IN CHRIST dead or alive report.

Atonement: Great White Throne: All those NOT IN CHRIST—only the dead report.

The "Nations" don't fall into either category.

They didn't receive Jesus, they are the corners not harvested for good or bad at the Judgment Seat of Christ.

They are not dead, so they are not judged for good or bad at the Great White Throne.

They are NOT HARVESTED, but allowed to live for up to 1,000 years with restricted treatment.

The restricted treatment becomes effective on Trumpets at the Judgment Seat of Christ.

The restricted treatment is: If one in the Nations sin, meaning breaking one of the laws of Jesus, they are instantly destroyed both soul and body by a Morning Star King/Judge.

If they die by natural causes, both body and soul dies. No eternal body is given.

Their judgment is they shall NOT LIVE more than 1,000 years.

They are not allowed entrance into the eternal kingdom. The Kingdom is *"not be left to other people"* and *"consume all these kingdoms."* (Daniel 2:44).

They are NOT part of the Marriage Supper or the Great White Throne judgment.

They fulfill the prophecy, *"the REST OF THE DEAD lived not again until the thousand years were finished."*

If they are resurrected at the end of the Millennium, it is only to destroy both body and soul.

They are the "corners of thy field." They are not reaped or judged, but die of natural causes unless they sin.

They have children, but their children receive the same treatment and eventual death of body and soul.

No eternal life for the nations nor their offspring.

LEVITICUS 23:22, "And when ye reap the harvest of your land, THOU SHALT NOT MAKE CLEAN RIDDANCE OF THE CORNERS OF THY FIELD when thou reapest, neither shalt thou gather any gleaning of thy harvest: thou shalt leave them unto the poor, and to the stranger ..."

The Nations do not receive eternal life, so upon body death, they also receive soul-death, be it by natural causes or Morning Star. They live until their first sin or the end of the Millennium whichever comes first. They fulfill the "rest of the dead" and when they die both body and soul dies. They are not allowed into the eternal kingdom. The last judgment is the Great White Throne. There is no judgment at the end of the Millennium. The Nations are given special treatment which starts at the Judgment Seat of Christ. These verses say they are ALL destroyed.

DANIEL 2:44, "And in the days of these kings shall the God of heaven set up a kingdom, which shall never be destroyed: and the kingdom shall NOT BE LEFT TO OTHER PEOPLE, [nations] *but it shall break in pieces and CONSUME ALL THESE KINGDOMS,* [only those in the book of life are eternal] *and it shall stand for ever."*

REVELATION 20:1-6, "And I saw an angel come down from heaven, having the key of the bottomless pit and a great chain in his hand. And he laid hold on the dragon, that old serpent, which is the Devil, and Satan, and bound him a thousand years, [pre-millennium] *And cast him into the bottomless pit, and shut him up, and set a seal upon him, that he should deceive the nations no more, till the thousand years should be fulfilled: and after that he must be loosed a little season.* [post-millennium Satan is loosed] [now we jump back to Trumpets, the Judgment Seat of Christ when all rewards to believers are received] *And I saw thrones, and they sat upon them, and judgment was given unto them: and I saw the souls of them that were beheaded for the witness of Jesus, and for the word of God, and which had not worshipped the beast, neither his image, neither had received his mark upon their foreheads, or in their hands; and they lived and reigned with Christ a thousand years.* [not the nations judgment is explained, the rest of the dead is the nations] *But the REST OF THE DEAD lived not again until the thousand years were finished.* [The nations are apparently resurrected to receive soul-death] [now we jump back to talking about the Marriage supper] *This is the first resurrection. Blessed and holy is he that hath part in the first resurrection:* [Pentecost Marriage of the Lamb] *on such the second death hath no power, but they shall be priests of God and of Christ, and shall reign with him a thousand years.* [They reign over the nations for 1,000 years because the nations only live for 1,000 years. Their reign ends at the end of 1,000 years because the nations all die at the end of 1,000 years.]*"*

Now the Bible jumps forward to the 7,000th year at the end of the Millennium with Satan being loosed. The Nations, dead and alive, both body and soul, are destroyed by the Morning Star from heaven. The Bible is not clear on this whole process, but we KNOW the Nations do NOT LIVE BEYOND 1,000 YEARS! That is the point to remember. They are the corners of the field left to the poor and NOT HARVESTED. They do NOT receive eternal life.

REVELATION 20:7-9, "And when the THOUSAND YEARS ARE EXPIRED, Satan shall be loosed out of his prison, And shall go out to deceive the nations which are in the four quarters of the earth, Gog, and Magog, to gather them together to battle: the number of whom is as the sand of the sea. And they went up on the breadth of the earth, and compassed the camp of the saints about, and the beloved city: and FIRE CAME DOWN FROM GOD OUT OF HEAVEN, AND DEVOURED THEM. [Morning Star]*"*

Remember the Bible, ESPECIALLY Revelation, is NOT CHRONOLOGICAL. The text backs up now to the Day of Atonement, the Great White Throne, at the pre-Millennial mark.

Notice the words "books" and "works." This is the judgment of the dead from the books based upon their works. All souls NOT in Jesus report for Judgment. Jesus is the RIGHTEOUS JUDGE with the KEYS OF HELL AND DEATH. Everything done in secret is made open and manifest, except those sins covered with a garment. The OLD heaven is done away with and the OLD earth is transformed into a new earth with no more sea.

REVELATION 20:11-15, "And I saw a GREAT WHITE THRONE, and him that sat on it, [Jesus] *from whose face the EARTH and the HEAVEN fled away; and there was found NO PLACE FOR THEM. And I saw the dead,* [Those NOT in Jesus] *small and great, stand before God; and the BOOKS were opened: and another BOOK was opened, which is the BOOK of life: and the dead were judged out of those things which were written in the BOOKS, according to their WORKS. And the sea gave up the dead which were in it; and death and hell delivered up the dead which were in them: and they were judged every man according to their WORKS. And death and hell were cast into the lake of fire. This is the second death. And whosoever was not found written in the BOOK of life was cast into the lake of fire."*

Every soul NOT in Christ reports to the Great White Throne and the bad fish are cast away. The goats are separated from the sheep. Five days later on the Feast of Tabernacles, we see "the tabernacle of God is with men." The old heaven and earth have been gone for five days. *"I make all things new"* is now in place.

HOSEA 4:3, "Therefore shall the land mourn, and every one that dwelleth therein shall languish, with the beasts of the field, and with the fowls of heaven; yea, *THE FISHES OF THE SEA ALSO SHALL BE TAKEN AWAY."*

REVELATION 21:1-3, "And I saw a new heaven and a new earth: for the first heaven and the first earth were passed away; and there was NO MORE SEA. And I John saw the holy city, NEW JERUSALEM, COMING DOWN FROM GOD OUT OF HEAVEN, prepared as a bride adorned for her husband. And I heard a great voice out of heaven saying, 'Behold, the tabernacle of God is with men, and he will dwell with them, and they shall be his people, and God himself shall be with them, and be their God.'"

Trumpets is the Judgment Seat of Christ. All IN JESUS dead or alive report. Jesus judges.

Atonement is the Great White Throne. All dead <u>NOT</u> IN JESUS report. Jesus judges.

How do we know every person back to Adam is judged on the pre-Millennial Day of Atonement?

As with Matthew 25, the following verse says BOTH GOOD AND BAD are judged at the same time on the same day. The point is that there is NOT a judgment in which ONLY the good show up or another judgment in which ONLY the bad show up.

The Judgment Seat of Christ on Trumpets and the Great White Throne on Atonement both have good and bad judged. The difference is those dead or alive IN CHRIST appear at the Judgment Seat of Christ and stand before Jesus whereas those dead NOT IN CHRIST appear before the Great White Throne and stand before Christ. The Nations do not appear for judgment and are not harvested and receive no eternal life. But from Trumpets forward, if they sin body and soul are destroyed, and they are informed of this "rod of iron' rule at Trumpets.

REVELATION 1:7, "Behold, he cometh with clouds; and EVERY EYE SHALL SEE HIM, and they also which PIERCED HIM: and ALL KINDREDS OF THE EARTH shall wail because of him. Even so, Amen. [Good and Bad]"

SUMMARY OF JUDGMENTS
FEAST OF PENTECOST
WEDDING SUPPER
Most IN Christ admitted
Receive Wedding Garment
White Horse
Become Bride of Christ
Wedding Garment is works
No works—cast into outer darkness

Feast of Trumpets
Judgment Seat of Christ

Those IN Christ report

All who accepted Jesus, dead or alive

Jesus Judges

Judgment by fire

Some works may be burned up

All rewards received, crowns, fine linen garments

No talents used, no fruit, no salt, no oil, no light no eternal life

Cast into outer darkness, weeping and gnashing of teeth

Feast of Atonement
Great White Throne

Judgment of the dead NOT in Christ

Jesus Judges

Judgment of works written in books

Book of Life opened

Those not in the Book of Life cast into the Lake of Fire

Chapter 16
PARABLES

The parables of Jesus are more meaningful when we know the setting, whether it is the Marriage Super or the Judgment Seat of Christ.

Let's study the Scriptures of the Barley and Wheat rejoicing at the Marriage Supper so we will recognize the setting at the Marriage Supper of the Lamb. This is when Jesus is changed from "Prince" to "King" and from "Lamb" to "Lion." We are changed from "Mud" to "Spirit" and from "Sin" to "Holiness."

We are given Wedding Garments made of fine linen, our righteous works for Jesus. Those invited to the Marriage Supper are washed in the Blood of the Lamb and see Jesus face to face! From Revelation 7:9, 7:13-19; 19:6-9; 20:6—Those invited to the Wedding Supper are holy and washed in the Blood of the Lamb. We will see in Matthew 22 some arrive with their sins washed away, but have no works. The fine linen garment is our works. Some are cast into outer darkness. This means the Wedding is in part judgment, but mostly rejoicing as we are wed to the Bridegroom!

REVELATION 7:9, 10, "After this I beheld, and, lo, a GREAT MULTITUDE, [Barley and Wheat] which no man could number, *[the Barley is 144,000 but when the Wheat is added no man can number them]* of all nations, and kindreds, and people, and tongues, stood before the throne, and before the Lamb, clothed with white robes, and palms in their hands; And cried with a loud voice, saying, 'Salvation to our God which sitteth upon the throne, and unto the Lamb.'"*

REVELATION 7:13-17, "And one of the elders answered, saying unto me, 'What are these which are arrayed in white robes? and whence came they?' And I said unto him, 'Sir, thou knowest.' And he said to me, 'These are they which came out of great tribulation, [don't have to live in the tribulation, but are resurrected in the tribulation] *and have WASHED THEIR ROBES, and made them white in the BLOOD OF THE LAMB. Therefore are they before the throne of God, and serve him day and night in his temple: and he that sitteth on the throne shall dwell among them. They shall hunger no more, neither thirst any more; neither shall the sun light on them, nor any heat. For the Lamb which is in the midst of the throne shall feed them, and shall lead them unto living fountains of waters: and God shall wipe away all tears from their eyes.'"*

REVELATION 19:6-9, "And I heard as it were the voice of a GREAT MULTITUDE, and as the voice of many waters, and as the voice of mighty thunderings, saying, 'Alleluia: for the Lord God omnipotent reigneth. Let us be glad and rejoice, and give honour to him: for the MARRIAGE OF THE LAMB is come, and his wife hath made herself ready. And to her was granted that she should be arrayed in FINE LINEN, clean and white: for the fine linen is the righteousness [works] of saints.' And he saith unto me, 'Write, Blessed are they which are called unto the

THE SECRET DOOR TO UNDERSTAND BIBLE PROPHECY 113

marriage supper of the Lamb. [meaning not all are called to the marriage]'"

REVELATION 20:6, *"Blessed and holy is he that hath part in the FIRST RESURRECTION:* [Marriage supper] *on such the second death hath no power, but they shall be priests of God and of Christ, and shall reign with him a thousand years."*

PARABLES SPEAKING OF THE MARRIAGE OF THE LAMB ON PENTECOST

The parable of "Bidden to the Wedding" is speaking of the Marriage of the Lamb. The Marriage occurs on Pentecost and is all about Jesus, but a little correction is given for those without a garment. We see the man who made it into the Wedding. Jesus calls him "friend," but because he had no garment, he is tossed into outer darkness.

The Bible doesn't talk much about outer darkness, or whether one can leave it and return to the light. The Bible doesn't tell us if after a space of correction, after being beaten with stripes at the proper time and the proper way, they might be allowed to return to the light. We would like to think so, but there is no Scripture I've found for it. It is always best to serve Jesus faithfully. Don't take a chance.

LUKE 12:47, 48, "And that servant, which knew his lord's will, and prepared not himself, neither did according to his will, shall be BEATEN WITH MANY STRIPES. But he that knew not, and did commit things worthy of stripes, shall be beaten with FEW STRIPES. For unto whomsoever much is given, of him shall be much required: and to whom men have committed much, of him they will ask the more."

BIDDEN TO WEDDING

The parable "Bidden to the Wedding" is an overview from the offer of salvation, rejection by the Israelites, Jerusalem being sacked and burned in 70 AD and the Gospel being given and accepted by the Non-Israelites, and concluding with the Marriage Supper of the Lamb, and when some are removed from the wedding.

MATTHEW 22:2-13, "The kingdom of heaven is like unto a certain king, which made a MARRIAGE for his son, And sent forth his servants to call them THAT WERE BIDDEN to the wedding: and they would not come. [Gospel rejected by Jews] *Again, he sent forth other servants, saying, 'Tell them which are bidden, 'Behold, I have prepared my dinner: my oxen and my fatlings are killed, and all things are ready: come unto the marriage.' But they made light of it, and went their ways, one to his farm, another to his merchandise: And the remnant took his servants, and entreated them spitefully, and slew them.* [Jews crucified Jesus] *But when the king heard thereof, he was wroth: and he sent forth his armies, and destroyed those murderers, and BURNED UP THEIR CITY.* [Jerusalem destroyed in 70 AD] *Then saith he to his servants, 'The wedding is ready, but they which were bidden were not worthy. Go ye therefore into the highways,* [Gospel offered to the Gentiles] *and as many as ye shall find, bid to the marriage.' So those servants went out into the highways, and gathered together all as many as they found, BOTH BAD AND GOOD: and the WEDDING was furnished with guests.* [Marriage Supper of the Lamb] *And when the king came in to see the guests, he saw there a man which had NOT ON A WEDDING GARMENT:* [no fruit, no salt, no oil, no light no eternal life] *And he saith unto him, 'Friend, how camest thou in hither not having a wedding garment?' And he was speechless. Then said the king to the servants, 'Bind him hand and foot, and take him away, and cast* him into outer darkness, there shall be weeping and gnashing of teeth.'"

Report to: Marriage of the Lamb they accepted Christ.

Judgment: No talents used, no fruit, no salt, no oil, no works, no light and no eternal life.

Punishment: Cast into outer darkness, weeping and gnashing of teeth.

TEN VIRGINS WITH LAMPS

This parable speaks of virgins IN Christ. It even says they go out to meet the Bridegroom, they know Jesus. Yet, Jesus says some are not ready to enter the Marriage on Pentecost. Perhaps four months later they will have some works or a garment at the Judgment Seat of Christ on Trumpets!

Why are five admitted and five not? What does oil represent? Oil burns and gives off light. Jesus is the *"Light of the world,"* so they had fallen asleep and had not worked. They had stopped watching and their excitement for Christ and His Gospel had grown cold, and they went to sleep. Even if we have asked Jesus into our heart, if we have no works, Jesus doesn't know us! And we are locked out of the Marriage Supper and are in danger of being castaways at the Judgment Seat of Christ on Trumpets. The last four words are scary, *"I know you not."*

In that it says, *"Go ye out to meet him"* is telling us they are living in Israel and alive on Pentecost when Jesus is walking around on Mt. Zion. (Revelation 14:1-4). Hopefully, they see Jesus and realize they have no works. They see Jesus and the Barley and Wheat arise to the Wedding and they are left. Hopefully, they get busy and work and are ready four months later at the Judgment Seat of Christ. After all, the whole purpose of the shout, *"Behold the Bridegroom Cometh"* is to get those asleep without works awakened and to have works. They know Christ, but are not ready. Because, *"strait is the gate, and narrow is the way, which leadeth unto life, and few there be that find it."*

MATTHEW 25:1-12, "Then shall the kingdom of heaven be likened unto ten VIRGINS, which took their LAMPS, and went forth to meet the BRIDEGROOM. And five of them were wise, and five were foolish. They that were FOOLISH took their lamps, and took NO OIL with them: But the wise took OIL in their vessels with their lamps. While the bridegroom tarried, they all slumbered and slept. And at midnight there was a cry made, 'Behold, the bridegroom cometh; go ye out to meet him.' Then all those virgins arose, and trimmed their lamps. And the foolish said unto the wise, 'Give us of your oil; for our lamps are gone out.' [They received the light, accepted Jesus, but had no fruit, salt, nor oil to give light] *But the wise answered, saying, 'Not so; lest there be not enough for us and you: but go ye rather to them that sell, and buy for yourselves.'* [go do your own works] *And while they went to buy, the bridegroom came; and they that were ready went in with him to the marriage:* [Marriage of the Lamb on Pentecost] *and the door was shut.* [They had no works and were not worthy to go to the Marriage] *Afterward came also the other virgins, saying, 'Lord, Lord, open to us.' But he answered and said, 'Verily I say unto you, 'I KNOW YOU NOT.'"*

Please note some simply had no oil and were not ready. We want to think missing the Marriage scared them to get to work. Others never knew Him, even though they apparently thought they did. Don't take a chance. Stay awake and serve in His vineyard.

THE SECRET DOOR TO UNDERSTAND BIBLE PROPHECY

The Wise Virgins with oil: Invited

The incident happens on Pentecost at the Marriage Supper. Christians with oil and works went in.

Reports to: Marriage Supper because virgins have accepted Christ, *"went forth to meet the bridegroom."*

Judgment: They slept, but had oil, light, fruit, salt *"... they that were ready went in ..."*

Punishment: None

Foolish Virgins with NO oil: Rejected

Reports to: Missed the Marriage supper so they report to the Judgment Seat of Christ.

Judgment: Slept and had no works, no oil, no light, no fruit, no salt *"...I know you not..."*

Punishment: They are virgins, so they are IN Christ, but they miss the wedding, hopefully will enter at Trumpets

PARABLES at THE JUDGMENT SEAT OF CHRIST on TRUMPETS
EVIL SERVANT:

The evil servant accepted Jesus but lost sight of him and turned to the world and got in fights and became an alcoholic as we would say today. His correct judgment is with the hypocrites. He is a hypocrite. His punishment is very bad—weeping and gnashing of teeth, but he is not tossed into the Lake of Fire. We don't want to find out what happens after the gnashing of teeth. The message to us is to serve the Lord with all our heart.

MATTHEW 24:46-51, "Blessed is that servant, whom his lord WHEN HE COMETH shall find so doing. Verily I say unto you, 'That he shall make him ruler over all his goods. But and if that EVIL SERVANT shall say in his heart, 'My lord delayeth HIS COMING;' And shall begin to smite his fellowservants, and to eat and drink with the drunken; The lord of that servant shall come in a day when he looketh not for him, and in an hour that he is not aware of, And shall CUT HIM ASUNDER, AND APPOINT HIM HIS PORTION WITH THE HYPOCRITES: there shall be weeping and GNASHING of teeth."

Report to: Judgment Seat of Christ, "Servant" he accepted Jesus, but lived like a sinner"... when he cometh ..."

Judgment: Evil works: drinks, fights, stops watching

Punishment: Numbered with the hypocrites, weeping and GNASHING of teeth.

A Hypocrite is a person who accepted Jesus, but lives like a sinner so the evil servant reports to the Judgment Seat of Christ. He not only has no good works, but has evil works and is given weeping and GNASHING of teeth. Not Lake of Fire.

SALT

This person has lost his salt. He has crawled into a shell and forgotten his call to be a light, to bring fruit into the Kingdom. He is worthless in terms of the Kingdom.

MATTHEW 5:13, "Ye are the SALT of the earth: but if the salt have lost his savour, wherewith shall it be salted? it is thenceforth good for nothing, but to be cast out, and to be trodden under foot of men."

Report to: Judgment Seat of Christ because salt has accepted Jesus

Judgment: Lost savor, tree without fruit, salt without saltiness, virgin without oil, man with light under a bushel

Punishment: Cast out trodden under foot

LIGHT

When the sun goes out in the fifth vial it never relights. Jesus is literally the light of the world. Here Jesus admonishes us to spread the light of the Gospel, if we are truly In Christ. If we are truly a Christian, everyone around us will know it because we have done all we can to see they are all Christians.

MATTHEW 5:14-16, "Ye are the light of the world. A city that is set on an hill cannot be hid. Neither do men light a candle, and put it under a bushel, but on a candlestick; and it giveth LIGHT unto all that are in the house. Let your LIGHT so SHINE BEFORE MEN, THAT THEY MAY SEE YOUR GOOD WORKS, and glorify your Father which is in heaven."

Reports to: Judgment Seat because they have light, they accepted Jesus

Judgment: No talents used, no fruit, no salt, no oil, no light no eternal life. Spread the light of Jesus

Punishment: None listed for those who have light, a tree with fruit, salt with saltiness or a virgin with oil.

NET CAST INTO SEA

We know this is the Judgment Seat of Christ on Trumpets because angels don't gather the living at Atonement. Atonement is the judgment of the dead. Notice the judgment is instant. No books, the angel separates the tares from the Wheat, and the tares are cast into the fire. The Morning Star sword misses those in Christ and hits those NOT in Christ. The Wheat see the Morning Star as lightning, shining from the east to the west as the tares are destroyed.

PSALM 91:7, "A thousand shall fall at thy side, and ten thousand at thy right hand; but it shall not come nigh thee. ONLY WITH THINE EYES shalt thou behold and see the reward of the wicked."

MATTHEW 13:47-50, "Again, the kingdom of heaven is like unto a net, that was cast into the SEA, and gathered of every kind: Which, when it was full, they drew to shore, and sat down, and gathered the good into vessels, but cast the bad away. So shall it be at the end of the world: the ANGELS SHALL COME FORTH, and SEVER THE WICKED FROM AMONG THE JUST, And shall CAST them into the furnace of FIRE: there shall be wailing and GNASHING of teeth."

MATTHEW 24:27, "For as the LIGHTNING cometh out of the east, and shineth even unto the west; so shall also the coming of the Son of man be."

Report to: Judgment Seat of Christ, "Angels don't sever the wicked from among the just" at Atonement, this is Trumpets

Judgment: By fire, no salt, no fruit, no good works, no oil for light, no eternal life

Punishment: Wicked cast into the fire

TALENTS

The one talent or gift every new believer receives the moment Jesus comes into our heart is salvation. Salvation is the ONE talent. The wicked servant is one who accepted Jesus, but did nothing to share the light. They put their light under a bushel; they were given salt, but never used it, like a tree that has leaves, but no fruit. The worthless, the servant that doesn't serve, the soul-winner that doesn't win souls has no fruit. There will be weeping and gnashing teeth. Notice there is no talk of the Lake of Fire.

MATTHEW 25:14-30, "For the kingdom of heaven is as a man travelling into a far country, [Jesus in heaven for 2,000 years] *who called his own SERVANTS, and delivered unto them his goods. And unto one he gave five talents, to another two, and to another one; to every man according to his several ABILITY; and straightway took his journey. Then he that had received the five talents went and traded with the same, and made them other five talents. And likewise he that had received two, he also gained other two. But he that had received one went and digged in the earth, and HID HIS LORD'S MONEY.* [tree without fruit, salt without saltiness, virgin without oil, man with light under a bushel] *After a long time* [Jesus left for 2000 years] *the lord of those servants cometh, and reckoneth with them.* [Trumpets, Day of the Lord] *And so he that had received five talents came and brought other five talents, saying, 'Lord, thou deliveredst unto me five talents: behold, I have gained beside them five talents more.' His lord said unto him, 'Well done, thou good and faithful servant: thou hast been faithful over a few things, I will make thee ruler over many things: enter thou into the joy of thy lord.' He also that had received two talents came and said, 'Lord, thou deliveredst unto me two talents: behold, I have gained two other talents beside them.' His lord said unto him, 'Well done, good and faithful servant; thou hast been faithful over a few things, I will make thee ruler over many things: enter thou into the joy of thy lord.' Then he which had received the one talent came and said, 'Lord, I knew thee that thou art an hard man, reaping where thou hast not sown, and gathering where thou hast not strawed: And I was afraid, and went and HID THY TALENT IN THE EARTH: lo, there thou hast that is thine.' His lord answered and said unto him, 'Thou wicked and slothful servant, thou knewest that I reap where I sowed not, and gather where I have not strawed: Thou oughtest therefore to have put my money to the exchangers,* [If you can't spread the light give to one who can] *and then at my coming* [Judgment Seat of Christ on Trumpets] *I should have received mine own with usury. TAKE THEREFORE THE TALENT* [eternal life] *FROM HIM, AND GIVE IT UNTO HIM WHICH HATH TEN TALENTS. For unto every one that hath shall be given, and he shall have abundance: but from him THAT HATH NOT* [tree without fruit, salt without saltiness, virgin without oil, man with light under a bushel] *shall be TAKEN AWAY EVEN THAT WHICH HE HATH. And CAST YE THE UNPROFITABLE SERVANT INTO OUTER DARKNESS: THERE SHALL BE WEEPING AND GNASHING OF TEETH.'"*

Talent: Gifts and abilities given to each person, the first gift was life eternal

Report to: Judgment Seat of Christ he was a servant of Christ

Judgment: No talents used, no fruit, no salt, no oil, no light, might not be eternal life

Punishment: Cast into outer darkness, weeping and gnashing of teeth

WHEAT AND TARES

This is one of the most important parables because this confirms Wheat is speaking of those IN Christ.

When the wheat and tares grow together it is almost impossible to tell them apart. They sit in the pews together, attend the Bible studies and say, "Praise the Lord." When the harvest is ripe the wheat farmer can walk into his field of wheat and spot the tares easily. They are the ones with what looks like no fruit. The seeds of the tares are smaller and bitter. If just one seed gets into the wheat flour it makes it bitter and unusable. The farmer must be very diligent to get every one of the tares out. The wheat is easy to spot because their seeds are much bigger, fuller, heavier and cause the top of the wheat to bend over.

The farmer walks through the field carefully pulling EVERY ONE of the tares out. He then burns the tares making sure not one seed gets into the wheat. Likewise, the angels with sharp sickles go through and slash the grapes, Jesus using the Morning Star burns the tares, taking great care not to hurt the wheat and not to miss a tare. This is the DAY of the Lord, Trumpets, Judgment Seat of Christ, the Judgment by fire, the day all IN Christ receive their rewards.

MATTHEW 13:36-43, "Then Jesus sent the multitude away, and went into the house: and his disciples came unto him, saying, 'Declare unto us the parable of the tares of the field.' He answered and said unto them, 'He that soweth the good seed is the Son of man; The field is the world; the good seed are the children of the kingdom; but the tares are the children of the wicked one; The enemy that sowed them is the devil; the harvest is the end of the world; and the reapers are the angels. As therefore the tares are gathered and burned in the fire; [Trumpets, day of the Lord] *so shall it be in the end of this world. The Son of man shall send forth his angels, and they shall gather out of his kingdom all things that offend, and them which do iniquity;* [Trumpets, armies of the New World Order attack Jerusalem] *And shall cast them into a furnace of fire:* [Jesus burns tares with Morning Star] *there shall be wailing and gnashing of teeth. Then shall the righteous shine forth as the sun in the kingdom of their Father.* [Trumpets, Judgment Seat of Christ, Barley and Wheat receive all rewards and glorified glowing body.] *Who hath ears to hear, let him hear.'"*

Wheat: those IN Christ

Report to: Judgment Seat of Christ he was a servant of Christ

Wheat Judgment: Morning Star does NOT burn, they have talents, fruit, salt, oil, light, servant and eternal life. *"A thousand shall fall at thy side, and ten thousand at thy right hand; but it shall not come nigh thee. Only with thine eyes shalt thou behold and see the reward of the wicked."*

Rewards: Crowns, fine linen is the righteous acts of the saints, Mansions on Tabernacles.

Tares: those NOT in Christ

Report to: Nowhere, their judgment is instant—being hit by the Morning Star, destroying both body and soul in ashes. The two angels with sharp sickles do slashing and the blood rises to the horse bridles.

UNLESS they have worshiped the Beast, his image, received his Mark or the number of his name.

Tares Judgment: Morning Star burns tares, evil, NOT IN Christ

Worshiped the Beast, his image, received his Mark or the number of his name: No soul-death for them, they are cast into the Lake of Fire with the Beast and False Prophet and Satan joins them 1,000 years later.

GREAT WHITE THRONE: SHEEP DIVIDED FROM GOATS:

This is a picture of the Great White Throne on Atonement. Notice there is no mention of Wheat, blood of Jesus or judgment by fire. This is a judgment of works as they are or are NOT written in the books. Notice the first thing Jesus says is, *"I was an hungred, and ye gave me meat,"* referring to how they treated the hungry, thirsty, naked, sick and those in prison. Those with good works get in, those without good works are cast into the Lake of Fire.

MATTHEW 25:31-46, "When the Son of man shall come in his GLORY, and all the holy angels with him, then shall he sit upon the throne of his glory: And before him shall be gathered all nations: and he shall separate them one from another, as a shepherd divideth his sheep from the goats: And he shall set the sheep on his right hand, but the goats on the left. Then shall the King say unto them on his right hand, 'Come, ye blessed of my Father, inherit the kingdom prepared for you from the foundation of the world: [judgment of works] *For I was an hungred, and ye gave me meat: I was thirsty, and ye gave me drink: I was a stranger, and ye took me in: Naked, and ye clothed me: I was sick, and ye visited me: I was in prison, and ye came unto me.' Then shall the righteous answer him, saying, 'Lord, when saw we thee an hungred, and fed thee? or thirsty, and gave thee drink? When saw we thee a stranger, and took thee in? or naked, and clothed thee? Or when saw we thee sick, or in prison, and came unto thee?' And the King shall answer and say unto them, 'Verily I say unto you, Inasmuch as ye have done it unto one of the least of these my brethren, ye have done it unto me.'* [tree without fruit, salt without saltiness, virgin without oil, man with light under a bushel] *Then shall he say also unto them on the left hand, 'Depart from me, ye cursed, into everlasting fire, prepared for the devil and his angels: For I was an hungred, and ye gave me no meat: I was thirsty, and ye gave me no drink: I was a stranger, and ye took me not in: naked, and ye clothed me not: sick, and in prison, and ye visited me not.' Then shall they also answer him, saying, 'Lord, when saw we thee an hungred, or athirst, or a stranger, or naked, or sick, or in prison, and did not minister unto thee?' Then shall he answer them, saying, 'Verily I say unto you, Inasmuch as ye did it not* [no works] *to one of the least of these, ye did it not to me. And these shall go away into everlasting punishment: but the righteous into life eternal.'"*

Report to: Great White Throne

Judgment: By works. Tree without fruit, salt without saltiness, virgin without oil, man with light under a bushel

Punishment: Punishment by fire. "Depart from me, ye cursed, into everlasting fire, prepared for the devil and his angels."

FALSE PROPHETS, RAVENING WOLVES AND EVIL FRUIT

This is a warning to Christian MINISTERS. Not all is right in Church leadership. It is also a warning to those who stir up trouble and know in their heart they are not called, not anointed, and not following the teachings of Jesus. They are not getting by with a thing. God not only knows what we do, but WHY we do it. Jesus is telling us how to spot those NOT in Christ. Jesus is saying we should watch their fruits not their lips! Just because they ask Jesus into their heart, use the Name Jesus, do miracles and works FOR Jesus does not mean they are IN Jesus. Those trees without good fruit are hewn down and cast into the fire at the Great White Throne. They asked Jesus into their heart, but Jesus says He doesn't know them, so they report to the Great White Throne. Notice they are not judged IN CHIRST, they are judged by their FRUIT or WORKS. The Great White Throne is the Judgment by WORKS not IN CHRIST.

MATTHEW 7:15-23, "Beware of FALSE PROPHETS, which come to you in sheep's clothing, but inwardly they are RAVENING WOLVES. YE SHALL KNOW THEM BY THEIR FRUITS. Do men gather grapes of thorns, or figs of thistles? Even so every good tree bringeth forth GOOD FRUIT; but a corrupt tree bringeth forth evil fruit. A GOOD TREE CANNOT BRING FORTH EVIL FRUIT, neither can a corrupt tree bring forth good fruit. EVERY TREE THAT BRINGETH NOT FORTH GOOD FRUIT IS HEWN DOWN, AND CAST INTO THE FIRE. Wherefore by their FRUITS ye shall know them. NOT EVERY ONE THAT SAITH UNTO ME, 'LORD, LORD,' SHALL ENTER INTO THE KINGDOM OF HEAVEN; but he that DOETH the will of my Father which is in heaven. Many will say to me in that day, 'Lord, Lord, have we not prophesied in thy name? and in thy name have cast out devils? and in thy name done many wonderful works?' And then will I profess unto them, 'I never knew you: depart from me, ye that work iniquity.'"

Please notice that Jesus speaks of grapes and figs. This confirms Jesus is speaking of Trumpets because grapes and figs are the last harvest and refer to Trumpets. These are they which worked at Christ, not for Christ, and thus report to the Great White Throne, not the Judgment Seat of Christ.

FALSE PROPHETS, RAVENING WOLVES AND EVIL FRUIT

Report to: Great White Throne, Christ never accepted them

Judgment is: Jesus never accepted them; they worked as false prophets, ravening wolves with evil fruit.

Punishment: *"I never knew you: depart from me, ye that work iniquity."*

GOOD TREES:

Report to: Great White Throne

Judgment is: by fruit or works

Punishment: hewn down and cast into the fire

Chapter 17
OVERCOMERS vs. REMNANT

I want to be an Overcomer and NOT a part of the Remnant. Here is why:

Unwalled villages: a place for the woman to flee ...

When we find the massive amounts of oil in Israel, I want to ask Israel for some unused desert land in southern Israel. I want to build the "land of unwalled villages" and bring the Christians and Israelites by the millions from around the world to Israel. I also want to participate in preparing the place in the wilderness for the woman to flee. (Revelation 12:6, 14)

That is two different places. The land of unwalled villages is today not built yet, but with the help of Israel and God, will be built in southern Israel. Whereas the place for the woman to flee will be somewhere in what is today Saudi Arabia, but by then will be Israeli territory after WWIII.

EZEKIEL 38:11, 12, "... the land of UNWALLED VILLAGES ... to them that are at rest, that dwell safely, all of them dwelling without walls, and having neither bars nor gates, ... the desolate places that are now inhabited, and upon the people that are gathered out of the nations, which have gotten cattle and goods, that dwell in the midst of the land."

There are many prophecies saying masses of Christians and Israelites from around the world will move to Israel. The way I suspect it may happen is: After the Russians destroy America and WWIII rages and destroys most of the western world, there will be millions of people needing a new place to live.

I believe many of them will move from the war-torn western nations to the new "blessed nation," which is now Israel. Israel will become the "New America." Many today who have no idea or interest in moving to Israel will move there for safety. It will be the last, safe-place for believers to live, but then the Antichrist shows up even there!

A side note to further confirm that Moses is one of the Two Witnesses: This part of the Song of Moses was a prophecy of the Last Days! Remember, Moses and John the Revelator are the Two Witnesses.

DEUTERONOMY 30:1, "And it shall come to pass, when all these things are come upon thee, the blessing and the curse, which I have set before thee, and thou shalt call them to mind among all the nations, whither the LORD thy God hath driven thee, And SHALT RETURN UNTO THE LORD THY GOD, and shalt obey his voice according to all that I command thee this day, thou and thy children, with all thine heart, and with all thy soul; That then the LORD thy God will turn thy captivity, [Wealth] and have compassion upon thee, and will return and GATHER THEE FROM ALL THE NATIONS, whither the LORD thy God hath scattered thee. If any of thine be driven out unto the outmost parts of heaven, FROM THENCE WILL THE LORD THY GOD GATHER THEE, AND FROM THENCE WILL HE FETCH THEE: And the LORD thy God will BRING THEE INTO THE LAND which thy fathers possessed, and thou shalt possess it; and he will do thee GOOD, AND MULTIPLY THEE ABOVE THY FATHERS. And the LORD thy God will circumcise thine heart, and the heart of thy seed, to love the LORD thy God with all thine heart, and with all thy soul, that thou mayest live. And the LORD thy God will put all these curses upon thine enemies, and on them that hate thee, which persecuted thee. And thou shalt return and OBEY THE VOICE OF THE LORD, and do all his commandments which I command thee this day. And the LORD thy God will make thee PLENTEOUS IN EVERY WORK of thine hand, in the fruit of thy body, and in the fruit of thy cattle, and in the fruit of thy land, for good: for THE LORD WILL AGAIN REJOICE OVER THEE FOR GOOD, as he rejoiced over thy fathers:"

Enoch and Elijah were NOT given any prophecies of the Last Days.

In the middle of the Tribulation the Antichrist will sit on the Ark of the Covenant and proclaim himself to be God. When he does, those familiar with Matthew 24 will recognize the act as the Abomination of Desolation. Jesus warned people when they see the Abomination to flee Jerusalem. When they flee, the Dragon casts water out of his mouth to drown the woman.

2 THESSALONIANS 2:3, 4, "... that MAN OF SIN be revealed, the son of perdition; Who opposeth and exalteth himself above all that is called God, or that is worshipped; so that he as God SITTETH IN THE TEMPLE OF GOD, shewing himself that he is God."

MATTHEW 24:15-18, "When ye therefore shall see the ABOMINATION OF DESOLATION, spoken of by Daniel the prophet, stand in the holy place, (whoso readeth, let him understand:) Then let them which be in Judaea FLEE INTO THE MOUNTAINS: Let him which is on the housetop not come down to take any thing out of his house: Neither let him which is in the field return back to take his clothes."

The Bible says that the earth helps the woman and swallows up the flood. The woman will flee to a place prepared of God where she is supernaturally protected by God for the last 3 ½ years of the Tribulation.

REVELATION 12:6-17, "And the woman [Those that keep the commandments of God and have the testimony of Jesus—the Church] fled into the wilderness, where she hath a place prepared of God, that they should feed her there a thousand two hundred and threescore days. And there was war in heaven: [Middle of the Tribulation] Michael and his angels fought against the dragon; and the dragon fought and his angels, And prevailed not; neither was their place found any more in heaven. And the great dragon was cast out, that old serpent, called the Devil, and Satan, which deceiveth the whole world: he was cast out into the earth, and his angels were cast out with him. [mid-tribulation] ... And when the dragon saw that he was cast unto the earth, he persecuted the woman [Israel] which brought forth the man child. [Jesus] And to the woman were given two wings of a great eagle, [Like leaving Egypt, not an airplane-Deuteronomy 32:11] that she might fly into the wilderness, into her place, where SHE IS NOURISHED for a TIME, AND TIMES, AND HALF A TIME, [last 3 ½ years] from the face of the serpent. And the serpent cast out of his MOUTH WATER AS A FLOOD AFTER THE WOMAN, that he might cause her to be carried away of the flood. And the earth helped the woman, and THE EARTH opened her mouth, and SWALLOWED UP THE FLOOD which the dragon cast out of his mouth. And the dragon was wroth with the woman, and went to make war with the REMNANT of her seed, [those who did not flee south as Jesus told them to do] which

THE SECRET DOOR TO UNDERSTAND BIBLE PROPHECY

keep the commandments of God, and have the testimony of Jesus Christ."

In general, there will be two groups of people on the earth on the day of the LORD, the day of Trumpets, the day of Armageddon. The believers, which will be mostly living in Israel, and the tares and grapes, living mostly in the rest of the world. Many, many believers will move to Israel.

> ISAIAH 43:5-7, "Fear not: for I am with thee: I will bring thy seed from the EAST, and gather thee from the WEST; I will say to the NORTH, Give up; and to the SOUTH, Keep not back: bring my sons from far, and my daughters from the ends of the earth; EVEN EVERY ONE THAT IS CALLED BY MY NAME ... "

Not every believer will move to Israel. There will be pockets of believers outside of Israel, but by this time most believers and ALL Israelites will have moved to Israel. All Israelites? Yes, all Israelites.

> EZEKIEL 39:28, "Then shall they know that I am the LORD their God, which caused them to be led into captivity among the heathen: but I HAVE GATHERED THEM UNTO THEIR OWN LAND, and HAVE LEFT NONE OF THEM ANY MORE THERE."

People have said, "Why would you want worthless desert land to build the unwalled villages on?"

Because at the right time our plan is to send out prayer warriors, prayer walkers, and those who know how to release curses from the land to pray and anoint the land, casting off the curses. When the curses are released the land will blossom like a rose. Israel will once again become a blessed land! You will recall that is the reason Lot chose to go south, because the land was well-watered.

DEUTERONOMY 11:10, 11, "For the land, whither thou goest in to possess it, is NOT AS THE LAND OF EGYPT, from whence ye came out, where thou sowedst thy seed, and WATEREDST IT WITH THY FOOT, as a garden of herbs: But the land, whither ye go to possess it, is a land of hills and valleys, and DRINKETH WATER OF THE RAIN OF HEAVEN:"

Please note the verses below are NOT speaking of the time after Jesus returns. We know this because in these verses they are still looking for the return of Jesus! *"Be strong, fear not: behold, your God will come with VENGEANCE, even God with a RECOMPENCE; he will come and save you."* Almost every time the word "vengeance" is used it is almost always speaking of the Day of the LORD! The time stamp on this is just PRIOR to the return of Messiah Jesus.

This is saying the land of Israel will once again blossom like a rose!

> ISAIAH 35:1-10, "The wilderness and the solitary place shall be glad for them; and the desert shall rejoice, and BLOSSOM AS THE ROSE. It shall BLOSSOM ABUNDANTLY, and rejoice even with joy and singing: the glory of Lebanon shall be given unto it, the excellency of Carmel and Sharon, they shall see the glory of the LORD, and the excellency of our God. Strengthen ye the weak hands, and confirm the feeble knees. Say to them that are of a fearful heart, 'Be strong, fear not: behold, your God will come with VENGEANCE, even God with a RECOMPENCE; he will come and save you.' Then the eyes of the blind shall be opened, and the ears of the deaf shall be unstopped. Then shall the lame man leap as an hart, and the tongue of the dumb sing: for in THE WILDERNESS SHALL WATERS BREAK OUT, AND STREAMS IN THE DESERT. AND THE

PARCHED GROUND SHALL BECOME A POOL, AND THE THIRSTY LAND SPRINGS OF WATER: in the habitation of dragons, where each lay, shall be grass with reeds and rushes. And an highway shall be there, and a way, and it shall be called The way of holiness; the unclean shall not pass over it; but it shall be for those: the wayfaring men, though fools, shall not err therein. No lion shall be there, nor any ravenous beast shall go up thereon, it shall not be found there; but the redeemed shall walk there: And the ransomed of the LORD shall return, and come to Zion with songs and everlasting joy upon their heads: they shall obtain joy and gladness, and sorrow and sighing shall flee away."

Israel will go through occupation by the Antichrist, but compared to the devastation of the rest of the world, it will still be one of the best places on earth to live, if you know when to leave Jerusalem.

Mt. Sinai:
A place for the woman to flee from the Antichrist ...

It is strange how some teachings sound so good when we first hear them until we discover they are NOT correct. Many Christians refer to the "Remnant" as those people who were faithful to stick with Jesus even in the face of trouble. It sounded like being part of the "Remnant" was a good thing, but being an Overcomer is much better!

The Bible specifically is speaking to those living in "Judaea," which is southern Israel, including Jerusalem. Those living just south of Judea will also flee. Basically, anyone in Israel who has read Matthew 24:15-18 will flee. Hopefully, those reading this book will have spotted the Antichrist early and left months earlier and avoided the panic.

REVELATION 12:9-17, "And the great dragon was cast out, [Middle of the Tribulation] *And when the dragon saw that he was cast unto the earth, he persecuted the woman which brought forth the man child. And to the woman were given two wings of a great eagle, that she might fly into the wilderness, into her place,* [Mt. Sinai?] *where she is nourished for a time, and times, and half a time, from the face of the serpent. ... And the dragon was wroth with the woman, and went to make war with the remnant of her seed, which keep the commandments of God, and have the testimony of Jesus Christ."*

I believe the Overcomers will run 216 miles straight south of Jerusalem to the Split Rock discovered by Jim and Penny Caldwell to the real Mt. Sinai in Saudi Arabia **http://splitrockresearch.org**. They will not offer sacrifices of animals, but rather SACRIFICES OF PRAISE. Because they believe in Jesus, they don't sacrifice animals.

JEREMIAH 33:11, "The voice of joy, and the voice of gladness, the voice of the bridegroom, and the voice of the bride, the voice of them that shall say, 'Praise the LORD of hosts: for the LORD is good; for his mercy endureth for ever: and of them that SHALL BRING THE SACRIFICE OF PRAISE INTO THE HOUSE OF THE LORD. For I will cause to return the captivity [Former state of prosperity] *of the land, as at the first,' saith the LORD."*

In 1991, my wife, Leslie, and I went on a two-week Biblical Archaeological tour with Ron Wyatt to see his discoveries. One of the places he showed us was what Ron believed was the Ancient Biblical city of Gomorrah. I have a box full of Sulphur balls from marble to baseball-size we picked up walking around the city. From looking at the evidence, we believe Ron found one of the cities of the plain, destroyed by God and believe this is probably the city of Gomorrah.

From time to time, Leslie and I take people on tours to Israel and show them these amazing places. In that part of the country there are deep ravines with high unclimbable walls caused by years of floods washing all through the area. If several thousand people were in one of those ravines during a hard rain, they could easily all be drowned with no escape.

When the Christians flee Jerusalem, heading south to the real Mt. Sinai, on their way the Bible says the Devil sends a flood trying to drown the Christians, but a crack opens in the earth and saves the woman. In prophecy the Church of believers is often referred to as a woman, and on some future Pentecost we all want to become the Bride of Christ.

I can easily see a group of several thousand people heading south. I can imagine them in one of those dry river beds and a big rain sent by the Devil, causing a massive flood with potential for drowning them all! But the earth will open and swallow the water. Then the Antichrist sees the hand of God is protecting them and leaves the OVERCOMERS and returns to Jerusalem and creates problems for the REMNANT, those who did NOT flee!

Being an Overcomer doesn't necessarily mean they died for Jesus. It means the OVERCOMERS disobeyed the Beast and OBEYED Jesus and fled Jerusalem. Therefore, the Bible calls them "Overcomers." The Bible calls those who did NOT resist the Beast and STAYED in Jerusalem the "REMNANT." The remnant still has their name in the Lamb's book, but they missed some of the blessings given to the overcomers, unless of course they take the Mark or worship the Beast.

The OVERCOMERS are simply those who REFUSE to comply with the demands of the Beast. The REMNANT are those people who didn't resist and DIDN'T follow the warning of Jesus to flee south.

By now you have noticed, I am NOT one who believes the name of Yod Hay Vav Hay or Yahweh is too Holy to speak or write. I think that is a ploy from the Devil that would love to see God's people NEVER use or speak His name and never use the power of His name! The more we use His name, the better. By speaking His name and speaking of Him and His commandment, we remember Him.

DEUTERONOMY 6:5, "And thou shalt love the LORD thy God with all thine heart, and with all thy soul, and with all thy might."

DEUTERONOMY 6:12, "Then BEWARE LEST THOU FORGET THE LORD, which brought thee forth out of the land of Egypt, from the house of bondage."

MATTHEW 21:9, "And the multitudes that went before, and that followed, cried, saying, 'Hosanna to the son of David: Blessed is he that cometh in the NAME of the Lord; Hosanna in the highest.'"

MATTHEW 12:21, "And in his NAME shall the Gentiles trust."

Because Revelation 12:14 mentions "wings of an eagle" many people think these people might get on a modern AIRPLANE and fly to safety. Not so. Revelation 12:14 says the Overcomers are given, *"TWO WINGS OF A GREAT EAGLE."* This is not an airplane, but as before the same hand of God that took the children of Israel out of Egypt in the days of Moses are once again guided out of Jerusalem back to the original

Mt. Sinai to have their final experience with Jehovah God and Jesus. (See Exodus 19:4). It is simply saying that God will be with those Overcomers who flee from Jerusalem from the Beast.

> EXODUS 19:4, "... I bare you on EAGLES' WINGS, and brought you unto myself."

> REVELATION 12:6, "And the WOMAN fled into the wilderness, where she hath A PLACE PREPARED OF GOD, that they should feed her there a thousand two hundred and threescore days."

> REVELATION 12:14, "And to the woman were given TWO WINGS OF A GREAT EAGLE, that she might fly into the wilderness ..."

In my opinion, the best to place to live if you want to try and survive the Tribulation is Jerusalem or Israel, if you know when to flee.

However, my plan is NOT to try to survive to the end. I want to go to the Marriage Supper of the Lamb. I want to see Jesus crowned KING OF KINGS, and the only way we get that invitation is to be dead, ready, and IN Jesus before the last Pentecost! That probably will be easy. Just stay faithful to Jesus and the Beast will help you to your goal!

My plan is to win thousands upon thousands of souls to the Kingdom and get the greatest rewards possible. I want to be an Overcomer Judge, given many crowns and the Morning Star who is privileged to sit on one of the thrones of Revelation 20:4. Why not go for the best in eternity? It also helps the most people.

> REVELATION 19:9, "And he saith unto me, 'Write, BLESSED ARE THEY WHICH ARE CALLED UNTO THE MARRIAGE SUPPER OF THE LAMB.' And he saith unto me, 'These are the true sayings of God.'"

> REVELATION 20:4, "And I saw THRONES, AND THEY SAT UPON THEM, and judgment was given unto them:"

> REVELATION 20:6, "BLESSED AND HOLY IS HE THAT HATH PART IN THE FIRST RESURRECTION: ON SUCH THE SECOND DEATH HATH NO POWER, BUT THEY SHALL BE PRIESTS OF GOD AND OF CHRIST, AND SHALL REIGN WITH HIM A THOUSAND YEARS."

I plan to be an Overcomer and "keep His works to the end," and receive the Morning Star. I will serve the Lord as long as I am physically able.

If my plan were to survive till Jesus returns, I would live in the city of Jerusalem and spot the Antichrist early and move ahead of the crowd to the city where the woman will flee. That would give me the highest probability of survival to the very end.

> REVELATION 2:26, "And he that OVERCOMETH, and KEEPETH MY WORKS UNTO THE END, to him will I give power over the nations: And he shall rule them with a rod of iron; as the vessels of a potter shall they be broken to shivers: even as I received of my Father. And I WILL GIVE HIM THE MORNING STAR."

SUMMARY:
OVERCOMER vs. REMNANT

The Overcomer resists and disobeys the Antichrist and flees at the sight of the Abomination of Desolation. The Remnant complies to a certain degree and does not flee.

Fleeing at the first sight of the Beast before the Abomination of Desolation is best. If you flee, you are not only protected by God for the last 3 ½ years, but receive greater rewards for being an OVERCOMER and *"keeping my*

THE SECRET DOOR TO UNDERSTAND BIBLE PROPHECY

works to the end." We get to play harps on the sea of glass mingled with fire and sing the Song of Moses and the Lamb!" Pretty good! Being the REMNANT and staying in Jerusalem and obeying the Beast only puts one in more danger and gives them no additional rewards. It also increases their chances of taking the Mark!

A person can be an overcomer and live anyplace in the world. The requirements to be an overcomer as Revelation describes are:

You must live at the same time as the Antichrist. You must be given the opportunity to take his Mark, worship his image or receive the number of his name and REFUSE! When you refuse the Beast, you become an overcomer. Which is different than being an overcomer as the Gospels describe. The difference in the overcomers of the New Testament verses Revelation is this.

Revelation is speaking specifically of the last seven years. It describes being an overcomer as one who overcomes the Beast. As you can see in the following New Testament verses being an overcomer is simply overcoming the world. There is a difference in OVERCOMING THE BEAST compared to OVERCOMING THE WORLD. It appears that those who overcome the Beast/Antichrist receive a special reward above simply having their name in the Book of Life.

REVELATION OVERCOMER:
Overcoming the Beast

REVELATION 2:7, "To him that overcometh will I give to eat of the tree of life, which is in the midst of the paradise of God."

REVELATON 2:11, "He that overcometh shall not be hurt of the second death."

REVELATION 2:17, "To him that overcometh will I give to eat of the hidden manna, and will give him a white stone, and in the stone a new name written, which no man knoweth saving he that receiveth it."

REVELATON 2:26, "And he that overcometh, and keepeth my works unto the end, to him will I give power over the nations:"

REVELATION 3:5, "He that overcometh, the same shall be clothed in white raiment; and I will not blot out his name out of the book of life, but I will confess his name before my Father, and before his angels."

REVELATION 3:12, "Him that overcometh will I make a pillar in the temple of my God, and he shall go no more out: and I will write upon him the name of my God, and the name of the city of my God, which is new Jerusalem, which cometh down out of heaven from my God: and I will write upon him my new name.

REVELATION 3:21, "To him that overcometh will I grant to sit with me in my throne, even as I also overcame, and am set down with my Father in his throne."

REVELATON 11:7, "And when they shall have finished their testimony, THE BEAST that ascendeth out of the bottomless pit shall make war against them, and shall overcome them, and kill them. [They fought and lost to the Antichrist, but because they did not take the Mark, they are still overcomers.]"

REVELATION 13:7, "And it was given unto HIM [The Beast] to make war with the saints, and to overcome them: and power was given him over all kindreds, and tongues, and nations. [The saints lost the battle, but won the war to overcome the

Beast by resisting and not taking the Mark nor worshiping his image.]"

REVELATION 17:14, "These shall make war with the Lamb, and the Lamb shall overcome THEM: for he is Lord of lords, and King of kings: and they that are with him are called, and chosen, and faithful. [Here the Lamb overcomes the tares and grapes. That is the point. Revelation is all speaking of overcoming the Beast!]*"*

REVELATION 21:7, "He that overcometh [The Beast] *shall inherit all things; and I will be his God, and he shall be my son."*

NEW TESTAMENT OVERCOMER:
Overcoming the World

JOHN 16:33, "... In the world ye shall have tribulation: but be of good cheer; I have overcome the WORLD."

JOHN 12:21, "Be not overcome of evil, but overcome evil with good. [The battle is simply overcoming evil, not the Beasts]*."*

1 JOHN 2:13, "I write unto you, fathers, because ye have known him that is from the beginning. I write unto you, young men, because ye have overcome the wicked one ..."

1 JOHN 4:4, "Ye are of God, little children, and have overcome them: because greater is he that is in you, than he that is in the WORLD. [Overcoming the world]*."*

1 JOHN 5:4, "For whatsoever is born of God overcometh the WORLD: and this is the victory that overcometh the world, even our faith."

1 JOHN 5:5, "Who is he that overcometh the WORLD, but he that believeth that Jesus is the Son of God?"

One of the many benefits of being a Revelation Overcomer is singing the Song of Moses on the sea of glass mingled with fire.

REVELATION 15:2-4, "And I saw as it were a SEA OF GLASS MINGLED WITH FIRE: and them that had gotten the victory over the beast, and over his image, and over his mark, and over the number of his name, stand on the sea of glass, having the HARPS of God. And they sing the song of Moses the servant of God, and the song of the Lamb, saying, 'GREAT AND MARVELOUS ARE THY WORKS, LORD GOD ALMIGHTY; JUST AND TRUE ARE THY WAYS, THOU KING OF SAINTS. WHO SHALL NOT FEAR THEE, O LORD, AND GLORIFY THY NAME? FOR THOU ONLY ART HOLY: FOR ALL NATIONS SHALL COME AND WORSHIP BEFORE THEE; FOR THY JUDGMENTS ARE MADE MANIFEST." [The Song of Moses is my favorite part of Revelation!]

Chapter 18
SEVEN EARLY SIGNS TO SPOT THE BEAST / ANTICHRIST

Everyone knows—the easiest and most obvious way to spot the Beast is when he sits on the Ark of the Covenant and requires worship.

Where is the Ark of the Covenant today? The Ark was kept in the Holy of Holies in the past. The correct answer from me is, "I don't know."

Once again, in 1991, on the Archeology Tour, Ron Wyatt claimed he found the Ark of the Covenant and believed at the right time God would bring it out once again, and I believe him. That is an easy prediction, since the Bible says the Antichrist will sit on it.

2 THESSALONIANS 2:1-4, "Now we beseech you, brethren, by THE COMING OF OUR LORD Jesus Christ, and by our gathering together unto him, LET NO MAN DECEIVE YOU by any means: for that day shall not come, except there come a falling away first, and that MAN OF SIN BE REVEALED, the son of perdition; Who opposeth and exalteth himself above all that is called God, or that is worshipped; so that he as God SITTETH IN THE TEMPLE of God, SHEWING HIMSELF THAT HE IS GOD."

The Ark will once again be revealed to the public. It removes all doubt when we see some man sit on it proclaiming himself to be God. That will be the Antichrist! At that time those living in Jerusalem and Israel in general are commanded to run! However, wouldn't it be nice to spot this guy four to seven months before the moment? Perhaps even years ahead of the crowd?

If you live in Jerusalem, as many Christians will by this time, if you wait until the masses recognize the Antichrist, you will be caught up in the frantic mass panic fleeing Jerusalem with no provisions. However, what I am about to tell you will help you to spot the Antichrist early!

The Bible warns us to watch and not be deceived. When the Beast is *"given a mouth speaking great things ... and blasphemies"* and *"given power to make war against the saints and to overcome them,"* blood shed on a massive scale will take place. Overcomers aren't worried because our fear is not of this world; our home is eternal. We realize this is all a test to determine our eternal blessings. We are not going to fall to the deception.

Warning Christians!!! Warning!!! When people begin to say, "This is the man! This is divinity, the man-god." Don't believe it.

MATTHEW 24:23-27, "Then if any man shall say unto you, 'Lo, here is Christ, or there; believe it not. For there shall arise false Christs, and false prophets, and shall shew great SIGNS AND WONDERS; insomuch that, if it were possible, they shall DECEIVE THE VERY ELECT. For as the lightning cometh out of the east, and shineth even unto the west; so shall also the coming of the Son of man be.'"

First ... watch for the World Government to arise, probably after America falls.

The first event to watch for is the fall of the old Bible-based world empire headed by the United States and the rise of the final Novus Ordo Seclorum, the secular or godless world government described by Daniel and Revelation. We probably won't see the Beast or at least be able to spot the Beast until the world government is formed.

These wealthy elite, mostly international bankers, think they are so clever and have fooled the whole world by secretly working behind the scenes to form a world government. Yet, God put it all in their hearts from their beginning! They are following His plan to draw them down upon the mountains of Israel for their destruction. They think world government is good. When Jesus heads it up it will be good, but it will bring the tares and grapes to their destruction! *"God hath put in their hearts to fulfil his will, and to agree, and give their kingdom unto the beast, until the words of God shall be fulfilled."* Like a moth to the flame, God has a plan to bring evil to an end, and *"none of the wicked shall understand."*

DANIEL 12:10, *"Many shall be purified, and made white, and tried; but the wicked shall do wickedly: and NONE OF THE WICKED SHALL UNDERSTAND; but the wise shall understand."*

REVELATION 13:1, 2, *"And I stood upon the sand of the sea, and saw a beast [world government] rise up out of the sea [people], having seven heads and ten horns [The seven continents divided into ten global regions], and upon his horns ten crowns [ten global-regional leaders], and upon his heads the name of blasphemy [Each leader blasphemes God]. And the beast which I saw was like unto a leopard [Muslims], and his feet were as the feet of a bear [Russia], and his mouth as the mouth of a lion [England]: and the dragon [Lucifer] gave him his power, and his seat, and great authority."*

The leopard represents the Muslims, the bear the represents Russians, and the lion represents England. This world government is a combination of Arabs, Russians and the English.

First sign: World government

Second sign: Deadly wound healed!

Notice the text does NOT say this man is WOUNDED in the HEAD. It says ONE of the TEN HEADS, meaning ONE of the ten global leaders will be WOUNDED. Once the world government is formed, they divide the seven continents into ten global regions. Each global region has a head or ruler over it. The Beast will be ONE of those heads. How or where he is wounded is not the point. The Bible is not specific whether he dies or appears to die. But in that he wants to become Christ and sit on the Ark of the Covenant, his best chance to get people to believe he is the Messiah is to fulfill the prophecies of the Messiah. The Beast wants to at least appear to die for three days and resurrect, proclaiming himself to be the Messiah. It is sad to say that most will believe him.

REVELATION 13:3, 4, *"And I saw one of his heads AS IT WERE wounded to DEATH; and HIS DEADLY WOUND WAS HEALED: and all the world wondered after the beast. And they worshipped the dragon which gave power unto the beast: and they worshipped the beast, saying, 'Who is like unto the beast? who is able to make war with him?'"*

First sign: World government

Second sign: Deadly wound healed!

Third sign: Mouth speaking against Christ!!!

This is one of the earliest and easiest prophecies to spot in this guy! In America there is sort of an unwritten

THE SECRET DOOR TO UNDERSTAND BIBLE PROPHECY

rule. "Don't say anything bad about Jesus." It is not even a good idea to speak against Christians or Churches. Just not a good idea. But the Beast is specifically given a mouth FROM GOD to say all manner of evil AGAINST the Bible, the people of the Bible, heaven, the Church and everything good!

REVELATION 13:5-8, "And there was given unto him A MOUTH SPEAKING GREAT THINGS AND BLASPHEMIES; and power was given unto him to continue forty and two months. And he OPENED HIS MOUTH IN BLASPHEMY against God, to BLASPHEME HIS NAME, AND HIS TABERNACLE, AND THEM THAT DWELL IN HEAVEN. And it was given unto him to MAKE WAR WITH THE SAINTS, AND TO OVERCOME THEM: and power was given him over ALL kindreds, and tongues, and nations. And ALL that dwell upon the earth SHALL WORSHIP HIM, whose names are not written in the book of life of the Lamb slain from the foundation of the world."

He will probably not curse nor use profanity, but most likely appear to be a man of peace with great intelligence. He will understand dark or evil sentences, he will cause craft [evil] to prosper. He won't be a diplomat; he will be a great orator-leader such as the world has never seen. No one will have control over him.

DANIEL 8:25, "And through his policy also he shall cause craft [evil] to prosper in his hand; and he shall magnify himself in his heart, [I am God] and by PEACE SHALL DESTROY MANY ..."

The "in crowd," the "intellectuals, college professors, and atheists" will be the first to fall in love with him. He will use words of high thought and repute. He will be instantly liked by all the wealthy, professors, leaders, Presidents, and governors. They will all say, "Finally, a man who sounds like us and speaks to our heart!" He will have a way to put hatred for Jesus, the Bible, Heaven and all Christians in their place. Stinging words of high rebuke! The Christians will not have an answer and will begin to hide. The elite will cheer, all to their own eventual destruction! No one will be able to stand before him! A great orator the likes we have never seen! All his words sound like a stinging truth against all that is called God. The world will rejoice that a man finally stands up for them and puts down Jesus and His Church. People will flock to him so fast it will make the days of Hitler's popularity look small in comparison! Masses upon masses will all be deceived at once and loving it, absolutely loving the deception. They can't get enough of him. All television stations turn to him 24 hours a day.

In May of 2000, Prophecy Club had Ken Peters speak about a dream he had twenty-five years earlier about the night God called him to be a Prophet. The title of the DVD is *I Saw the Tribulation*. He tells of how he lived through the first three and one-half years of the Tribulation until he was beheaded for Christ. Out of 330 titles made over 25 years it is still to this day one of our most popular DVDs. He said some amazing things, and no one I know doubts it is true.

Both Ken Peters in *I Saw the Tribulation* and Daniel Daves in *I Saw the Dollar Dead* saw large-thin-screen-televisions that covered the entire side of tall, skyscraper-type buildings. They describe them as Televisions as thin as Mylar, which broadcast the Antichrist around the clock. (DVD disks available at **www.ProphecyClub.com** or watch instantly at **www.WatchProphecyClub.com**)

All the global elite and Presidents endorse him! Hollywood elite, Kings, Queens, all the leaders both small and great say, "This is God, this is the man, everyone must accept him as God. This will solve our problems. No more anger over different religions, no more war!"

All nations give him their military power and authority. Almost all people of every nation and language say, "Let him rule the world! He will solve all our problems! He will do away with all national names boundaries, militaries and currencies! No more multiple Gods." The world can be as one, as John Lennon told us. We can all be at peace. No more war, no more fussing and fighting! Just give allegiance to the Beast! Whatever name he goes by, it won't be "Beast," but those who know their God will be strong and do exploits.

REVELATION 17:17, "For GOD HATH PUT IN THEIR HEARTS to fulfil his will, and TO AGREE, AND GIVE THEIR KINGDOM UNTO THE BEAST, until the words of God shall be fulfilled."

At first, resistors will be labeled as rebels, outcasts and trouble makers. Tolerance for other gods and other ideas will soon be gone. Soon it turns to violence. Those convinced the Beast is the God-man begin to say, "These rebels are holding back society from growing and progressing." Their patience begins to run out. The Beast steps up his call for global unity. Soon resistors are not just beaten, but the crowd turns to acceptance of a unifying mark for all people— a way to know who is with them and who is not. Soon, almost all people have agreed to form this new global society and accepted the new leader as 'God' and taken his Mark.

It may be that beings other than human will mingle their seed with men causing super-men, and of course, they will be best used to enforce the will of the Beast. It may be that people accepting the new leader and his mark and worshiping his image may also receive the "injection of life." They may promise this injection will cure all diseases and give eternal life, only to discover later it causes horrible malignant sores, and the time comes when people want to die to escape the new leader's world, only to discover they can't die. They want to die, but can't die!

DANIEL 2:43, "And whereas thou sawest iron mixed with miry clay, THEY SHALL MINGLE THEMSELVES WITH THE SEED OF MEN: ..."

REVELATON 9:6, "And in those days shall men seek death, and shall not find it; and shall desire to die, and death shall flee from them."

REVELATION 16:2, "And the first went, and poured out his vial upon the earth; and there fell a NOISOME AND GRIEVOUS SORE UPON THE MEN WHICH HAD THE MARK OF THE BEAST, and upon them which worshipped his image."

As the Beast and False Prophet rise, the Two Witnesses (Moses and John the Revelator) show up and refute everything these two liars say. These are the days of Elijah fulfilled for the last time. All people on earth must choose which God is their God—the Beast and False Prophet OR Jesus! As in the days of Elijah the one true God will answer one final time by fire! It will be the fire of the Morning Star. As with the 450 prophets of Baal, all those NOT in Christ will be killed. Except the nations.

The False Prophet and three other demons released from the Euphrates begin using miracles. These will be mighty miracles, including calling

THE SECRET DOOR TO UNDERSTAND BIBLE PROPHECY

down lightning from the sky, trying to convince people that they are the true God.

> REVELATION 16:13, 14, *"And I saw three unclean spirits like frogs come out of the mouth of the dragon, and out of the mouth of the beast, and out of the mouth of the false prophet. For they are the SPIRITS OF DEVILS, WORKING MIRACLES, which go forth unto the kings of the earth and of the whole world, TO GATHER THEM TO THE BATTLE of that great day of God Almighty* [gathering the tares for the burning.]*"*

First sign: World government

Second sign: Deadly wound healed!

Third sign: Mouth speaking against Christ!!!

Fourth sign: "Wonder!!!"

This was one of the insights I saw in memorizing Revelation. "Wonder" appeared several times and I came to understand that this "wonder" is something special. Magicians all try to "dazzle" their audience with tricks, stunts and illusions. However, the Beast will perform WONDERS far above them all!

How much would a man impress the world that was declared dead for three days like Jesus, then in the sight of all the world, he comes back to life!? That is the kind of "wonder" the Bible is speaking of. Not just jaw-dropping wonder, but the kind of wonder that convinces all people, nations and languages to forsake their god or no-god and choose to worship him and appoint him the world ruler! Wonder so strong they begin to kill all that are rebellious of their new ideas of global change and the Antichrist. Those who WONDER after the Beast become so loyal they kill all who resist worshiping him, like many today that are intolerant of other people and their ideas!

> REVELATION 13:3, *"... and his deadly wound was healed: AND ALL THE WORLD WONDERED AFTER THE BEAST."*

Even when John the Revelator saw the woman drunken with the blood of saints he "wondered with great admiration!" The angel rebuked John for "wondering" over the woman. If John the Revelator wondered, how much more will a normal person? The answer? They will totally be taken by this guy! They will fall for him like no one in history! By the millions all people, nations and languages! They will say, "Never a man speaks like this man!"

Remember, I love my Catholic Brothers and Sisters who diligently follow Jesus, but they must understand their church is going to be hijacked by the False Prophet and many will fall down, slain for the name of Jesus. Those who know their God will be strong and faithful and do great exploits! But *"some of them of understanding shall fall, to try them, and to purge, and to make them white." The Beast "shall do according to his will; and he shall exalt himself, and magnify himself above every god, and shall speak marvellous* [Lies about Jesus] *things against the God of gods, and shall prosper till the indignation be accomplished:"* This Beast *"shall* [not] *regard the God of his fathers, nor the desire of women, nor regard any god: for he shall magnify himself above all."*

> REVELATION 17:1-8, *"And there came one of the seven angels which had the seven vials, and talked with me, saying unto me, 'Come hither; I will shew unto thee the judgment of the great whore* [The hijacked Catholic Church] *that sitteth upon many waters: With whom the*

kings of the earth have committed fornication, [Caused the world to fall away from Christ] *and the inhabitants of the earth have been made drunk with the wine of her fornication.' So he carried me away in the spirit into the wilderness: and I saw a woman sit upon a scarlet coloured beast, full of names of blasphemy, having seven heads and ten horns.* [The world government built upon seven continents divided into ten global regions.] *And the woman was arrayed in purple and scarlet colour,* [The Pope gives the crowns and power and authority to most of the European leadership.] *and decked with gold and precious stones and pearls, having a golden cup in her hand full of abominations and filthiness of her fornication: And upon her forehead was a name written, MYSTERY, BABYLON THE GREAT, THE MOTHER OF HARLOTS AND ABOMINATIONS OF THE EARTH.* [There are many Catholics in America. I think this part is specifically speaking of America and the names of the forehead should be: "MYSTERY BABYLON" "THE GREAT," and I think President Donald Trump gave America the name "The GREAT" in his first candidacy for President when he came up with the campaign slogan, "Make America GREAT Again." He gave America the name "GREAT."] *And I saw the woman drunken with the blood of the saints, and with the blood of the martyrs of Jesus:* [I am aware of the millions the Catholic Church has killed in the past, but Revelation is not speaking of the past. This is speaking of the last seven years before Jesus' return. This is speaking specifically of America. Once she falls when the Russians defeat her in a surprise nuclear attack. The conquering nations with the help of evil people in America set a goal to clean the globe of all other religions. Most religions cooperate; those who resist are called rebels and resistors and are eliminated beginning first in America.] *and when I saw her, I WONDERED with great admiration.* [wonder means the world is stunned, and mesmerized by the Beast] *And the angel said unto me, 'Wherefore didst thou MARVEL?' ... and they that dwell on the earth shall WONDER, whose names were not written in the book of life from the foundation of the world, when they behold the beast that was, and is not, and yet is."*

Seemingly no one is able to resist the captivating message of the Beast—except those whose names are in the Book of Life. That is the WONDER of the Antichrist! It won't be easy to refuse which is why those who do are very blessed!

First sign: World government

Second sign: Deadly wound healed!

Third sign: Mouth speaking against Christ!!!

Fourth sign: "Wonder!!!"

Fifth sign: His appearance

Ken Peters said the Antichrist was "the most handsome man I have ever seen," and he had olive-colored skin. The Scriptures tell us he looks different than normal humans. Perhaps it is because he is genetically different than us.

> DANIEL 7:20, 21, *"And of the ten horns that were in his head, and of the other which came up, and before whom three fell; even of that horn that had eyes, and a mouth that spake very great things, whose LOOK WAS MORE STOUT THAN HIS FELLOWS. I beheld, and the same horn made war with the saints, and prevailed against them;"*

DANIEL 8:23-25, *"And in the latter time of their kingdom, when the transgressors are come to the full, a king of FIERCE COUNTENANCE,* [Strong face. He looks different.] *and understanding dark sentences, shall stand up. And his power shall be mighty, but not by his own power:* [Power of Lucifer] *and he shall destroy WONDERFULLY,* [He is amazing.] *and shall prosper, and practise, and shall destroy the mighty and the holy people.* [Will make war against the saints] *And through his policy also he shall cause craft* [evil] *to prosper in his hand; and he shall magnify himself in his heart, and by peace* [He says world government with him heading it shall bring peace, but it kills most Christians.] *shall destroy many: he shall also stand up against the Prince of princes; but he shall be broken without hand.* [He shall be destroyed on the day of Trumpets at Armageddon when the Beast and False Prophet are cast into the Lake of Fire. Revelation 19:19]."

Based on the following five sets of verses, it appears that this Beast army has been genetically modified. Jesus said:

MATTHEW 24:37, *"But as the days of Noe were, so shall also the coming of the Son of man be."*

What were they doing in the days of Noah? They were mixing "other" DNA with human DNA—their offspring became giants.

GENESIS 6:4, *"There were GIANTS IN THE EARTH in those days; and also after that, when THE SONS OF GOD CAME IN UNTO THE DAUGHTERS OF MEN, and they BARE CHILDREN TO THEM, the same became mighty men which were of OLD, men of renown."*

The word in the Bible for "old" means eternal. Meaning these half-breeds did not inherit the death-seed of Adam and were not dying. This is another reason God had to destroy the world before the flood.

DANIEL 2:43, *"And whereas thou sawest iron mixed with miry clay, THEY SHALL MINGLE THEMSELVES WITH THE SEED OF MEN ..."*

We can conclude the Beast will be a half-breed; half-man/half-fallen angel, possessed with the spirit and power of Lucifer and have a difference in APPEARANCE. Apparently, genetics by this time will have progressed to the point of full regenerative powers, giving them instant healing! He will probably be a resurrected Nebuchadnezzar.

JOEL 2:6-8, *"Before their face the people shall be much pained: ALL FACES SHALL GATHER BLACKNESS. They shall run like mighty men; they shall climb the wall like MEN OF WAR; and they shall march every one on his ways, and they shall not break their ranks: Neither shall one thrust another; they shall walk every one in his path: and WHEN THEY FALL UPON THE SWORD, THEY SHALL NOT BE WOUNDED."*

REVELATION 9:6, *"And in those days SHALL MEN SEEK DEATH, AND SHALL NOT FIND IT; AND SHALL DESIRE TO DIE, AND DEATH SHALL FLEE FROM THEM."*

First sign: World government

Second sign: Deadly wound healed!

Third sign: Mouth speaking against Christ!!!

Fourth sign: "Wonder!!!"

Fifth sign: His appearance

Sixth Sign: Mark of the Beast

By the time we reach the sixth sign, it won't be difficult to spot the Beast. He is they guy that all the world is required to worship and receive his Mark. Ken Peters said the Mark of the Beast was about the size of a nickel. It was located in the web between the thumb and first finger and looked like the yellow Mexico sun with another hand in the middle of the sun. He saw no chip associated with it, just a tattoo.

REVELATION 13:16, *"And he causeth all, both small and great, rich and poor, free and bond, to receive A MARK IN THEIR RIGHT HAND, OR IN THEIR FOREHEADS:"*

REVELATION 15:2, *"And I saw as it were a sea of glass mingled with fire: and them that had gotten the victory over the BEAST, and over his IMAGE, and over his MARK, and over the NUMBER of his name, stand on the sea of glass, having the harps of God."*

It appears that those who are beheaded and refuse the mark in the time of the Beast become judges and sit on thrones.

REVELATION 20:4, *"And I SAW THRONES, and THEY SAT UPON THEM, and JUDGMENT WAS GIVEN UNTO THEM: and I saw the souls of them that were BEHEADED FOR THE WITNESS OF JESUS, and for the word of God, and which had not worshipped the beast, neither his image, neither had received his mark upon their foreheads, or in their hands; and they lived and reigned with Christ a thousand years."*

First sign: World government

Second sign: Deadly wound healed!

Third sign: Mouth speaking against Christ!!!

Fourth sign: "Wonder!!!"

Fifth sign: His appearance

Sixth Sign: Mark of the Beast

The Seventh and Final Sign: Abomination of Desolation!

2 THESSALONIANS 2:3, 4, "Let no man deceive you by any means: for that day shall not come, except there come a falling away first, and that man of sin be revealed, the son of perdition [hell]; Who opposeth and exalteth himself above all that is called God, or that is worshipped; so that he as God SITTETH IN THE TEMPLE OF GOD, SHEWING HIMSELF THAT HE IS GOD."

The worst punishment our souls could ever receive surprisingly is not being tossed into the Lake of Fire which is soul-death. It is being tossed into the Lake of Fire and not dying, but being tormented forever. Satan, the Beast and the False Prophet are tossed into the Lake of Fire, but for them it is NOT soul-death. It is even worse; it is eternal torment day and night. Here is the final warning, *"NOT TO WORSHIP THE BEAST OR HIS IMAGE OR RECEIVE HIS MARK OR THE NUMBER OF HIS NAME!"*

REVELATION 14:9-11, "... If any man WORSHIP THE BEAST AND HIS IMAGE, AND RECEIVE HIS MARK IN

HIS FOREHEAD, OR IN HIS HAND, The same shall drink of the wine of the wrath of God, which is poured out without mixture into the cup of his indignation; and HE SHALL BE TORMENTED WITH FIRE AND BRIMSTONE in the presence of the holy angels, and in the presence of the Lamb: And THE SMOKE OF THEIR TORMENT ASCENDETH UP FOR EVER AND EVER: AND THEY HAVE NO REST DAY NOR NIGHT, who worship the beast and his image, and whosoever receiveth the mark of his name."

REVELATION 20:10, "And the devil that deceived them was cast into the lake of fire and brimstone, where the beast and the false prophet are, and shall be TORMENTED DAY AND NIGHT FOR EVER AND EVER."

REVELATON 20:14, 15, "And death and hell were cast into the lake of fire. This is the second death. And WHOSOEVER WAS NOT FOUND WRITTEN IN THE BOOK OF LIFE WAS CAST INTO THE LAKE OF FIRE."

SUMMARY:
Spot the Beast early!

First: World government is in place

Second: The Beast's deadly wound is healed

Third: Given a mouth speaking great things and blasphemies – speaks against Jesus Christ, Prophets, and Heaven

Fourth: Wonders! and signs, lying wonders all the world is amazed!

Fifth: Appearance, looks stout, fierce countenance

Sixth: Mark, Image, Name or number of his name—666

Seventh: Commits the Abomination of desolation, sits on the Ark of the Covenant /Throne of God

Chapter 19
DO ALL PROPHECIES FROM GOD COME TO PASS?

In my younger days of Bible prophecy, I read:

> DEUTERONOMY 18:21, 22, *"And if thou say in thine heart, 'How shall we know the word which the LORD hath not spoken?' When a prophet speaketh in the name of the LORD, IF THE THING FOLLOW NOT, NOR COME TO PASS, THAT IS THE THING WHICH THE LORD HATH NOT SPOKEN, but the prophet hath spoken it presumptuously: thou shalt not be afraid of him."*

I concluded that the test of a prophet was whether they could foretell the future and NOT miss. Through the years, as I began to learn more about the heart of the LORD and His plan for man, I discovered that He doesn't have to prove He spoke. He is quite willing to use one of His servants for His bigger plan. He is willing to give a warning with plans to turn people from their sin and then relent from His judgment. The prophet delivers it, but the prophecy doesn't come to pass. It means not every prophecy from God will come to pass, nor is it even the plan of God that it should come to pass, but rather His plan is to fill His Kingdom with as many people as possible.

WAS JONAH A HERO OR FALSE PROPHET?

We all agree Jonah heard from God; yet, his prophecy of the destruction of Nineveh didn't come to pass in forty days. God had a bigger plan. I began to learn that with some prophecies if we looked closely God is telling us "this one WON'T CHANGE," "this one WILL come to pass," as to others they are "warning prophecies," intended to change our course; not intended to come to pass. Some WILL come to pass as with Nineveh; the destruction hit 40 years later, but it was delayed from 40 days to 40 years later. God's purpose is not to prove that He can foretell the future, but to fill His Kingdom.

If the word says,

> REVELATION 19:9, *"... And he saith unto me,' THESE ARE THE TRUE SAYINGS OF GOD.'"*

> REVELATION 21:5, *"... And he said unto me, 'Write: for these words are TRUE AND FAITHFUL.'"*

> REVELATION 22:6, *"And he said unto me, 'THESE SAYINGS ARE FAITHFUL AND TRUE ..."*

> DANIEL 2:45, *"... THE DREAM IS CERTAIN, AND THE INTERPRETATION THEREOF SURE."*

We know these prophecies WILL come to pass, and no amount of praying and fasting will stop them. I still want to believe that we can bring a softening and delay, but that is not a promise.

People are unsure when to believe God is speaking. They want to trust the word of God. Many say, "I only accept what is written in the Bible." The problem is some are not following this rule, because there are over 400 different versions of the Bible! That brings us back to, "How do we know the Word which the Lord hath spoken?" People are confused.

In 1987, I was teaching a class on Bible prophecy at our local church.

THE SECRET DOOR TO UNDERSTAND BIBLE PROPHECY

I had determined that I was going to believe what is in the KJV Bible. Just believe the Bible. But again, "What Bible?" From what perspective? And what do you do when people bring you these different perspectives? I stuck to my principles with only a few course corrections.

A person seeking truth must be willing to offend others, do and say things politically incorrect and go against the grain to bring 100 percent pure truth. It isn't easy. Most Old Testament Prophets were stoned, sawed in half or boiled in oil. To bring the true Word of God is a very dangerous assignment! I was and am still willing to do that. Specifically, it appeared to me that Revelation 18 had to be speaking of America.

I used to play chess. I discovered sometimes getting up from the table and walking around the chess board and looking at the same pieces from a different angle helped. Such is the case with Bible prophecy. We must be willing to look at prophecies from different perspectives, always seeking truth with our whole heart. I was seeking truth.

I looked at Revelation 18 from every possible angle, but the pieces still didn't move, so neither did my opinion. From those early days of teaching Bible prophecy up to 2018 my opinion has only become more certain. I think because I told my prophecy class that I believed Revelation 18 must be speaking of America, I received a very big blessing. God introduced me to one of his greatest modern prophets, Dumitru Duduman!

When do we believe the message is from God?

One Sunday in February, 1988, after the prophecy class I was teaching, I was handed an audio tape and the lady said, "I believe you will be interested in this." It was a Pastor from Romania, telling how God had sent him to America, because God had decided to punish America. He said, "Revelation 18 is speaking of America!" I invited him to speak at the Full Gospel Businessmen's Fellowship in Lawrence, Kansas. I didn't know what a blessing I had been given. I was about to meet the greatest prophet to ever set foot in America in the opinion of those who knew him. I had been allowed to meet a real prophet on the order of John the Revelator!

Why do we believe Moses?

He had many supernatural experiences with God. He was part of delivering 10 plagues before Pharaoh, leader of the world at that time. All Israelites heard God's voice from the heavens. Moses came down from Mount Sinai with his face aglow. He was used by God to give them water from a rock, parting the Red Sea and involving them in many other supernatural experiences. However, beware, as the devil will deceive mankind in the last days by causing fire to come down from heaven on the earth in the sight of men. We must be aware of his plans.

Why do we believe Paul?

Paul had letters from the High Priest authorizing him to arrest, beat and stone Christians when he saw a light and heard a voice and was blinded for three days. He did not eat nor drink for three days until Ananias prayed for him:

> ACTS 9:17, "And Ananias went his way, and entered into the house; and putting his hands on him said, 'Brother Saul, THE LORD, EVEN JESUS, THAT APPEARED UNTO THEE IN THE WAY as thou camest, hath sent me, that thou mightest receive thy sight, and be filled with the Holy Ghost.'"

It was a supernatural experience from God that convinced the people to believe Paul was called of God. When we have over 400 different Bible translations, how do we know the accurate word of God? Miracles should convince us more than some group of people who decided to include some text in their version of a Bible.

Why do we believe Cornelius and Peter to give the Gospel to the Gentiles?

Cornelius had an angel tell him to go to Peter. Peter had three visions of a sheet filled with abominable animals and was told not to call unclean what God had called clean. As the vision ended, three men from Cornelius were knocking on the door!

According to *Foxe's Book of Martyrs*, John the Revelator was boiled in oil and banned to the island of Patmos. An angel visited him and gave him the Book of Revelation. We believe John in part because he survived boiling in oil, a great test from God.

> REVELATION 1:1, "The Revelation of Jesus Christ, which God gave unto him, to shew unto his servants things which must shortly come to pass; and he sent and signified it by his angel unto his servant John:"

> REVELATION 1:13, "And in the midst of the seven candlesticks one like unto the Son of man, clothed with a garment down to the foot, and girt about the paps with a golden girdle."

Why do I believe Dumitru Duduman?

I am going to include part of Dumitru Duduman's testimony in this book. I met him, I have been in his house, and he in mine on two occasions. I know him or knew him as he is with the Lord now. But how do YOU know if you can believe this warning is from God? It is not in the Bible.

Here is the reason a person should believe this warning. It is backed by Scriptures in the Bible, but Dumitru was severely tested by God as were Paul, John and many of his other messengers.

Dumitru Duduman smuggled Bibles for 30 years into Romania and Russia. He was arrested, tortured for five months, culminating in them putting him on the electric chair twice!!! That should be enough.

There is more. The angel told him the year, month, day and hour he would be exiled to America. It came to pass exactly as he was told.

When he arrived in America, the angel showed him the warning for America, then told him four specific things that would happen to him the next day. They all came to pass exactly and preciously as he was told. If these had happened to anyone 1,000 years ago there would be no question this is the hand of God. Today, we are more modern. Some say God doesn't speak like this to us today. God says He is the same, *"yesterday today and forever, neither do I alter that thing which has gone out of my lips."* If God proved His messengers of Matthew, Mark, Luke, and John the Revelator and Christians 2,000 years ago were smart enough to recognize the voice of God in His servants, surely in our modern computer age we are at least as smart as His servants 2,000 years ago!

> PSALM 89:34, "My covenant will I not break, nor alter the thing that is gone out of my lips."

> HEBREWS 13:8, "Jesus Christ the same yesterday, and to day, and for ever."

We must be careful to run after truth and grab it when we find it, knowing truth is probably NOT what our flesh wants to hear.

I met Dumitru for the first time in March 1988

I picked up Dumitru and his grandson and interpreter, Michael, and was driving from Kansas City to Topeka, Kansas. My wife was unpacking as we had just moved to our new house in Omaha, Nebraska. Dumitru turned to me and said, "This woman in your life ..."

"Yes, my wife."

"You tell her, 'First she must pray for strength for herself, before she prays for other people.' She is praying for others, and their problems are coming back on her."

When we arrived at the restaurant, I called Leslie in Omaha and told her what Dumitru said. "Does this speak to you?"

She started crying, saying, "Yes, yes, I have been opening boxes and praying for anyone who comes to mind, and I am exhausted. Yes, I must pray for strength for myself before praying for others!"

I was shocked! What manner of man do I have in my car???? He hit it! How can a man on the freeway in Kansas know the secret, private prayers of my wife in Omaha? I began to watch him very carefully.

If we believe Moses, Paul, Peter and John the Revelator, we MUST believe Dumitru Duduman!!!

Here is his testimony as brief as I can make it. (The full version is available at **handofhelp.com**)

Dumitru Duduman's Testimony: Twice on the electric chair

I was born in a Christian family. My father was a pastor of a Pentecostal Church. At the age of 17 I ran away from home. I went to marine school. I stayed there for about four and a half years.

I became a marine officer. They gave me about 80 recruits. They shipped me out on the Black Sea. The Communist government told me to search the ships coming in from foreign countries. If I found any Bibles, confiscate them and arrest the Missionaries.

They said, "Dumitru, if you do this we will advance you quickly." When I heard I could become a big man, I started searching the ships faithfully.

God Called

One morning a ship from Holland came. I took eight men with me. In checking the ship, under a crate of cookies, I found a great quantity of Bibles. I asked the Captain of the ship whose Bibles, they were.

He said, "I don't know." I told him, "Don't worry. You will know." I saw a man crying and praying to God. It was a missionary from Holland. He worked with Open Doors. I went to him and I asked him for his passport.

I asked him, "Are these your Bibles?"

He said, "No."

I said, "Who do they belong to then?"

He said, "They belong to your brothers and your sisters."

When he said this, it was like putting a knife into my heart. Then I heard a voice in my ear saying, "What are you doing Dumitru? I put you here. Don't confiscate those Bibles. Don't you know your dad is a pastor? Don't you know your brother is a Christian?" I looked around to see who was talking to me. And when I saw there was nobody, I started shaking. I didn't know what was wrong with me. I was embarrassed that I was shaking in front of the missionary. I went into another compartment. I stuck my fingers in my ears, so I would not hear the voice any more. It got even louder.

"Go, give him his passport or I will punish you."

I went to the missionary, shaking. I told him, "Here is your passport. Your God answered your prayers. He spoke to my ear and told me to give your passport back. I will even send some men to protect you from the police." As I gave him the passport the voice stopped, and I felt a peace in my heart. Then I realized it was the voice of God. Then I said, "Every man has an angel. The angel of God is near you."

I stayed on the Black Sea for two years. As many Missionaries came through, they came through without fear. I was put there by God, and I would help them.

The Electric Chair!

Now let's fast forward thirty years. He was not caught with Bibles. God blinded their eyes, so they couldn't see the Bibles, but he was arrested. God was about to test him before giving him his greatest task and greatest blessing that would win millions of people to Jesus! He was about to tell him America's future, but could America spot the hand of God?

They put him through all kinds of tortures.

"They would tell me to confess where I got the Bibles. Who brought me the Bibles? How I took them to Russia? Who helped me to take them" In my ear was the same voice [Angel] from the ship. "Dumitru, don't tell. Don't confess."

After five months of torture, they took me into a room. There they had a very unusual chair. They said, "Do you see this chair? We brought it from Germany especially for you! Tell us now or you are going to die on that chair."

I said, "Even if I die. I have nothing to tell you." They tied my hands behind the chair. They tied my feet around it. Then they put something under my feet. They tied something over my heart. They stuck a big bowl on my head. Then they stuck two things in my ears.

They said, "Think about those Bibles. You are going to die now." They plugged it in. I felt such a powerful shock through all of my body; it felt like pins and needles were going through it. I couldn't see any more. I thought, "I am going to die." When I thought, "I am going to die, the same light appeared."

It said, "Dumitru. Don't be afraid, you won't die. Plead the blood of Jesus."

I started saying, "The blood of Jesus, the blood of Jesus." When I woke up, I was laying down. My eyes and mouth were full of blood. They were throwing cold water on me and slapping me around.

Electric Chair Again!

The next day they put me on the electric chair once again. They did the same thing with me. They turned the power up even higher. When I thought I was dead, again, the angel of God came.

"Dumitru, don't be afraid. YOU WON'T DIE, plead "the blood of Jesus." YOUR ENEMY WILL DIE. You will live. You have to go through one more powerful torture, and then I will take you out of their hands."

Then I began to plead, "The blood of Jesus." When I woke up, I woke up the same way, full of blood. They slapped me around again and poured cold water on me. Then they said, "Now, we have everything." Again, I heard my voice, "the blood of Jesus, the blood of Jesus." They couldn't kill him!

Dumitru told me that the next morning he woke up and all his teeth had fallen out! The electricity had killed all his teeth. This he did for Jesus!

1980 Judgment Upon America is Spoken

Three months later the angel came to me again and said, "You have four more years to carry Bibles. The police will follow you step-by-step, but I will be with you. I will blind their eyes. They won't catch you. When they see they can't catch you, they will kick you out of your country."

He said, *"YOU WILL BE EXILED, JULY 22, 1984, AT 10:00 AM. YOU ARE GOING TO AMERICA TO GIVE THEM A MESSAGE FROM GOD."* [That was 1980].

For four years I carried Bibles into Russia. I WOULD PULL UP TO THE BORDER CHECKPOINT WITH SO MANY BIBLES IN MY CAR, THERE WAS NO ROOM FOR ANYONE TO SIT. THE BORDER GUARD WOULD SAY, "DUMITRU, WHAT DO YOU HAVE IN THE CAR?"

I would say, "Bibles!"

He would say, "Stop making fun of us! Go on, get out of here." They couldn't see them!

The day I was kicked out of Romania, all my family was watching the time. JULY 22, 1984, AT EXACTLY 10:00 AM THE AIRLINE STEWARDESS PICKED UP THE PLANE'S MICROPHONE AND SAID, "WELCOME TO FLIGHT NUMBER ...," IT HAPPENED JUST AS THE PLANE WAS DEPARTING FROM THE GATE, EXACTLY AS THE ANGEL OF GOD HAD TOLD ME.

With the help of God, and the help of the American Embassy in Italy, I came to California. I didn't know anybody, and I was accepted very badly. They took me to an apartment. The apartment was very dirty. Dogs had lived there before. The carpet stunk badly. There was no bed, no table, no chair, nothing. I was in despair. I didn't know what to do.

My wife and daughter were crying. The children had fallen asleep on the suitcases. I walked around the building saying, "Why, God, did you punish me? Why did you bring me to this country? I can't understand anybody. If I ask anybody anything, I can't understand them." (DVD available at **ProphecyClub.com** or watch instantly on **WatchProphecyClub.com**). I suggest you order the "Wake-up America Gift offer" as that is the package of items specifically designed to bring you up to date with the warning to America.

The Message: The Fall of America

It was late at night, and I couldn't stay inside because of the smell. I was sitting outside on a rock. A light came toward me. The fear of cars came within me. The Romanian police tried to run over me with cars. That's why I jumped up to run. The light surrounded me. Out of the light I heard the same voice. The angel said, "Dumitru, why are you so despaired?"

I said, "Why did you punish me? What did I do that was so rotten that you brought me to the United States? I have nowhere to lie my head down upon. I can't understand anybody."

He said, "Dumitru, didn't I tell you that I am here with you also? I brought you here to this country because this country will burn."

"Then why did you bring me here to burn? Why didn't you let me die in my own country?"

"Dumitru, have patience, and I will tell you. Get beside me."

I got beside the angel. He showed me all of California. He showed me all the cities of California. Then he showed me Las Vegas, Nevada.

"You see what I have shown you. This is Sodom and Gomorrah. In one day it will burn."

He said, "Its sin has reached the Holy One."

He showed me another great city. He said, "Do you know what city this is?"

I said, "No."

He said, "This is New York City. This is Sodom and Gomorrah. In one day it will burn."

He showed me Florida. He said, "This is Florida. This is Sodom and Gomorrah. In one day it will burn."

He said, "I brought you to this country. Dumitru, I want to wake up a lot of people. I love this country. I love the people. I want to save them. America will burn."

"How can I save them? I can't even speak their language? Who knows me here? How will they call me?"

He said, "Don't worry. I will be ahead of you. I will make great healings among the American people. You will go to television stations, radio stations, and churches. Tell them everything I tell you. Don't hide anything. If you try to hide anything, I will punish you. America will burn."

"How will America burn? It is so powerful."

He said, "The Russian spies have discovered where the most powerful nuclear missiles are in America."

The Fall of America

"The fall of America will start with an internal revolution in America, started by the Communists. Some of the people will start fighting against the government. The government will be busy with internal problems. Then, from the oceans, Russia, Cuba, Nicaragua, Central America, Mexico, and two other countries which I cannot remember, will attack! The Russians will bombard the nuclear missiles in America. America will burn."

I said, "What will you do with the church?"

He said, "The church has left me."

I said, "How? Don't you have people here?"

He said, "People in America honor people. The honor that should be given to God, they give to other people. Americans think highly of themselves. They say, 'I serve God,' but they don't. In the church there is <u>divorce, adultery, fornication, sodomy, abortion, and all kinds of sin</u>. Jesus Christ doesn't live in sin. He lives in HOLINESS." I brought you here, so you could cry out loud. Don't be afraid. I am with you. Tell them to stop sinning. God never stops forgiving. Tell them to repent. He will forgive them. Tell them to start preparing themselves, so I can save them in the day of trouble."

I said, "How will you save the church, if America will burn?"

He said, "Tell them as I tell you. As he saved the three young men from the oven of fire, and Daniel from the mouth of the lion, that is how I will save them. Tell them to stop sinning and repent.

I have blessed this country because of the Jews that are here. I have seven million Jews here. They haven't tasted war or persecution. God blessed them more than anyone else. Instead of thanking God, they started sinning and doing wickedly. Their sins have reached the Holy One. God will punish them with fire.

Israel doesn't recognize the Messiah, because they place their trust on the power of the Jews in America.

When God will hit America all the nations will be terrified.

God will raise up China, Japan, and many other nations, and they will beat the Russians. They will push them back to the gates of Paris. There they will make a peace treaty, but they will make the Russians their leader. All the nations with the Russians as their leader go against Israel. It's not that they want to. God makes them.

Israel doesn't have the help of the Jews in America anymore. In their terror, when they see what is coming. They call upon the Messiah. The Messiah will come to help Israel. Then the church of God will meet him in the clouds." He himself will fight against all the nations.

I said, "If you are the angel of God. Everything you tell me has to be written in the Bible. If it is not, then I can't tell the Americans."

"Tell them to read Jeremiah 51: 8-15, he names it THE MYSTERY BABYLON, THE GREAT ADULTERESS. Also, REVELATION CHAPTER 18, the whole chapter. There it says clearly what will happen to America."

"Why did he name it **THE MYSTERY BABYLON?**"

"Tell them because all the nations of the world immigrated into America, and America accepted them. America accepted Buddha, the devil church, the Sodomite church, the Mormon church, and all kinds of wickedness. America was a Christian nation. Instead of stopping them, they went after their gods. Because of this, he named them THE MYSTERY BABYLON.

So you know that I truly have been sent by God, tomorrow, at 9:00 AM, someone will come to give you a bed. At 10:30 AM, someone will come to pay your rent. At noon, someone will bring you a car, and give you a bucket of honey."

BROTHERS, IT HAPPENED AS THE ANGEL HAD SAID. AT 9:00, SOMEONE RANG MY DOORBELL AND SAID, "I BROUGHT YOU A BED. I COULD NOT SLEEP ALL NIGHT LONG. GOD TOLD ME THAT YOU WERE FROM ROMANIA, AND THAT YOU NEED A BED." AT 10:30, SOMEONE ELSE RANG MY DOORBELL AND HANDED ME A CHECK FOR $500 AND SAID, "GOD TOLD ME TO BRING YOU $500!" AT NOON SOMEONE CAME AND GAVE ME A CAR AND A BUCKET OF HONEY!

You might say, "Why would God do this to America? We trust in God! We have God on our side! On our dollar bill it has "We trust in God." How are our lives? We go after the foreign gods. The American church has adultery, fornication, sodomy, divorces, and abortions. If we repent with all of our hearts, and call Jesus to help us, we will stop sinning. We know that when Jesus comes, we will meet him in the clouds.

The angel also said, "BEFORE THE INTERNAL PROBLEMS BEGIN IN AMERICA YOUR COUNTRY (ROMANIA) WILL HAVE A REVOLUTION. FULFILLED DECEMBER 22, 1989. (DUMITRU TOLD ME ABOUT THE REVOLUTION IN MARCH OF 1988, OVER A YEAR BEFORE IT OCCURRED!)

Is this prophecy for America one which will come to pass? Yes, I believe with prayer, fasting and repentance, it might be softened or delayed, but not stopped and here is why.

Dumitru was told, "Tell my people the days are numbered, and THE SENTENCE HAS BEEN PASSED." Meaning this one will not be prayed away.

Daniel was told the dream is certain, and the interpretation sure, meaning this WILL come to pass.

> DANIEL 2:45, "... the great God hath made known to the king what shall come to pass hereafter: and the DREAM IS CERTAIN, AND THE INTERPRETATION THEREOF SURE."

John was told these words are "true and faithful" and "faithful and true," meaning the Book of Revelation will also come to pass. Likewise, Dumitru was told, "THE SENTENCE HAS BEEN PASSED."

> REVELATION 21:5, "And he that sat upon the throne said, 'Behold, I make all things new.' And he said unto me, 'Write: for these words are TRUE AND FAITHFUL.'"

> REVELATION 22:6, "And he said unto me, 'These sayings are FAITHFUL AND TRUE: and the Lord God of the holy prophets sent his angel to shew unto his servants the things which must shortly be done.'"

After the initial warning to Dumitru, God continued to speak to Dumitru. Here is a selection of the most important messages. A complete list is at www.handofhelp.com.

The Bear Awakes

The last of three final messages given to Dumitru in April of 1997.

I knelt beside my bed to pray, as I do every night before I go to sleep. After finishing my prayer, I opened my eyes, but I was no longer in my room. Instead, I found myself in a forest. I looked around, and to my right I saw a man, dressed in white, who pointed his finger and said, "See and remember." It took me a while to find out what he was pointing at. It was a small bear who seemed half dead, lying on the ground. As I continued to watch this bear, it began to breathe deeper. With every passing minute it seemed to revive itself, and as I watched, it also became angrier. It then began to grow. Soon it was larger than the forest floor, and as it grew larger, it continued to become angrier. It then began to paw the ground, so that when its paw would hit the ground, the earth would shudder. The bear continued to devastate all that stood in its path until it came upon some men with sticks trying to fend it off. By this time the bear had grown so large that it simply crushed the men underfoot and continued to rampage. I was stunned by what I saw and asked the man standing beside me, "What does this mean?"

"At first, they thought the great bear was dead," the man said. "As it will begin to stir once again, they will consider it harmless. Suddenly it will grow strong once more with purpose and violence. God will blind the eyes of those who CONTINUE TO TRAMPLE ON THE SACRIFICE OF CHRIST'S BLOOD until the day the bear will strike swiftly. This day will catch them unprepared, and it will be just as you saw." The man then said, "TELL MY PEOPLE THE DAYS ARE NUMBERED, AND THE SENTENCE HAS BEEN PASSED. If they will seek My face and walk in righteousness before Me, I will open their eyes that they may see the danger approach. If they only look to the approaching danger, they too will be caught up and trampled underfoot. Only in righteousness will they find safety."

Suddenly, I was once again by myself in my room, on my knees, with sweat covering my face.

The Mountain

Dumitru Duduman—June 1989.

I was staying with a pastor in Oregon. I awoke about 1:00 AM in the morning and could not find Danny (the hired interpreter). I woke-up the pastor. Neither of us could find him. I told the pastor to go to his room and pray, and I would also pray. We asked God to show us where Danny was. God revealed to me that he was at a bar. I cried to God. I said, "God, I cannot work with a wicked man." I went down and told the pastor that God revealed to me that Danny was at a bar. As we were talking, God gave me a vision.

I saw trees and houses and the ground all explode into fire.

I heard a voice saying, "Dumitru, quick get on the mountain or you will burn."

I looked and saw a very tall mountain. The bottom half had trees and the top half was bare. I started climbing the mountain. I called out for my family. Michael was having a hard time climbing the mountain, and I went and helped him up the mountain. The climb was very difficult. I noticed that from out of the fire came all kinds of people trying to climb the mountain. The children ran up the mountain quickly and easily. Some of the people could climb using the trees. When there were no more trees, they fell back into the fire. The climb was difficult. At times we had to crawl and pull each other up. We finally reached the top of the mountain.

An angel came to me and said, "Come with me. I will show you what it will be like when America burns."

He took me down to the backyard of the pastor's house. All around me the trees and houses were exploding! Fire erupted from the ground. The natural gas pipes exploded.

He said. "This is what it will be like when America burns."

Then he continued. "Do you know what the mountain is?"

"No."

"The mountain is Jesus!" He said. Then he asked, "Do you know why the children went up the mountain so fast?"

"No."

He answered, **"Because they have no sin."** Then he said, "Do you know who the people were who only made it halfway up the mountain, then fell back into the fire?"

"No."

"They are the people who backslid away from Jesus."

Then the vision ended. I was back in front of the pastor once again.

Black Army

Dimitru Duduman, May 7, 1993.

One night, while in Oregon, I dreamed the sky was getting dark. Then suddenly it turned pitch black! It was as if the whole world had gone dark at that moment! All the people were in frenzy! They became disoriented, and some were even screaming. After some time, we heard the sound of an army approaching. Soon, we saw them coming out of the black mist. All were dressed in black, except one. That one seemed to be their leader. He was dressed in a red robe with a thick black belt over his waist. On his head, he had a sign. As I looked, I saw that in his hand he held the same kind of sharp spear as everyone else in his army.

"I am Lucifer!" he exclaimed. "I am the king of this world! I have come to make war against the Christians!"

It looked as though all the Christians were huddled together in one big group. Some began to cry when they heard this. Others began to tremble, while some just stood without saying anything. Lucifer continued to speak. "All of those that want to fight against my army and think they can be victorious; go to the right. Those that fear me; go to the left."

Only about a quarter of the group stepped to the right. All the others went to the left. Then Lucifer ordered his army, "Destroy those on the right!"

The army began to advance and quickly surrounded the Christians on the right. As they began to close in on us, a powerful light appeared and encircled us. Then, an angel of the Lord spoke. "Take out your swords and fight. Defend yourselves and be victorious over the enemy."

"What swords?" a man in the group asked.

"The Word of the Lord is your sword," the angel answered. When we understood what the angel meant, we began to quote verses from the Bible. Then suddenly, as if we were one voice, we began to sing a song. Our voices thundered so loudly, that the Dark army began to retreat in fear. They did not have the courage to come against us anymore.

Lucifer, then filled with rage, turned to those on the left. "You, who all of your life have been trying to please two masters, because you could not stand against me; I have the power to destroy you."

He then ordered his army to attack. It was a total massacre. The ones on the left could not defend themselves. One by one they all fell. This killing seemed to go on for a long time. After a while we could actually smell the stench of the dead.

"Why could they not be protected also?" someone asked.

The angel answered, "Because all their life they have been lukewarm. Because of their hypocrisy, the true church has been blasphemed. They have brought disrespect to the Word of God. They were not clean."

As we continued to look, we saw the sun coming over the horizon. The black clouds began to break up. Then they disappeared. Only one was left— on which Lucifer and his army stood. Lucifer looked at me shaking his fists and said, "I will destroy you even if I have to throw my spear at you from here!" Then that cloud disappeared too.

As I looked around I began to see faces that I recognized among our group. I saw a pastor from Bellflower— another from Indiana— one from Michigan— as well as many of my American friends. This strengthened me greatly. Then I awoke. The first thought that came to my mind as I awoke was that this had been the last fight of the devil against the church. If we remain faithful, we will be victorious.

When will America fall?

These were messages given to my wife, Prophet Leslie Johnson. By the way, as we don't call female Pastors Pastoresses, likewise the word in the Greek can also be interpreted—Prophet or Prophetess—either is correct. We prefer to call Leslie a Prophet, not a Prophetess. It is a small thing.

Fortunately, God has given us some signs. My wife Leslie is a reluctant Prophet. I like that. She didn't ask for nor wants the job and is very slow to release prophecies. Once given, that is the last time we hear of the prophecy. As her husband, I do not know of one prophecy out of the over 5,000 she has given that has missed. I trust her more to hear from God than anyone alive now.

Arafat in the Hospital

On April 15, 2002, Prophet Leslie Johnson was given a dream called "Arafat in the Hospital." It was published it in the

THE SECRET DOOR TO UNDERSTAND BIBLE PROPHECY

Crusader magazine, the website **www.prophecyclub.com** and read on radio. It is also available in the *"Wake-up America"* Gift Offer at **prophecyclub.com**.

It gave several events leading to the next war in the Middle East.

They were:

1. ARAFAT WOULD GO INTO THE HOSPITAL. Fulfilled two years later 11/11/04 at 3:30 AM.
2. ISRAEL WOULD GIVE THE PALESTINIANS A STATE.
3. THE PALESTINIAN STATE WOULD BE A TEMPORARY MEASURE TO ALLOW THE ISRAELIS TIME TO STRENGTHEN THEIR MILITARY.
4. OIL WOULD BE DISCOVERED IN ISRAEL.
5. OIL WILL MAKE THE JEWS WILLING TO FIGHT FOR THEIR LAND.
6. ISRAEL AND AMERICA WILL GO AGAINST MOST OF THE ARAB WORLD.

Leslie had the following dream which gave us the newspaper headlines leading to the fall of America.

Future Headlines

Given to Leslie Johnson, January 22, 2006:

I heard the audible voice of God in the night speak the words: *Israel Refuses to Help America.* Then I heard the following headlines in my heart. This was the order in which I heard them. Not necessarily the order in which they will happen. We believe these are future newspaper headlines, and they have been confirmed. They are from God.

ISRAEL REFUSES HELP TO AMERICA

OLMERT USHERS IN PALESTINIAN STATE [She heard it pronounced; it sounded like "Omer;" she is not sure of the spelling Omer or Olmert.]

CATASTROPHE HITS AMERICA

ONE OF AMERICA'S GREATEST TIMES OF NEED

ISRAEL IS ATTACKED, AMERICA SENDS TROOPS

CHAOS REIGNS AS AMERICANS PROTEST HELP TO ISRAEL

"IT WILL START WITH AN INTERNAL REVOLUTION ..."

Americans became furious. They were mad at the U.S. Government, Jews, and the Muslims.

She said, "Then I heard Stan's voice quoting the Angel who spoke to Dumitru Duduman, 'It will start with an Internal Revolution in America started by the communists. Some of the people will start fighting against the government. The government will be busy with internal problems. Then from the oceans, Russia, Cuba, Nicaragua, Central America, Mexico and two other countries will attack and defeat America.'"

Prophecy of Massive Amounts of Oil in Israel

In 1982, a group of businessmen invited Hayseed Stephens a part-time pastor and fulltime oilman out of Willow Park, Texas, to go to Israel with them to meet Prime Minister Menachem Began. While he was there, he said the Lord spoke to his heart and said, **"The world's largest oil field is located at the South-West end of the Dead Sea."** He found 17 prophecies in the Bible saying in the last days massive amounts of oil will be found in Israel.

In 1995 he started an oil company to gather the funds to go and drill for oil in Israel.

In 1998, I invited Hayseed Stephens to make a DVD called *Oil the Road to Armageddon*. (DVD available at **ProphecyClub.com** or watch instantly on **WatchProphecyClub.com**).

The Prophecy Club put him on our 10-city speaking tour, casting his vision to drill for the oil the Bible said would be discovered in Israel in the Last Days. That speaking tour blew financial life into his vision.

Looking back, God had been preparing me for my journey in oil. I say that because my wife, Leslie Johnson, was given a dream on Oct. 26, 2001, in which she was shown on the map where the river of oil flows underneath Israel. At the time we didn't know why this was revealed to us and not Hayseed; he was the man in the oil business, not us.

We were given motivation when, on Dec. 16, 2002, just before drifting off to sleep, I said, "Lord, I love you more than my wife, children or my life." I guess that was what God was waiting to hear from me, because that night was the first time God ever spoke to me. I heard the audible voice of God say: "I'm giving you part of the harvest of the seeds sown by Billy Graham." In my dream, a two-edged sword appeared in my hands, representing The Word of God, and a 2-foot by 2-foot piece of paper appeared. I swung and cut off about one-third of the paper, while thinking, God is going to give me about one-third the number of souls he gave Billy Graham. I think some of them will come from meetings in sports stadiums.

This confirmed a prophecy I received on Dec. 7, 1987, that said, "You are a soul-winner, a fisher of men and you will save thousands upon thousands." I started praying and asking God how He was going to give me money to win so many souls. On May 6, 2003, I got my answer. Just as in ...

JOB 33:15, 16, "In a dream, in a vision of the night, when deep sleep falleth upon men, in slumberings upon the bed; Then he openeth the ears of men, and SEALETH THEIR INSTRUCTION ... "

God had answered my question. The financial foundation I will stand on, which allows me to take Bible prophecy to the world and to tell America she is the Mystery Babylon is— OIL! Oil will finance the Gospel reaching the world. God had already told my wife, Leslie, that one day The Prophecy Club will be the No. 1 prophecy ministry in the world; now we knew the financial foundation to make it happen would be oil.

I was excited and took my dream to mean that Hayseed would find oil and give us the money to spread the Gospel. I called his wife and made an appointment to see him upon his return from Israel. He was there gathering funds to drill, but I never got the chance to share the dream with him because upon his return he died on May 15, 2003.

His son took over, and unfortunately, things didn't go as planned. On the evening of Hayseed's funeral, I had another prophetic dream wherein I was driving around a desert (I believe to be Israel) in an SUV with Hayseed's son in the passenger seat, looking for ANOTHER place to drill, another oil well. In my lap was a huge steak. In my right hand were the steering wheel and a

THE SECRET DOOR TO UNDERSTAND BIBLE PROPHECY

knife, and in my left hand a fork. As we drove, I would cut off a piece of steak from time to time and eat it. My interpretation is: The steak represented the finances to drill. I brought the finances and was in charge. Sitting in the back seat was an intercessor for our church with her hands on our backs, intently praying. God was bringing me into the oil business.

I still didn't get it. I did not see God was suggesting that I would be involved with oil in Israel! As a small investor in the vision personally, I was frustrated with the lack of progress under the new leadership and considered selling my stock and washing my hands of it. I put God to the test. I had never been on a drilling rig in my life, so I prayed, "God, if you want me to stay involved with the vision to find oil in Israel, show me in a dream what it's like to be at an oil well when it comes in."

Sure enough, that night I dreamed I was standing on a drilling rig floor, looking at a tree of pipes when somebody shouted: "Thar she blows," like in the movie *Moby Dick*, and I felt the ground shake. Under tremendous pressure, air began screaming out of the top of the pipe, then the pressure dropped to nothing, the ground shook and a fountain of oil the color of brown sugar shot up. I took this to mean God wanted me to stay involved with the vision for oil in Israel, but I still didn't see what was coming.

Hayseed's old company had ground to a near halt, and on Nov. 27, 2007, Hayseed's former attorney called and asked if I would be willing to start a new company to continue the vision to find oil in Israel. I told him, "Thanks, but no thanks," that I grew up in the oil business and wanted nothing to do with it. I promised to pray about it, but insisted it was unlikely I'd change my mind.

In an effort to get out of this invitation that night I prayed, "Lord, you know I don't have an extra $5,000 lying around to give that attorney to start some new oil company. If you want me to do this, send the money, in Jesus Name."

I thought, "There you go." I got out of that pretty easy and scarcely gave it a thought until a woman called the Prophecy Club the next day, asking me to return her call about oil in Israel. I thought, "Great, why are these people calling me?" About that time somebody said, "She's been a faithful $50 a month supporter of the ministry for over 10 years; you ought to call her back." Of course, I was going to call her anyway, but that erased all doubt.

When I spoke with her she said, "Two days ago God woke me in the middle of the night and told me to give you $30,000 to continue the vision to find oil in Israel!" She couldn't have known of my prayer the night before. Impossible! No way! I had to take this as an answer to my prayer, an arrangement by God to continue the vision to find oil in Israel. And so, on Jan. 1, 2008, we started Prophetic Oil, Inc.

Hayseed had found 17 verses in the Bible which say massive amounts of oil will be found in Israel. Hayseed was a Pastor, whereas I am a Bible prophecy teacher and soul-winner. So, I dedicated myself to do my own Bible study into oil in Israel, and including what Hayseed had found, increased the total to over 30 Scriptures confirming in the last days massive amounts of oil will be discovered in Israel.

I have also found 5 verses which identify which one of the over 30 maps on the internet showing the layout of the land of the 12 tribes is the CORRECT map.

I have also found what I believe is THE SINGLE VERSE that identifies where the oil is located, not to mention in a dream Leslie was shown where the oil is located in Israel.

I made three DVD's on my discoveries in Bible prophecy about oil in Israel. (DVD's available at **ProphecyClub.com** or watch instantly on **Watch-ProphecyClub.com**)

I believe massive amounts of oil will build up Israel's military, because the Bible says Israel will be victorious and get back her land from the Euphrates to the Nile—probably including all of Saudi Arabia. I discovered that the Bible—in Genesis 49:25; Deuteronomy 33:13; Isaiah 45:3— says the oil will be yellow, deep and double the amount given to the Arabs. If you have questions about the vision of the company Stan started to drill for oil in Israel visit **www.propheticoil.com**. Nothing in this book is an attempt to sell securities.

You recall when Moses was standing in front of the burning bush God said:

> EXODUS 3:8, "And I am come down to deliver them out of the hand of the Egyptians, and to bring them up out of that land unto a good land and a large, unto a land FLOWING WITH MILK AND HONEY ... "

> DEUTERONOMY 32:13, "He made him ride on the high places of the earth, that he might eat the increase of the fields; and he made him to SUCK HONEY OUT OF THE ROCK, AND OIL OUT OF THE FLINTY ROCK;"

In my research, I have researched crude oil in five colors. The most widely used black crude oil provides most of the world's energy. The green crude oil looks black until you hold it against the light, showing a slight green hue. There is the red color such as the oil that squirted out in the Gulf from the Deepwater Horizon accident in April, 2010. Another oil color was made famous by the Beverly Hillbilly's theme song, *Oil, that is, black gold, Texas tea.* The reason they call this crude oil "Texas tea" is simple. When you pour it into a clear glass, it looks just like tea! That brings me to my point. The fifth and most valuable color of oil is yellow. The higher the viscosity, the more energy is in the crude, thus the more valuable the crude oil. The lower the viscosity, or the closer the crude is to tar, like they use to make highways, the less energy and the more it costs to extract the energy so the price is lower. The highest priced oil in the world I am told is "Bonny Light" which is yellow-colored crude oil. That sounds just like God to give His people yellow crude oil, the most valuable oil on the planet!

Around 1973, Andy Sorrell drilled a series of wells in Israel. One of them was the deepest oil well ever drilled in Israel, and he said he found yellow crude oil. Unfortunately, a length of pipe about 300 feet long was dropped down the well and killed the well.

Later he drilled some shallow gas wells as the report goes, and hit a light showing of natural gas in sand "as white as table salt." As white as table salt ... I believe that white sand represents the "milk" in the prophecy to Moses. So "milk" may be natural gas. When God told Moses He was going to send Moses into a land flowing with milk and honey, He may have been saying oil and natural gas! The white sand producing the natural gas representing the "milk" and yellow-colored crude oil being the "honey."

When you pour yellow-crude oil in a glass it looks like honey! I mean you

CAN'T tell it from honey by looking at it. I believe when we drill for oil in Israel, what we will find is yellow crude oil! I believe oil will provide the money for Israel to build their military for their victory in WWIII. They will get back all their land from the Euphrates to the Nile, including much of Saudi Arabia. God will raise Israel up to be one of the wealthiest nations on earth.

At last check, since 1953, over 500 holes have been drilled in Israel seeking oil, and only about seven are producing crude oil—a dismal failure—and the worldly reason for so much failure is either drilling was done in the wrong place or not deep enough. I believe Psalm 81:13-16 holds the spiritual answer.

PSALM 81:13-16, "Oh that my people had HEARKENED UNTO ME, and Israel had WALKED IN MY WAYS! I should soon have SUBDUED THEIR ENEMIES, and turned my hand against their adversaries. The haters of the LORD should have submitted themselves unto him: but their time should have endured for ever. He should have FED THEM also with the finest of the wheat: and with HONEY OUT OF THE ROCK SHOULD I HAVE SATISFIED THEE."

Our goal is to increase the number of souls in the Kingdom of God and give Israel her greatest financial blessing as Genesis 27:28; Jeremiah 33:7, 9 and 14; Deuteronomy 32:13 prophesied to Jacob, Moses, and the house of Israel and Judah.

In March of 2007, we were tour hosts on another tour to Israel. I asked one of our guests to take a picture of me praying at the Western (Wailing) Wall of the temple and handed him my camera. I got on my knees and prayed the same five-point prayer I have been praying for years, "Lord, give me the money and open doors to take your end-time, soul-winning Gospel to the world." Looking back, it was strange that I would pray at the Wall, strange that I kneeled and even stranger that I asked for a picture to be taken, but that picture and that act of prayer turned out to be momentous!

"Unknowingly at the time, I fulfilled the requirements to get Solomon to pray in agreement with me when, on Sunday, March 18, 2007, I prayed on my knees at the Wailing Wall of Solomon's Temple in Jerusalem and prayed!

I believe my prayer fulfilled the requirements of 1 Kings 8:41 of a "stranger not from Israel," because I came from a faraway country for His Name's sake to pray at the Western Wall, asking to take His Name around the globe. Solomon's prayer was asking God to give me what I need to accomplish my request: money and open doors! Eight months later, it was not a coincidence that I was asked to start Prophetic Oil. It was the hand of God.

1 KINGS 8:41-43, "Moreover concerning a stranger, that is not of thy people Israel, but cometh out of a far country for thy name's sake; ... when he shall come and pray toward this house; Hear thou in heaven thy dwelling place, and do according to all that the stranger calleth to thee for: that all people of the earth may know thy name, to fear thee, as do thy people Israel; and that they may know that this house, which I have builded, is called by thy name."

My plan is not to move to Israel at first. We will hire people to supervise it. A man has already called me, and we both believe it is a Divine connection. He will serve as the middleman and supervise the oil operation. I am just a vehicle through which the mission will be put into place. My objective is to win thousands upon thousands of souls like God has promised me on four occasions. This will be a soul-well to fund soul-winning and Israel's expansion and victory in WWIII!

Purpose:

I want to find and present the oil to Israel. We believe God has told us the oil will be used to build Israel's military for their WWIII victory. The Bible says they will get back all their land.

I want to us the oil money to bring back the exiles and Christians to Israel, build the land of unwalled villages and a place for the woman to flee.

I think the oil will serve to build Israel to be the richest strongest nation on the earth.

I believe God has told me the oil will also finance global radio and television taking the end-time prophecies and the name of Jesus to the world. We will organize meetings in sports stadiums. God will fill them with people, giving their heart to Jesus! Seven-fold miracles will be present. Not just double-portion, but miracles seven times greater than anyone has ever seen.

> JOHN 14:12, *"Verily, verily, I say unto you, 'He that believeth on me, the works that I do shall he do also; and GREATER WORKS THAN THESE SHALL HE DO; because I go unto my Father.'"*
>
> JEREMIAH 16:19, *"O LORD, my strength, and my fortress, and MY REFUGE IN THE DAY OF AFFLICTION,* [a date stamp putting this prophecy happening near the tribulation] *the Gentiles shall come unto thee from the ends of the earth, and shall say, 'Surely OUR FATHERS HAVE INHERITED LIES, vanity, and things wherein there is no profit.'* [they will see that their gods are all false] *SHALL A MAN MAKE GODS UNTO HIMSELF, AND THEY ARE NO GODS? Therefore, behold, I will this once cause them to know, I WILL CAUSE THEM TO KNOW MINE HAND AND MY MIGHT; AND THEY SHALL KNOW THAT MY NAME IS THE LORD.* [God will show them his seven-times miracles to convince them he is real. After all that is the real purpose of the Two Witnesses, to refute the Beast and False Prophet and prove Jesus is Lord.]*"*

I was asked, "Do you worry that you may not find oil in Israel?"

No. I didn't call the attorney and ask him to start me an oil company. I didn't decide to do this for me. God called me to do this for Him. One more thing. I didn't sit down and decide I was going to write a book on Bible prophecy either. I just determined that I was going to memorize the book of Revelation, and this book is the blessing I was given as a result. No one has learned as much from this book as I have in writing it! Thank you, Lord! Before starting to memorize Revelation, I knew NONE OF THIS IN THE BOOK! I learned as well.

We look at it like this: If God does not want oil to be found there is no way it will be found, but since God has told us He will give us the $50 million necessary to drill for oil in Israel, we believe He will see it through. After all, it is His project, His money, His well, His souls for His glory! My plan is to hold meetings in sport stadiums. My heart is to see thousands pouring out of the bleachers onto the field giving their heart to Jesus!

We estimate the first hole will cost around $50M. I suppose when God gives $50M, the money to drill, we will have a pretty good idea of where it is going!

DISCLAIMER: We can't guarantee we will find oil in Israel. This is not an effort to sell or offer to sell securities or stock. This is ONLY a discussion on Bible prophecy. This is for entertainment purposes only.

The only way we can discuss this with interested parties is for them to request a prospectus from Prophetic Oil, Inc. Here are a few of the moments of encouragement the Lord has given me concerning oil in Israel.

Vision of Sports Stadium

On May 5, 1997, Dumitru Duduman died. I was more than just a little upset. Not only had I lost a friend, but also an important mentor. I was so upset I went out to a cabin in the woods to fast and pray for a week. I drank only distilled water and read my Bible and prayed. On the morning of the sixth day, as I was waking up, I saw this vision. This was my first vision.

I was standing in the parking lot of a large sports stadium. It was dusk, I saw cars streaming in for miles! I had just been on TV talking about this meeting. The secular media had helped to get the word out through interviews with me. The hidden plan was to take the license plates of the attendees. The attendees knew their license plates would be taken and there would be consequences, but they wanted Jesus!

I organized the meeting and was in charge. I would be one of several speakers and the message would be hard repentance and based on Dumitru's warning. I knew thousands would fall on their faces and give their hearts to Jesus at the meeting.

Chapter 20
MY TESTIMONY

"... to the intent that the living may know that the most High ruleth in the kingdom of men, and giveth it to whomsoever he will, and SETTETH UP OVER IT THE BASEST OF MEN" (DANIEL 4:17).

I am just another ordinary guy with ordinary skills who was saved by grace to whom the God of heaven looked down and gave an opportunity to serve Him, and I took it and ran with it to the best of my ability!

I wasn't born in a manger wearing swaddling clothes, but I didn't start as a winner either. I failed the fourth grade. Looking back, I think I had a mild case of attention deficit disorder. That is a fancy term for learning books was not easy for me, I preferred to play outside. So, I never thought I would be writing a book!

It wasn't funny anymore when school started the next year and all my friends went down the hall to the next classroom. Not only did I stay in the same room, I sat in the same desk, used the same books, and had the same teacher for another year! You cannot imagine how humiliating it was to have to tell all my friends that I failed and had to repeat the fourth grade.

This caused a terrible inferiority complex problem I still deal with today. I determined that, "I will never fail again!" I covered up my inferiority with arrogance. I would compare my strengths to other people's weaknesses to make my miserable, lowly-self feel less like a failure. I was looking for ways to compensate for this terrible feeling of failure.

I could take you to the very spot on the playground and show you where the Lord spoke to my heart in the fourth grade. He said, "You will be a sought-after public speaker!" Is that any kind of a phrase that a fourth grader would make up? No. Perhaps God spoke to give me hope.

Whatever is good in this book, attribute that to the Lord. I own whatever is ridiculous.

God prepares us for what He wants us to do. I spent 13 years teaching public-speaking courses!

How I Got Started in Bible Prophecy

It was 1987, and I was selling heat and smoke detectors door-to-door. Remember, I had a terrible secret. I had a confidence problem, so I HAD to become an over-achiever and HAD to win to feel normal! I won just about every sales award there was to win.

I knocked on a man's door one evening. He made a deal with me. He said, "I will watch your presentation if at the end you listen to my presentation." Arrogant Stan thought, "Okay bub, you got a deal because you don't know a five-time national sales champion just walked in your door. You are sold, and you don't even know it yet!" I think back now, "What a foolish young man I was!"

He didn't buy, but he tried to lead me to Jesus. Of course, I was raised in church and was already saved. Then he changed my life. In one moment he changed my life! He handed me an audio tape. A pastor was telling about a time in the future in which buzzards were going to eat people killed in the greatest battle of all time! I was hooked! I didn't know the Bible foretold the future, but thinking back, I did hear people talking about the future times at church, but it didn't stick with me. It probably just wasn't time for me to begin my journey into Bible prophecy yet.

I grabbed my Bible and began to devour all the parts about Bible prophecy. God arranged for me to start a Bible study in my home. Later, I was teaching Bible prophecy at my local church.

My next big life-change happened on December 7, 1987. After some study, I concluded that the Spirit baptism and water baptism were two separate baptisms. The water for salvation, the Spirit for boldness, power and witnessing. I wanted it. My wife and two ladies prayed for me and BOOM! I GOT IT! It changed my life again! I think this was the event that got God's attention. This is where God seemed to take notice of me and began to put His hand on my life.

My next big life-change happened January, 1988. I attended a meeting of FGBMFI: Full Gospel Businessmen's Fellowship meeting in Lawrence, Kansas. Charles Doss was speaking. I went up for prayer and BOOM! He prophesied from the throne of God. He said some things that still, to this day, shape my life. He said, "Put your hands up, son; God has a special, double anointing for you, a double blessing. You are going to be a soul-winner, a fisher of men. You are going to save thousands upon thousands. The LORD wants you to know that all your sins are forgiven!"

February 1988: The next month after the class in Bible prophecy, a lady handed me an audio tape saying, "I believe you will be interested in this." It was Dumitru Duduman's testimony.

June 1993: A radio station manager called and asked me to do a radio program on Bible prophecy. I called it the Prophecy Club.

May 5, 1997: Dumitru Duduman died. I fasted, nothing but distilled water for seven days. On the sixth day I had a vision of me speaking in a SPORTS STADIUM. I knew that many would be falling down and giving their heart to Christ. I am a soul-winner for Christ. He bought and paid for me with a terribly high price, it is my pleasure to serve Him to the death. He overpaid.

Tips on Memorizing Scripture

Please do not think I am smarter or have more intelligence than you and that is the reason I was able to memorize the Book of Revelation. You can do it too! I will give you some tips, but please understand that the knowledge is not stored on your hard drive, but upon the hard drive of our Savior!

All wisdom comes from Jesus, and if you persevere and stay with it, you can memorize large blocks of the KJV Bible also. Other versions are up to you. You are on your own, but if you use the KJV, God will help. God is no respecter of persons. What He has done for one, He will do for another under the same conditions.

> PHILIPPIANS 4:13, "I can do all things through Christ which strengtheneth me."

In the process of memorizing Revelation, I did learn some techniques that will help make it easier, but understand, they are only temporary. Once the Word got into my heart, the memory techniques no longer were necessary and by default went away. But they were helpful to start.

In my life, I have memorized a Scripture but it was years later before

I got the "revelation understanding." We tend to think we "understand" before we have researched the Scripture. I have discovered that if we simply read it, we understand very little of the complete meaning. Then, since we think we "understand" it, we don't think we need to memorize it and move on. Big mistake.

I have discovered I don't really know what a verse is saying until I DO memorize it, and then there is no guarantee I got the full meaning.

As I memorized Revelation, I was shown 30 revelations and two visions. I began to see deeper in the Spirit of the true meaning.

We see the black ink on white paper, but do we have the deep revelation understanding? For example, Jesus said, "I have the keys of hell and death."

The word "Keys" we know, "hell" we know, "death" we know, but what is He really saying? He is saying He decides who goes to hell, who dies, who lives, and when they die. Just because we can quote the Scripture doesn't mean we understand it. By memorizing it, we get much closer to understanding it.

Sometimes revelation comes by memorizing. The kind of revelations I am speaking of in this book come in an instant, NOT from memorizing. I think memorizing Revelation is the reason the revelations and visions came and provided the ability to write this book.

You Can Memorize Scripture

If I can memorize, you can MEMORIZE! With Scripture, there is no such a thing as a good memory or a bad memory because God is no respecter of persons! He will help those who want to learn His Word! Here are my suggestions for memorizing Scripture.

Before I start I pray, "Lord, give me wisdom and help me to memorize Your Word and never forget it. Give me revelations from on high. Show me the deep and secret things within Your Word. In Jesus' Name, Amen."

I first used a yellow pad. Don't use yellow pads. The yellow makes certain highlighters and ink unusable. I use a spiral-ring white, good quality, wide-ruled notebook of 120 pages or more. Some people like 3 x 5 cards. I don't like them because they are easily lost, crumpled up or soiled. They are good for a verse or two, but not for multiple verses. I like a spiral ring notebook because it gives me room for the text plus notes. In many places, I made more notes than text. It gives me a permanent place to store all my memorized verses.

I write the chapter number at the top of the page and the date I started the chapter.

I number each verse slightly in the margin and use my very, very best penmanship as if I was trying to win a neatness writing contest.

You may have noticed the verses you like are also the ones that are the easiest to memorize. That is a key. Love the Word to memorize it.

As I write, I think ... "I love this text," and I try to show it in every letter I write. I prefer cursive, but printing will do. I try to form my letters perfectly as if I am in a writing contest for neatness. Nice, neat writing is easier to read, easier to read is easier to memorize. I form the letters about 1/3 larger than I would typically, specifically trying to make them easier to read.

I do NOT write fast. I am in the process of falling deeply in love with every word! That is another suggestion. I memorize the verses I love. AND I LOVE the verses I memorize, and it starts with writing them in my notebook.

I use a .07 gel pen that rolls easily. If it is jerky or hard to move, I find another one. I don't want to be distracted by anything like a television in the background or a pen that is difficult to use. I want to totally focus on every letter of every word. I am praying constantly, asking God to give me revelations on His Word.

I use black, blue, green or purple ink for normal text and red for special text.

If a mistake is made I mark it out with the same pen I was writing with. When I say mark it out, I mean I make it one big unreadable blotch on the paper totally unreadable. I don't want my attention to ever be stopped on that part of the paper. I am telling myself to totally ignore that place! Totally. Never look at it again. If I only run a line or two through it, I find my eyes stopping at it again.

After writing out the chapter, I use 6 to 8 colors of highlighters to go back over it and highlight the primary words I want to concentrate on in each sentence.

I want to own it. I never try to memorize looking at black type on the white paper of a Bible. I don't own that. I have not written on it and made my marks. I must own it. So, I mark it, underline it, make it my own. There are cases where past mistakes in writing the text become the Scripture I can't forget! I don't worry about mistakes. I concentrate on falling in love with the text and its author.

As I write, I try to fall in love with each letter, each word. I noticed that it is easier to memorize the parts I love the most, so I fall in love with each word! I memorize as I write.

I try to memorize as I write. I try to fall in love with the word as I write it. You are already noticing that I am repeating myself. That is done on purpose, because at the end of the day your best technique for memorizing is repeating and repetition, and reading it over and over, and listening to the audio over and over and over!

I bought an iPod and put the KJV on it. When my car starts so does my KVJ chapter–automatically! I immerse myself in the Word! I don't just write to write, but I write to memorize. I keep saying each sentence as I write it.

I listen to the chapters as I drive around. I am distracted often while driving, but it still helps to soak in.

I am careful to get every word included and spelled correctly. If I miss a word "written," it is to miss it "memorized." I write one thought per line. Paper and ink are cheap. I am not trying to get as much text per line or per page as possible. I write out ONE THOUGHT or ONE PHRASE per line. The typical verse will take two to four lines to write out.

I want to own the text. Anything to make it NOT black ink on white paper like a book. I highlight, underline, use different colors of ink and highlight. I draw squares, and circles. I try to make it mine! Anything to make it NOT just the same text, not just the same black ink on white paper! Yes, I know I am repeating, repeating myself, myself. Such is memorizing. Memorizing is not easy, but it has given me some of my greatest pleasure in life! It is wonderful! Even if you never have an occasion to quote it.

I have one notebook for Revelation and another one for Daniel.

I turn off the television early and get away from distractions. I read a verse out loud several times until I can recite it and quote it correctly. I go to the next verse when I have that one repeatable. I repeat that technique for the whole chapter.

I might write a book fully detailing all the techniques, but I will close with this one. The most effective one.

As I had completed the Book of Revelation, I was needing to have a partner to check me. I called my friend. It was late at night; the house was dim and quiet. I quoted through half of Revelation. The next day I arrived early at Church and stood behind the pulpit. I was going to practice quoting Revelation. It seemed like when I stood up my mind sat down! I stumbled badly.

I realized I had learned quoting Scripture while sitting down without distractions. Quoting Scripture while STANDING ON MY FEET behind the pulpit, was almost impossible for me, especially WITH DISTRACTIONS. They are two very different things! It was as if I had stored it in two different places in my brain. One was without distractions, and now I needed to copy it to the area of my brain that would quote it WITH distractions! I needed to learn to quote WITH DISTRACTIONS and ON MY FEET!

Now, I will tell you the final and best technique I found. I discovered this technique only works once I have the chapter down quotable without looking. I mean where I can quote it sitting down without having to look at the text.

In my opinion, at this point, I do NOT have it memorized yet. I don't have the chapter down until I can quote it standing up WITH distractions!

It is like pouring cement into the mold. It is only usable once it sets up and is hard. This next technique allowed the chapter to set up and harden in my memory. It got it to stick for months, not moments. After this, I could quote it driving, preaching or on the phone. If I can't quote a verse anytime, anywhere, I don't have it. If I roll my eyes, or even hesitate while quoting a verse, I don't have it down! This helps more than anything, but you can ONLY do this once you can quote the chapter without looking at the text.

I set my computer up to play the audio of the chapter. Using Windows Media player, I discovered if I click on the moving dot at the bottom and push the left arrow it backs up about 10 seconds. This is the best thing I have found to FINISH memorizing Scripture and to refresh Scripture!

I play the audio WHILE STANDING. I recite along with the audio text, and if I hesitate too long or if I miss in any word, I hit the back arrow and recite just that part again, while standing. I go over the text until I can quote it along with the person reading it. Generally, I had it down after three repeated times. I would do this until I could get all the way through the entire chapter. I was amazed to discover STANDING AND RECITING was very effective and the next day I could rip through that chapter faster than the guy reading it! It was great! But, I could only do it after I pretty much had the chapter down. It was not effective until I pretty much had the chapter down. Standing, reciting with audio was WONDERFUL!!! It cemented and hardened the verses in my heart.

From time to time I repeat this procedure to refresh. One or two times through it and the next day it is all back!

Benefits I Noticed By Memorizing Scripture

I feel closer to God, more like I am pleasing Him, or that He is pleased with my efforts. I feel like my prayers are answered more often and carry more power. Before, I used to just dread having to pray for someone. I used to think, "Why do I have to do this. It is uncomfortable and is pretty much a waste of my time. I am only doing this because I am forced to." I didn't really believe much was really going to happen. Maybe it did, but I hadn't seen many results.

Memorizing Scripture has allowed me to KNOW my Lord much, much better! Today, I feel much more confident and will immediately pray now, especially in a crisis!

JOHN 15:7, "If ye abide in me, and my words abide in you, ye shall ask what ye will, and it shall be done unto you."

I find I am using Scripture in my prayers more, great for worship!

DO NOT ...

DO NOT Try to memorize directly from a Bible from black ink on white paper—you don't own it—it all runs together—you miss seeing the pictures of the page—you miss the step of memorizing and worshipping as you write—you miss the step of falling in love with the Word as you write. It puts you at a distinct disadvantage.

DO NOT Use any other version other than King James. Why should God help you memorize words which are not His? (Watch the **ProphecyClub. com** DVD *King James or 400 Counterfeits by Adam Johnson*.) Almost all the people who memorize large portions of Scripture almost always memorize King James Version / KJV.

When you quote "conversational versions" these don't sound like Scripture, and people doubt you are quoting Scripture and won't listen.

When quoting KJV, even sinners know it is from the Bible. Quoting God's Word stops people, and they listen and do not interrupt.

It is my guess that people quoting other conversational versions are not only questioned but interrupted because it doesn't deserve their silence since it is not 100 percent God.

Yes, I recommend memorizing Scripture.

A great blessing!

If you want to place an order:
www.prophecyclub.com
P.O. Box 750234, Topeka, KS 66675;
785 266-1112

To watch instantly:
www.WatchProphecyClub.com

Inquiries about our vision to find oil for Israel:
www.propheticoil.com

If you have questions or comments the best response comes from the ask Stan email:
askstan@prophecyclub.com

Social Media

https://www.youtube.com/channel/UCXM5jmd0qxd3uLSrvJazfiw/videos
http://prophecyclub.sermon.net/main/main/21230590
http://www.prophecyclub.com/
https://www.facebook.com/ProphecyClub/
https://vimeo.com/prophecyclub/vod_pages
https://www.watchprophecyclub.com/

Watch instantly 300 videos:
https://itunes.apple.com/us/podcast/the-prophecy-club/id679162744?mt=2